PROBLEMS FOR COMPUTER SOLUTION

PROBLEMS
FOR COMPUTER SOLUTION

Fred Gruenberger

The RAND Corporation
Santa Monica, California

George Jaffray

Associate Professor of Mathematics
Los Angeles Valley College
Van Nuys, California

JOHN WILEY & SONS, INC.
New York · London · Sydney

PREFACE

It is assumed that a student, through an introductory course, has learned a good deal of what computers can do. At this point, he and his instructor should be concerned with what he can do—given access to a computer and various coding aids, and using his own ingenuity. The problems in this book, taken from a broad range of disciplines, should provide challenging problems to stimulate creative work and demonstrate competence.

The problems cover also a wide range of difficulty. Some are little more than exercises, while others could lead to term projects extending over a semester's time.

In most cases, a new topic is introduced by the brief statement of a problem. Then the student is guided into analyzing the problem; thus he is encouraged to develop good problem-solving techniques. This analysis frequently leads to other problems, some of which are shorter and simpler than the original problem and serve as preliminary exercises. The solution of the exercises broadens the student's understanding of the larger problem, until that problem is reduced to an exercise just a little more advanced than the work that the student has already accomplished.

The details of programming are usually left for the student. The solution of a computer problem is in an important sense the computer *routine*, rather than the answer to the problem question. In this sense, a computer problem does not have a unique solution. Any two students may develop strikingly different computer routines, and they *both* may solve the problem correctly and efficiently.

Problems for Computer Solution is intended to meet the needs of an instructor who must provide suitable problems for each member of his class. Ideally, the choice of problem should be made by the student, since the best problem to work on is the one the student is most interested in. The greatest danger, of course, is that in this selection process, the student will tend to select a problem that is too difficult for his capabilities, or

too long for him to complete. If the instructor is tempted to reject a problem because it seems to lack sufficient interest, be
too familiar, have too little significance, lack enough challenge,
be too difficult, involve too many new principles, require too
much special background, be too short, be too long, or for a
combination of these reasons, then we may ask for whom is it
too easy, too challenging, etc.?

Even in a class of highly selected students, there is a
tremendous range of interest, ability, and motivation for computing. The explosive increase in computing classes will surely
draw into computing many instructors who lack extensive experience and fairly large numbers of unexceptional students.
For some of these, it is difficult to say of a particular problem
that it is too familiar, too easy, or lacks challenge.

On the other hand, the increasing importance of computing
may be expected to bring into computing classes students with
very special interests in biology, linguistics, law, space flight,
nuclear structure, nursing, economics, or the like. Can we say
with certainty that for all of these a particular problem is too
difficult, frustrating, specialized, or time consuming?

Ideally, it is desirable to exclude any problem that cannot be stated in machine-independent terms. Practically, it is
very difficult to do so. A large number of excellent problems
are machine-specific and must be stated and explained in terms
of a specific computer. These include, for example, problems
related to loading routines, core dumping routines, and patho-
logical characteristics of a machine. Where a specific machine
has been necessary, we have used the IBM 1620 as the reference
machine. There are reasons for the choice: Both authors are
familiar with it and have used it in their own classes, and (at
this writing) it seemed likely to be the most widely installed
machine for student use. However, we appreciate that many
types of machines will be used for student needs. In particular,
many students will have access only to a large machine of the
computing center, and may have to submit their problems according to some operating system and monitor routine. For the
student who uses other than a 1620, the terminology and details
of the 1620 will have to be adjusted to those of his machine, but
that of itself is a fine problem for the student of computing.

We wish to thank Dr. Richard Hamming for his meticulous
commentary on the manuscript of this book. Special acknowl-

edgement is also due Professor Richard Andree, of the University of Oklahoma, whose keen insight revealed the need for a book of this type.

Fred Gruenberger
George Jaffray

Los Angeles
May, 1965

CONTENTS

Problem

Problem

INTRODUCTION

This book is addressed to the student of digital computing. Such a person presumably wishes to learn many things, among which are:

1. What is a digital computer?
2. How does it operate?
3. What is it used for?
4. How is it programmed?
5. What are its limitations?
6. What should we compute?

In the learning of any subject (tightrope walking, for example) there is a sharp distinction between theory and practice. Theory is fine up to a point, but there is no substitute for actual practice. To make the practice meaningful in a course in computing, the student should work independently on a problem, preferably one of his own choosing. He must avoid choosing too few problems, limiting himself to three or four grandiose problems. He should rather plan to do many of the easier exercises. He will find that he develops his problem-solving ability much faster by solving many apparently simple exercises. These prepare him for attacking the bigger problems. He can actually complete more big problems by first doing the easier exercises which lead up to them than he could accomplish by attacking those impressive problems directly.

The sixth question raised above (What should we compute?) thus becomes important. The question has a double meaning. In its smaller sense, it could mean the choice the student must make, to select a problem consistent with his capabilities that he can hope to complete in time. In its larger sense, it refers to a more fundamental problem; namely, what are the attributes of a good computer problem? In other words, what are the characteristics of any problem that is suitable for computer attack? These characteristics can be listed.

In the practical world, where computer time is measured in dollars per minute, an overriding attribute of a good computer problem is *usefulness*. With rare exceptions, industrial users of computing equipment are somewhat cool to the idea of extending tables in number theory, for example. In the atmosphere of the school, however, this requirement can be waived. Any problem that fits the other requirements is automatically useful for the training process.

From here on, we can develop criteria that apply to any use of a computer, whether practical or in a classroom.

1. Definition

The problem must be defined; that is, we must know precisely what the problem is. It is an "obvious" criterion, but many a man-hour has been wasted on a plunge into programming an undefined or ill-defined problem. Consider the warehouse manager who innocently asks to have his inventory problems "put on the computer." Or the student who asks, "Can we 'do' roulette on the machine?"

The old hand learns to keep asking, "What is the problem?" In a specific situation, he may ask it to the point of open rebellion on the part of the customer. He appears, to the customer, rather stupid; after all, it is perfectly clear to the customer what his problem is. Or is it? The short history of computing is already loaded with sad tales of people who never did get their problem properly defined.

It might be said that a problem is defined when everyone concerned with it understands it. Or, in computer terms, problem definition might end when all the inputs and outputs are stated.

So definition is necessary. It is hardly sufficient. Few problems are better defined, for example, than Fermat's last theorem (see any text on the theory of numbers or the same topic in an encyclopedia.)

If we know precisely what the problem is (and we should continually emphasize "precisely"), then we need a method.

To be high-sounding about it, we need an

2. Algorithm

In other words, we must know some way to solve the problem, with or without a computer. Note that we say *some* way. There are usually many ways. Here may be the first distinction between a computer solution to a problem and any other solution. We are privileged to keep in mind that a computer is fast; we may capitalize on this fact to seek, as a first cut, a brute force (or crowbar) method. As a criterion, the elegance of the method matters little. What is vital to understand is that we must have an algorithm that works, at least in theory.

Here, of course, is where the theorem of Fermat fails as a computer problem. We do not have a method, with or without a computer. Often a problem can be solved by exhaustion, by which we attempt to try all possibilities. This is frequently acceptable as a method to use on the computer.

So far so good; we know what our problem is and a way to solve it. We should now check for

3. Machine match

This sounds like the most trivial criterion of all; namely that our problem should fit the machine we propose to solve it on. It must fit in two ways: The instructions plus data must fit the storage capacity of the computer, and the running time to solution must fit what time is available. Brute-force methods may kill us here. Even in a classroom atmosphere (perhaps especially in that atmosphere), computer time is not unlimited and is almost never free.

In a well-run computer course, the student does many exercises. He should also do at least one problem. The distinction is this: An exercise relates to a specific technique, and the approach is usually spelled out. A problem, on the other hand, will involve a broad goal, using many techniques, and with very little spelled out.

The best situation of all is the one where the bright student selects a problem all his own; perhaps one never tackled before. The checklist we are developing might be of some help in testing whether an original problem, suggested by the student, is appropriate for computer solution.

4. Repetition

We make the statement categorically: A good computing problem has a large element of repetition. This rule has many exceptions, of course. The use of a computer for true one-shot calculations is fairly common, but that does not mean that one-shot problems (and particularly straight-line formula evaluations) are good computer problems. One thing a computer does well is repeat a sequence of instructions (with or without modification). A good problem, then, capitalizes on this capability.

5. Payoff

The fifth criterion refers to over-all efficiency. It does not intersect with the concept of usefulness. The question is this: Is a solution by computer more efficient, in some sense, than a solution by any other means? For a good computer problem, there should be a large payoff.

These, then, are five criteria that should be met by any problem that is proposed for computer solution. Considered as a checklist for how to get started, we can add two more principles.

6. Cut the problem down to size

This principle is emphasized again and again throughout this book. It can involve the idea of segmenting the problem; that is, breaking it down to a set of subproblems (usually in the form of subroutines). More often, it calls on the problem solver to try a cut-down, simplified version of the problem first. Many problems appear formidable at first glance. A simplified version not only offers a toehold, but usually lays out a correct plan of attack. It is a truism in computing that only when a routine is debugged and tested, and some production has been run, does the programmer really know how he should have attacked the problem in the first place.

7. Brains beat brawn

Experienced programmers can furnish countless examples of this principle, wherein over-all amounts of brainwork (at the desk, not at the console) can save large amounts of computer time. Principles 6 and 7 interact. Brute-force methods can be of service on cut-down versions of a problem.

Problem A1

EVALUATING A POLYNOMIAL

A very simple application of the principle that "there is always a better way" is made in finding the value of a polynomial involving a single letter for a given value of the letter. If we apply brute force to the polynomial

$$y = 5.142x^3 - 0.897x^2 + 3.145x - 7.250$$

for the value $x = 3.212$, we substitute 3.212 for x and make six multiplications:

$$y = (5.142)(3.212)(3.212)(3.212) - 0.897(3.212)(3.212) + 3.145(3.212) - 7.250$$

In evaluating a complete polynomial of tenth degree by the same brute force method, the number of multiplications would mount to forty-five. The "better-way" principle asks how many multiplications are actually needed.

By rearranging the order of operations, the evaluation of the cubic polynomial can be reduced from six to three; and the multiplications for a tenth-degree polynomial with no missing terms can be reduced from forty-five to ten:

$$y = 5.142x^3 - 0.897x^2 + 3.145x - 7.250$$

is written as

$$y = ((5.142x - 0.897)x + 3.145)x - 7.250$$

Since evaluating a polynomial is a fundamental operation in many applications of computers, it is worthwhile to make it brief, provided the programming is not made complicated by doing so. Actually, shortening the routine makes it simpler, as shown by the flow chart of Figure A1.1. It is assumed that the coefficients $a_1, a_2, \dots , a_{11}$ of the polynomial

1

$$y = a_1x^{10} + a_2x^9 + a_3x^8 + a_4x^7 + a_5x^6 + a_6x^5 + a_7x^4$$
$$+ a_8x^3 + a_9x^2 + a_{10}x + a_{11}$$

are already stored in consecutive ten-digit fields with five decimal places each. We shall call the typical coefficient A, so that A represents each coefficient in turn. We "advance A" by modifying its address in the instruction that forms the sum.

> EXERCISE 1.(a) Show that the number of multipli-
> cations required to evaluate a polynomial of the nth
> degree by the brute-force method is $n(n - 1)/2$;
> whereas only n multiplications are required by
> grouping the terms as shown. (b) Write a routine
> to evaluate a tenth-degree polynomial according
> to the flow chart in Figure A1.1.

The method just described for evaluating a polynomial is called the "nesting method."* If the student is familiar with synthetic division and the remainder theorem, he should verify that the nesting method is <u>exactly</u> equivalent to evaluating a polynomial by synthetic division.

> EXERCISE 2.(a) Using hand calculation, evaluate the poly-
nomial
>
> $$y = 5.142x^3 - 0.897x^2 + 3.145x - 7.250$$
>
> for $x = 1$ by synthetic division and also by the nest-
> ing method to show that exactly the same operations
> are performed in exactly the same order. (b) Mod-
> ify the routine of Exercise 1 so that you can specify
> the number of decimal places common to the coeffi-
> cients, the variable, and the answer. (c) Explain
> whether you consider it desirable to round off the
> products.

The student should note that the algebraic method used in evaluating a polynomial by synthetic division becomes very straightforward and natural when applied to computing. He should be alert to discover other algebraic processes in a new and simpler guise in his computing methods. For example, the

---

*Even the nesting method is not the <u>most</u> efficient way to evaluate a polynomial, but it is easy to code.

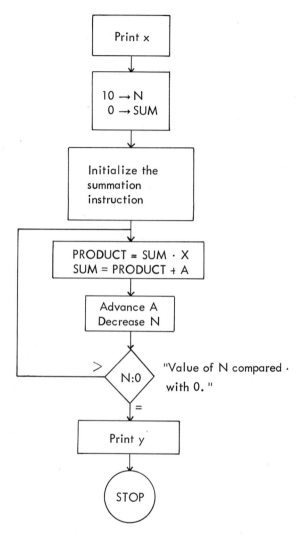

Figure A1.1: Evaluation of a tenth-degree polynomial.

scientific notation has a simplified counterpart in floating-point calculations, where the exponent (if positive) simply shows the number of digits to the left of the decimal point.

EXERCISE 3. Rewrite your routine for evaluating

a polynomial as a subroutine. Include in the calling sequence the address of the variable, the address of the leading coefficient, and the degree of the polynomial.

The nesting method for evaluating a polynomial for $x = b$ can easily yield the quotient of the polynomial divided by $x - b$.

EXERCISE 4. Extend your routine for Exercise 2 (slightly) so as to obtain the coefficients of the quotient at the same time.

EXERCISE 5. Write a routine in Fortran to evaluate a polynomial of any degree up to the tenth.

There should be error checks in any routine. These checks are especially important in a subroutine, which may be called on in many different situations with widely divergent data.

EXERCISE 6. (a) Discuss what action should be taken by the subroutines to evaluate a polynomial if the degree is given as zero. Note that this check must be added to Figure A1.1. (b) Consider the possibility that the polynomial does not exist, having no coefficients at all. If this is possible, what should the subroutine do? (c) Decide what should be done for the polynomial $y = 7$ (having no x terms) to be evaluated when $x = 7$. (d) Make any changes necessary to assure that your subroutines conform to the decisions in parts (a), (b), and (c).

The routine to evaluate a polynomial can be used repeatedly to find any particular root of a polynomial equation.

EXERCISE 7. (a) Write a routine to call upon your subroutine to evaluate a polynomial repeatedly with increasing values of x. Make the size of the steps in x a value to be read in from the typewriter. (b) Use your routine repeatedly to locate a root of the equation

$$5.142x^3 - 0.897x^2 + 3.145x - 7.250 = 0$$

to the nearest integer, then to the nearest tenth,
nearest hundredth, and nearest thousandth.

Another application of the nesting method is to find the
slope of a curved line at a given point, as will be required in
Newton's method for solving an equation in Problem A3. First
let us consider a straight line.

The slope of the straight line $3x - y = 5$, or $y = 3x - 5$, is
the ratio of the increase in y to the increase in x as we move
along the line. Or we can say it is the increase in y corresponding to a unit increase in x. The slope m of the straight line
in Figure A1.2 is 3.

An equation of degree higher than the first represents a
curved line. The average slope between two points on the line is
still the ratio of the increase in y to the increase in x. For the
equation $y = x^3 - 3x + 1$, the average slope of the curve from the
point $(1, -1)$ to the point $(2, 3)$ is 4, since y increases four units
while x is increasing one, as shown in Figure A1.3. Of course,
the curved line is changing direction continuously, so that the
exact slope at any particular point is different from the slope
at neighboring points. A straight line passing through a point on
the curve with the exact slope of the curve at that point is tangent to the curve.

The exact slope of the curved line representing a polynomial
is found in numerical work by applying the nesting method twice.*
To find the slope at the point $x_0 = 3.212$ on the curve of

$$y = 5.142x^3 - 0.897x^2 + 3.145x - 7.250$$

we divide by $x - 3.212$, using the nesting method to obtain the
quotient

$$5.142x^2 + 15.619x + 53.309$$

Then we evaluate the quotient for $x = 3.212$, again using the
nesting method. The result is the required slope.

---

*In calculus, the exact slope is found by differentiation, and the slope
is called the derivative of y with respect to x, written dy/dx, or sometimes indicated as y'. The reader who has studied calculus will see that
here again the numerical method is simpler than the traditional explanation, and helps to make the concept clearer. In particular, the numerical
method emphasizes the division involved in the idea of a derivative.

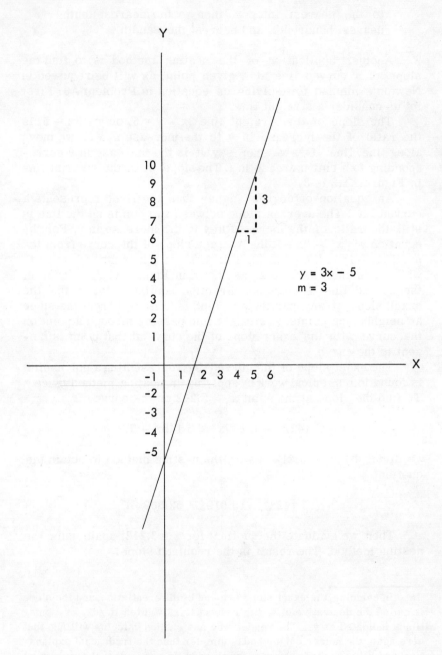

Figure A1.2: Slope of a line.

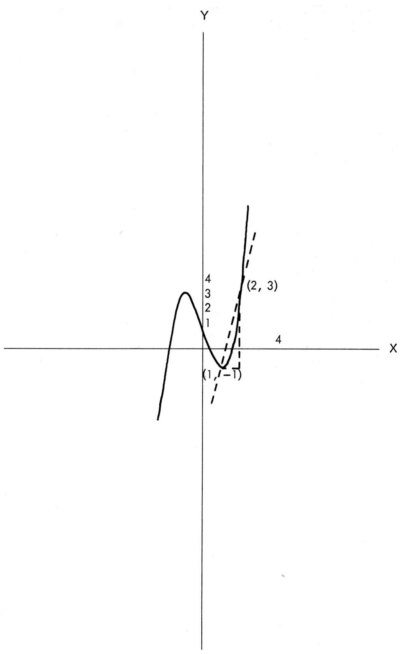

Figure A1.3: Average slope for the curve $y = x^3 - 3x + 1$

EXERCISE 8 (a) Write a routine to use the sub-routine of Exercise 4 twice: once to obtain the quotient, and a second time to evaluate the quotient for $x = x_0$. (b) Use the routine of part (a) to calculate the exact slope of the curve $y = 5.142x^3 - 0.897x^2 + 3.145x - 7.250$ for $x_0 = 3.212$.

The numerical method for finding the (exact) slope depends directly upon the definition for average slope from the point (x_0, y_0) to the point (x, y):

$$\text{Average slope, } m = \frac{y - y_0}{x - x_0}$$

When the nesting method is used to evaluate the polynomial, the work is exactly the same as dividing the polynomial by $x - 3.212$, obtaining $5.142x^2 + 15.618x + 53.309$ and a remainder of 163.979. The remainder is the value y_0 of the polynomial for x_0. The original polynomial minus the remainder is $y - y_0$. When we discard the remainder, we obtain the quotient $(y - y_0)/(x - x_0)$, which is the average slope of the curve from the point (x_0, y_0) to the point (x, y). If we substitute the value of x_0 itself for x in the quotient, we obtain the average slope from x_0 to x_0, that is, the exact slope at the point. The value of the quotient is found, of course, by the nesting method.

Problem A2

THE POPULATION PROBLEM

Assume that in 1960 the population figures for the United States and Mexico were 180,000,000 and 85,000,000 respectively. Assume also that the annual rate of growth for the United States was 1.23 per cent, and that for Mexico, 2.23 per cent. If these growth rates remain constant, in what year will the population of Mexico equal or exceed that of the United States? The flow chart of Figure A2.1 applies.

The second assumption made in this problem is dangerous. Consider similar data for the United States (180,000,000) and the state of California (15,700,000) for 1960, and growth rates of 1.23 per cent and 3.70 per cent. Applying the same routine, we would find a year in which the population of California exceeded the population of the United States, which is nonsense.

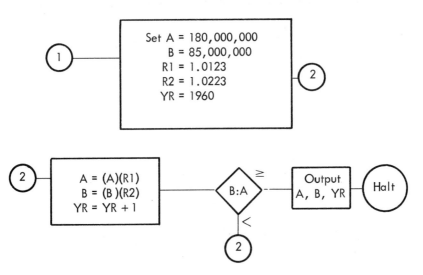

Figure A2.1: The population problem.

Modify the problem then (for the United States and Mexico figures), to include a different assumption. The growth rate for the United States was 1.23 per cent in 1960 but increases by 0.01 per cent each year. Similarly, the growth rate for Mexico was 2.23 per cent in 1960, but increases 0.001 per cent each year. Will the population of Mexico, then, ever exceed that of the United States?

Or try this version of the problem. In 1963, the United States consumption of motor fuel was 64,000,000 gallons, increasing 4 per cent per year. The consumption in California was 6,000,000 gallons, increasing 5.4 per cent per year. In what year will California consume more than the United States?

The principle illustrated by the last exercise is that of GIGO—"garbage in; garbage out." If the problem definition is intrinsically nonsensical, then the application of a computer to it will add no sense. Blaming the nonsensical result, then, on the computer is not fair, but we see examples of it frequently.

Problem A3

SOLUTION OF ALGEBRAIC EQUATIONS

The student is familiar with the formula for the roots of a quadratic equation.*

For $ax^2 + bx + c = 0$

$$x_1 = \frac{-b + \sqrt{b^2 - 4ac}}{2a} \qquad x_2 = \frac{-b - \sqrt{b^2 - 4ac}}{2a}$$

He will find it interesting and instructive to write a routine to solve quadratic equations.

> EXERCISE 1. (a) Write a routine to solve a quadratic equation that has real roots. Read a, b, and c into storage from the typewriter as 10-digit fields with 5 decimal places. Include a division subroutine and a square root subroutine as described in Problem A11. (b) Change the routine of part (a) to test for a negative radicand. Provide in this case for printing the real and imaginary parts of the roots separately.

Equations of third or higher degree usually do not need to be solved for all their roots, but only for the root in a certain neighborhood. If the left side of the equation

$$x^5 + 2.501x^4 - 1.250x^3 - 3.125x^2 - 2.251x - 5.615 = 0$$

is plotted as the curve

$$y = x^5 + 2.501x^4 - 1.250x^3 - 3.125x^2 - 2.251x - 5.615$$

the real roots of the original equation are the values of x where the curve crosses the x-axis, for at such points y = 0, as shown in Figure A3.1.

---

*Note that these formulas are mathematically correct, but they would need to be modifed for proper use with finite arithmetic.

11

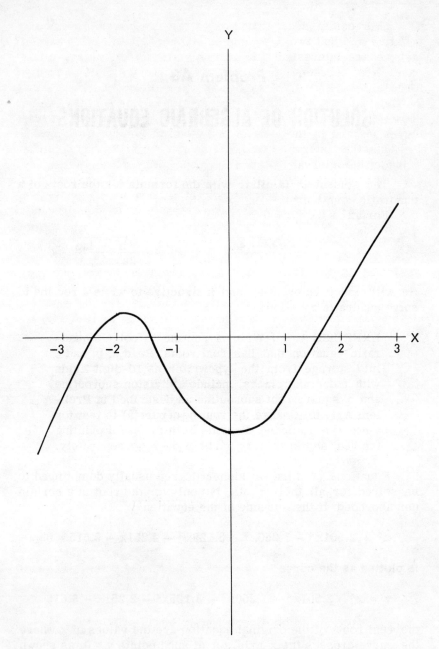

Figure A3.1. Graph for a fifth-degree equation

It is easily seen that two of the five possible roots are negative and that two are complex numbers. It will often happen that we are interested only in the positive root, which, in this case, lies between x = 1 and x = 2. A very simple or brute-force approach would be to test the value midway between 1 and 2. The value of y for this average value of x is positive, which shows in this case that x is still too large, since the curve slopes upward to the right in this vicinity. We therefore have a new, smaller interval that contains the root. We can continue to bisect the interval, determining the root approximately to any desired accuracy. This method seems very crude, but is easy to code. The student will find it profitable to code it.

We may write a recursion formula for the process:

$$x_{n+1} = \frac{1}{2} \left(a_n + b_n \right)$$

where a_n is the low end of the interval and b_n the high end. The flow chart in Figure A3.2 assumes that the curve is rising in the given interval. If this is not the case for the equation under consideration, it can be made true by multiplying the coefficients by −1.

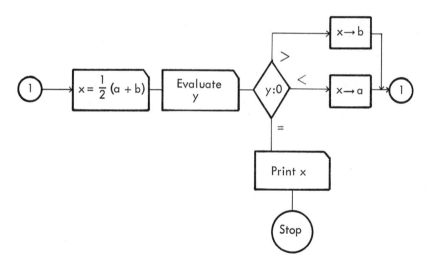

Figure A3.2. Bisection method for solving an equation

EXERCISE 2. Write a routine to solve the equation

$$x^5 + 2.501x^4 - 1.250x^3 - 3.125x^2 - 2.251x - 5.615 = 0$$

Assume that the coefficients are already stored in consecutive 10-digit fields with 5 decimal places, and that the values of x for the ends of the interval are stored in a similar way. Use the subroutine from Problem A1, Exercise 4, to evaluate the polynomial. According to the flow chart of Figure A3.2, the process is terminated when y = 0. It is not likely that the value of y will ever be precisely zero (using finite arithmetic); the test must be made for the difference (between y and zero) becoming smaller than some preassigned value such as 10^{-4}

The simple averaging method already described does not take into account the possibility that y may be much farther from the x-axis at one end of the interval than the other. This consideration leads to the interpolation method (or false-position method).

Suppose we have the equation

$$x^3 - x - 1 = 0$$

We plot the left side as $y = x^3 - x - 1$ by hand or with the aid of a plotting routine as described in Problem B1. We ask for the value of the root that lies between x = 1 and x = 2, as shown in Figure A3.3.

The rise in y is from −1 to 5, a total of 6. We need to go far enough to the right for y to rise to 0, about one-sixth of the total rise. Our estimate for x will be 1 1/6. If we represent the points A and B by (x_0, y_0) and (x_1, y_1), the average slope is $(y_1 - y_0)/(x_1 - x_0)$, as explained in Problem A1. The desired increase in y is from y_0 to 0, that is, $0 - y_0$. If we divide this by the average slope, we find the approximate increase in x. Hence,

$$x = x_0 + \frac{(0 - y_0)/(y_1 - y_0)}{x_1 - x_0} \quad \text{or} \quad x = x_0 - \frac{x_1 - x_0}{y_1 - y_0} \cdot y_0$$

We calculate the value of y corresponding to this value of x. If y is positive, we replace x_1 by x; if it is negative, we replace x_0 by x, as in the simple averaging method.

The interpolation method will converge much faster than the previous method, but it is harder to code.

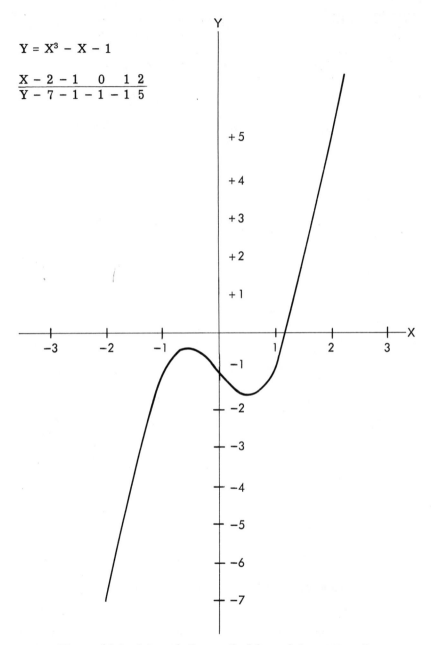

$Y = X^3 - X - 1$

X	-2	-1	0	1	2
Y	-7	-1	-1	-1	5

Figure A3.3. Interpolation method for solving an equation

EXERCISE 3. Write a routine to solve the equation $x^3 + 0 \cdot x^2 - x - 1 = 0$ by the interpolation method. Assume that the coefficients (including the coefficient of x^2) are already stored in consecutive ten-digit locations with five decimal places, and that the values of x_0 and x_1 are similarly stored.

The interpolation method for solving an equation can be represented by the recursion relation

$$x_{n+1} = x_n - \frac{y}{\text{slope}}$$

That method used the average slope over an interval containing the root. If the estimated value of the root is close to the actual value, using the <u>exact</u> slope might arrive at the root quicker. Newton's method is like the interpolation method except that it uses the exact local slope. In the equation

$$x^3 - 12x^2 + 44x - 49 = 0$$

we plot the graph of $y = x^3 - 12x^2 + 44x - 49$, as in Figure A3.4.

The root between $x = 2$ and $x = 3$ is close to 2, so that the exact slope at the point $(2, -1)$ is a better choice than the average slope between $x = 2$ and $x = 3$.

The exact slope is found as explained in Problem A1 by dividing y by $x - 2$ and evaluating the quotient for $x = 2$. The iteration can be continued until the second term in the recursion formula is zero.

EXERCISE 4. Write a routine to solve an equation of tenth degree or less, following Newton's method. Use the evaluation subroutine of Problem A1, Exercise 4, to calculate both y and the slope. We now have three methods for finding the root of an equation of higher degree than the second:*

Bolzano (bisection) method (simple averaging)

---

*A further discussion of these and other methods, including the determination of complex roots, can be found in any book on numerical analysis, for example, in <u>Numerical Methods and FORTRAN Programming</u> by D. D. McCracken and W. S. Dorn, John Wiley & Sons, New York, 1964, p. 150.

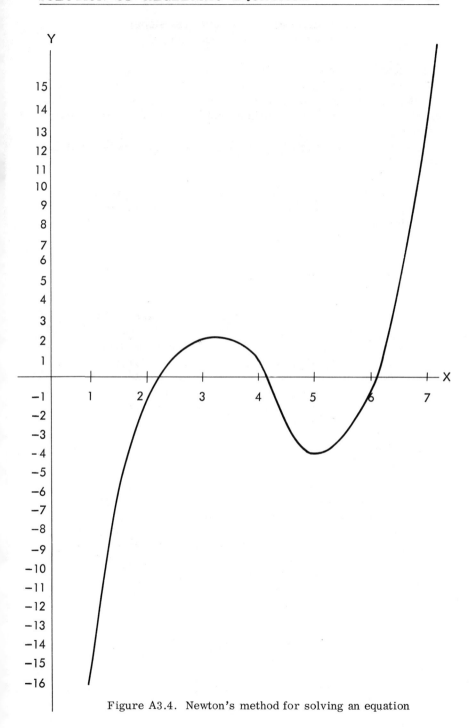

Figure A3.4. Newton's method for solving an equation

Interpolation method (average slope)
Newton's method (exact slope)

The Bolzano method is simple to code and takes advantage of the great speed of the computer to converge quickly to an accurate answer. It is intrinsically slow, but very safe. The other methods require fewer iterations, but demand more complicated routines.

Newton's method is often used to justify recursion formulas used in subroutines.

EXERCISE 5. (a) Show that Newton's method applied to the equation $x^2 - N = 0$ gives the recursion formula

$$x_{n+1} = x_n + \frac{N - x_n^2}{2x_n} = \frac{x_n^2 + N}{2x_n}$$

and show that this is equivalent to the formula $x_{n+1} = x_n + [(N/x) - x_n]/2$ used in Problem A11 for extracting square root. Perform the division and evaluation by hand in accordance with the discussion in Problem A1 to find an expression for the exact slope. (b) Show that Newton's method applied to the equation $x = (N)^{1/3}$ or $x^3 - N = 0$ gives

$$x_{n+1} = x_n + \frac{1}{3} \left[\frac{N}{x_n^2} - x_n \right]$$

as a recursion formula for extracting cube root. (c) Write a routine to extract cube roots by Newton's method. A suitable choice for x_n if N is greater than 1 is $(N/2000) + 2$. Be sure to do the necessary algebra before the computing; that is, rework the formula into the best form for computation.

Problem A4

HASTINGS' APPROXIMATIONS

Any person seriously interested in computing should become familiar with the remarkable polynomial approximations devised by Cecil Hastings, Jr., described in the book <u>Approximations for Digital Computers</u> (Published by Princeton University Press, Princeton, New Jersey, 1955). In the first half of this book, Hastings shows in detail how such approximations can be created; the second half contains 76 of them, together with an error analysis for each one. Although the directions for creating them are explicit, their creation is still an art rather than a science.

Let us illustrate with his Sheet 14, an approximation for $\sin(\pi/2)X$:

$$\sin\frac{\pi}{2} X = aX + bX^3 + cX^5$$

where

$$a = 1.5706268$$
$$b = -0.6432292$$
$$c = 0.0727102$$

and

$$-1 \leq X \leq 1.$$

It is obvious that this formula is correct at $X = 0$. By adding coefficients, we arrive at the value for $X = 1$; namely, 1.0001078. The absolute error (i.e., true value minus approximation) at $X = 1$ is thus 0.0001078.

EXERCISE 1. Write a routine to compare the values given by Hastings' approximation for $X = 0(0.05)1$ (meaning that X is to take the values from 0 to 1 in steps of 0.05) and the values in each case as given by a packaged routine for the sine of x. Notice that we may be doing absolutely nothing by this exercise,

19

since it is quite possible that the packaged sine function at your disposal <u>is</u> the same approximation. It is more likely, however, that the packaged function is Hastings' Sheet 15, which yields far more accuracy.

EXERCISE 2. Write a routine to calculate the relative error for each of the points used in Exercise 1; i.e., calculate

$$\frac{\text{approximation} - \text{function}}{\text{function}} = \text{relative error}$$

HALL PASS

WAYNE VALLEY HIGH SCHOOL

STUDENT: _____ GRADE: _____

DATE: _____ PERIOD: _____ TIME: _____

DESTINATION

_____

TEACHER: _____ ROOM: _____

10

	7745		Roll	.53
	7746		Roll	.69
	7747		Roll	.81
	7748		Roll	1.19
	7749		Roll	1.55

s: 1 1/2 "x500" - 20
Rolls/Carton.

	7810		Roll	1.75
	7811		Roll	2.55
	7812		Roll	2.85
	7813		Roll	3.45

TOTAL THIS PAGE

Problem A5

THE LEANING BRICKS

How many perfectly smooth, loose, 8-inch bricks are required to form a single pile with no part of the bottom brick under the top brick? How far can such a pile lean? How many bricks are required to cover a walk 24 inches (three bricks) wide?*

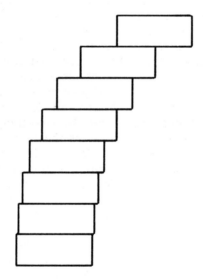

Figure A5.1. The pile of leaning bricks

By determining the center of gravity of the top two bricks, it is easy to show that the third brick can clear the top two by no more than one-fourth of its length, as shown in Figure A5.1. Similarly, the fourth brick can clear by no more than one-sixth, so that we have the series

---
*The situation posed by this problem can actually be demonstrated with a stack of punched cards.

$$\frac{1}{2} + \frac{1}{4} + \frac{1}{6} + \frac{1}{8} + \frac{1}{10} \cdots$$

In this series, each term is one-half of the corresponding term in the well known harmonic series

$$\frac{1}{1} + \frac{1}{2} + \frac{1}{3} + \frac{1}{4} + \frac{1}{5} + \frac{1}{6} + \frac{1}{7} + \frac{1}{8} + \cdots$$

But the harmonic series is easily shown to diverge; i.e., the sum can be made as large as you please by adding enough terms.*

> EXERCISE 2. (a) Write a routine to calculate the sum of 1,024 or more terms of the harmonic series by grouping the terms as in the footnote on this page. Print the number of terms in each group, the sum of each group, and the cumulative total of the series. (b) Use the routine of part (a) to show that the harmonic series is indeed divergent and to investigate the behavior of the sum more closely as the number, k, of terms increases. How does the sum of a group vary as k increases? What limit does it seem to approach? Justify this limit by reasoning. Devise an expression which represents the cumulative sum reasonably well when k is large. Discuss what is meant by saying that the sum of k terms of the series approaches the value of this expression asymptotically.

The harmonic series is celebrated for its simplicity and for the slowness of its divergence. Exercises 1 and 2 show that a great many terms must be added for the sum to reach as much as six. This enormous repetition forces us to consider the accuracy of our calculation. Suppose, for example, that we continue with Fortran programming that employs 8-digit floating-point arithmetic and truncates the results (by dropping the less significant figures). Then it is clear that although the Fortran subroutines can calculate the value of individual terms that are as

---

*Grouping terms, we have $1 + (1/2) + (1/3 + 1/4) + (1/5 + 1/6 + 1/7 + 1/8) + (1/9 + 1/10 + 1/11 + 1/12 + 1/13 + 1/14 + 1/15 + 1/16) + \ldots$, which is greater than $1 + 1/2 + 1/2 + 1/2 + 1/2 + \ldots$.

small as 10^{-50} or 10^{-99} (according to the limits of the particular floating-point system in use), they cannot ever add less than 10^{-7} to a sum which begins with 1.0000000. The sum will, therefore, reach a definite value and then stop increasing.

From this point of view, the divergence of the harmonic series appears to be only a sort of mathematical abstraction. When we attempt to calculate the value of the sum, we are forced to use finite arithmetic, and no matter how many decimal places we start with, our result always reaches some finite limiting value (and actually assumes that value). We therefore ask: What is the value calculated for the sum of the harmonic series if 8-figure Fortran arithmetic is used?

The student should consider this question carefully before rushing to the computer, or even before writing a single line of code. Does he plan to go on the machine with a simple routine and add, term-by-term, until he reaches the term that no longer alters the sum? If that term should be the millionth or ten-millionth term, how much machine time would be required? The student should instead apply the sixth principle given in the Introduction: Cut the problem down to size. He might decide after a little important analysis to start out with only five significant figures; or maybe, to assure his success, to limit his first calculations to four significant figures.

> EXERCISE 3. (a) Write a Fortran routine to add each term of the harmonic series to an arbitrary starting value a which can be read in from the typewriter; i.e., form a $1/1 + 1/2 + 1/3 + \cdots$. Provide for subtracting the starting value from the sum when the sum (as calculated by the computer) reaches the limiting value that is forced by the 8-digit arithmetic. (b) Use the routine of part (a) to find the limiting value for the calculated sum of the harmonic series when only 4-figure arithmetic is used. That is, calculate the sum of $10{,}000.000 + (1/1 + 1/2 + 1/3 + 1/4 + \ldots) - 10{,}000.000$. (c) Carry out an investigation similar to that of part (b) for 3-figure arithmetic, and also for 5-figure arithmetic. Estimate the time that would be required for 8-figure arithmetic.

Exercise 3 should have demonstrated clearly the futility of attempting to use the same method to find the limiting value of the calculated sum for the full 8-figure arithmetic of the Fortran

subroutines. The slowness with which the harmonic series di-
verges increases with number of terms. The student can easily
verify that there would be 500,000 terms each equal to 0.000001
if only 6 decimal places were counted.

EXERCISE 4. (a) Explain why only 6-decimal place
accuracy can result for the last half-million terms
of the calculated sum. Calculate by hand the sum of
these terms. (b) Make a calculation by hand or with
a desk calculator to determine the sum of the last
900,000 terms in the calculated sum for the series.
(c) Design a plan for calculating the sum of the harmonic series with full 8-figure Fortran arithmetic.
Write a routine to implement the plan by calculating
the sum of the terms less than 0.000100 but not less
than 0.000001. Modify the routine of Exercise 3 so as
to calculate the sum of the first 10,000 terms. Now
answer the question: What is the limiting value of
the sum calculated by adding the terms of the harmonic series in Fortran 8-figure arithmetic? (d)
Write a short but careful report of your investigations. Compare the situation with that for the con-
verging series for $\log_e 2$:

$$\log_e 2 = \frac{1}{1} - \frac{1}{2} + \frac{1}{3} - \frac{1}{4} + \frac{1}{5} - \cdots$$

and

$$\log_e 2 = 2\left(\frac{1}{1} \cdot \frac{1}{3} + \frac{1}{3} \cdot \frac{1}{3^3} + \frac{1}{5} \cdot \frac{1}{3^5} + \frac{1}{7} \cdot \frac{1}{3^7} + \cdots\right)$$

The divergence of the harmonic series dramatizes an aspect of finite arithmetic that often eludes the student's attention,
although it is a fundamental fact about computer (and most
other) calculations. In the case of the harmonic series, small
values are obtained for the sum by computer calculations, even
though it is known that the sum actually exceeds the largest
number that can be handled in the floating-point system of Fortran (10^{49} or 10^{99}, depending upon the system in use) or any
number that can be named. The student's experience with the
harmonic series should alert him to the possibility that the result of any long calculation with approximate numbers should
be carefully analyzed before it is accepted.

EXERCISE 5. (a) Write a Fortran routine to sum

the series

$$\Sigma \ \frac{n^3}{n^2 + (1.5)^n} \qquad \text{for } n = 1, 2, 3, \ \cdot \ \cdot \ \cdot$$

(b) Suggest a plan for obtaining the sum accurate to 6 decimal places.

EXERCISE 6. (a) Write a short Fortran routine to read in the first term a and the ratio r of a geometric progression. (b) Use the routine of part (a) to investigate truncation errors for various values of a and r, such as a = 10, r = 0.99.

Problem A6

A TABLE OF LOGARITHMS

The packaged function LØG is included in your Fortran system to calculate logarithms whenever they are needed. Contrary to the expectations of some beginners in programming, tables of logarithms (or other elementary functions) are almost never stored in computers for use in computation. The storage space is usually more urgently needed for other things, and even if we could spare the room in storage, we find it quicker to calculate the logarithm than to interpolate in a table.*

The fundamental formula for calculating natural logarithms is

$$\log_e (1 + x) = 1n (1 + x) = x - \frac{x^2}{2} + \frac{x^3}{3} - \frac{x^4}{4} + \cdots$$

This infinite series represents the logarithm exactly for $x \le 1$, but a very large number of terms may be required to give even moderate accuracy.

Your Fortran processor probably uses a polynomial of 4 or 5 terms to calculate logarithms. The following remarkable formula will give 10-figure results with only 5 terms. For x in the range

$$\frac{1}{\sqrt{2}} \le x \le \sqrt{2}$$

and $B = (x - 1)/(x + 1)$,

$$\log_2 x = C_1 B + C_3 B^3 + C_5 B^5 + C_7 B^7$$

where $C_1 = 2.885390072738$
$C_3 = 0.961800762286$

---

*The situation could change, of course, if very large random-access storage became available in our computers.

$C_5 = 0.576584342056$
$C_7 = 0.434259751292$

This approximation is Sheet 42 in the book Approximations for Digital Computers, by Cecil Hastings, Jr. (Princeton University Press, Princeton, N.J., 1955).

Although this formula contains only 4 terms, it is so accurate that the error involved in the approximation is less than 0.0000000002 in absolute value for the logarithm of any number in the given range.

Logarithms to any other base are proportional to the logarithms to the base 2; so that the former can be obtained from the latter simply by multiplying by a constant:

$$\log_{10} N = \frac{\log_2 N}{\log_2 10}$$

$$= 0.3010299957 \cdot \log_2 N$$

EXERCISE 1. (a) Write a short Fortran routine to calculate 4-place logarithms to the base 8. (b) Extend the routine in part (a) to convert the numbers N to octal representation. The logarithms remain in decimal representation, so that our table enables us to multiply or divide octal numbers by using decimal arithmetic. (c) Explain how to find the characteristic for use in your table. (d) Explain how interpolation in this table differs from interpolation in an ordinary table of logarithms.

Although desk calculators and computers have largely supplanted logarithms, practical problems often require the use of a table of logarithms. As a student, you might find it desirable to calculate such a table. Suppose, for example, you wish to calculate a 50-place table of natural logarithms for the integers from 1 to 1,000. This table might prove to be more appropriate for your work than any table that money can buy. In addition, you will have the pleasure of creating your own table.

It should be clear that the polynomial formula is not adequate for 50-place tables. We return to the fundamental series, which is converted for computing purposes to

$$\ln\ (N + 1) = \ln N + 2 \left(\frac{r}{1} + \frac{r^3}{3} + \frac{r^5}{5} + \cdots \right)$$

where $r = 1/(2N + 1)$.

The terms of this series decrease rapidly, so that it is much better suited for actual calculation than the fundamental series.

> EXERCISE 2. Calculate by hand or with a desk calculator the natural logarithms of 2, 3, and 4 to four decimal places. Verify in this way that only a few terms of the series are required. We say that the series "converges rapidly to its sum."

We start with the working part of the routine. In doing so, we define our symbols. We note that each term in the parentheses is equal to the previous power P, multiplied by r^2 and divided by a number D which increases by 2 from term to term. Hence we can start the working part of our routine as in Figure A6.1.

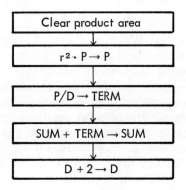

Figure A6.1.

We will need to initialize, and we should test to see when the term just calculated is zero, up to the number of decimal places being calculated. At that point we add twice the value of SUM to the logarithm of integer N to find the logarithm of the next integer, $N + 1$. The flow chart is then something like Figure A6.2.

Since the calculation may require several hours of machine time, it is vital to provide a restart procedure, as indicated.

Before writing the routine, the student should make a number of decisions.

1. How many digits should be reserved for each field? Since each result depends upon all the preceding results, the accumulated round-off error in the 1,000th result could amount

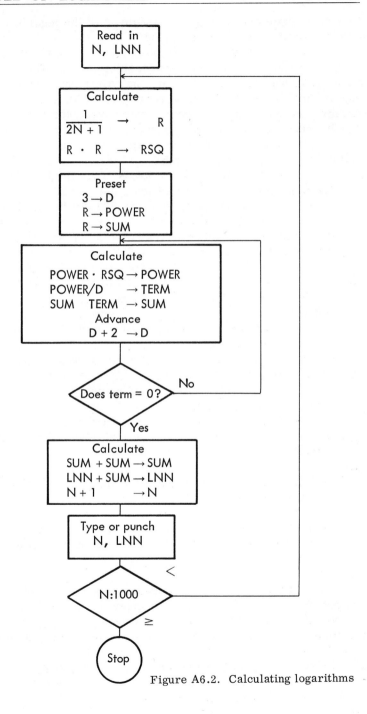

Figure A6.2. Calculating logarithms

to the equivalent of 500 in the last place of the logarithm. Several extra digits should be carried.

2. How many digits should be carried in the testing phase? Since 5-place tables are easily accessible,* a good choice would be 8 digits rounded off to 5 at the end. After thorough debugging and testing, the routine can be reassembled for producing logarithms with 50 decimal places. Alternatively, the length of field can be read in, with the routine making the necessary changes.

3. What kind of check can be made of the 50-place logarithms before starting a production run?

a. log (A · B) = log A + log B. Thus the log of 6 should check as equal to the sum of log 2 and log 3.

b. The logarithms of 960 and 972 can be obtained from $960 = 2^6 \cdot 3 \cdot 5$ and $972 = 2^2 \cdot 3^5$ as soon as the logarithms of 2 · 3 and 5 have been calculated. These values can be used to check a run from 960 to 972.

c. A short run can be made to produce 56-place (or greater) logarithms of numbers from 2 to 7. Then these can be combined to form logarithms as check points between 10 and 1,000.

4. Should provisions be made to calculate common logarithms under switch control?

5. Shall the results be typed at once, or would it be preferable to punch them for later typing?

a. Consider interruptions and control of printing format for 50 sheets of results.

b. Anticipate further use of a card deck for preparing additional tables with fewer decimal places, or in different format.

EXERCISE 3. (a) Write a routine to calculate 5-place natural logarithms of integers from 1 to 1,000. Allow storage space for easy extension to 50-place logarithms. (b) Extend the routine of part (a) so that common logarithms can be calculated under switch control.

The student who has prepared at least one table of logarithms for himself is ready to consider how to improve the method previously suggested to see whether large savings in machine time can be effected. By experimenting with various

---

*Mathematical Tables from Handbook of Chemistry and Physics, Chemical Rubber Publishing Company, Cleveland, Ohio, 1964.

substitutions for r, such as r = 3/(2N + 3), he will see how he can skip integers. For example, he might omit the logarithms of all even numbers, since these can easily be obtained from the others by adding the logarithm of 2. He might even limit his calculations to logarithms of primes.

> EXERCISE 4. (a) Devise a plan for calculating the logarithms of all numbers which are not divisible by 2 or 3, by sweeping the interval from 1 to 1,000 twice. This reduces the calculation two-thirds. (b) Extend the plan to complete the table by simple addition, punching out two new cards for each one in the original deck. Include a method for easily arranging the cards in sequence if a card sorter is not accessible. (c) The previous method has selected one-third of the integers including all the primes. Discuss several difficulties which would be encountered in trying to limit calculations to the primes alone, thus selecting about one-sixth of the integers from 1 to 1,000. Show that the point of diminishing returns seems to have been reached with one-third of the integers.

A somewhat different approach to the problem of improving the method for calculating a table of logarithms is to apply the series to obtain the logarithms for every twentieth integer and then to build up the table for intermediate integers by adding differences.

We think of the known logarithms as widely spaced points on the graph of y = ln N, as shown in Figure A6.3. We wish to complete the graph by plotting the intermediate points. By applying the methods described in Problem A1 to the fundamental logarithmic series, it can be shown that the exact slope of the curve for the point whose abscissa is N is $1/N$. By choosing small values of DN, we can proceed smoothly from one integer to the next by many small steps which follow the curve very closely. We continue in this way until a check point is reached.

Our procedure differs from that in building up a table of squares from second differences in an important way. In that problem the differences are exact, so that it is not necessary to calculate check points and interpolate the intermediate points. Here the interpolation is an approximation to the curve, so that the check points are important. Nevertheless, the idea of calculating values for a few points and then subtabulating has had

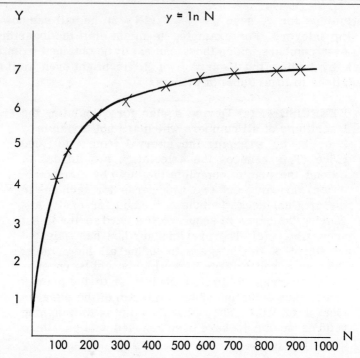

Figure A6.3. The logarithmic curve: (Every 100th point is shown, instead of every 20th point)

widespread application in the calculation of tables of many different kinds, and has resulted in tremendous savings in the time required to calculate tables.

EXERCISE 5. (a) Write a routine to calculate 5-place natural logarithms for every twentieth integer from 20 to 1,000. Then calculate points along the curve at intervals corresponding to DN = 0.1. Punch out cards for integral values of N. (b) Modify the routine to use the average of the slopes at successive points for the interval between those points.

Problem A7

FACTORIALS AND SUBFACTORIALS

Can you use the computer to prepare a table of factorials or subfactorials?

Each factorial, n!, can be expressed in terms of the preceding factorial; i.e., we have a recursion formula:

$$n! = n \cdot (n - 1)!$$

Thus we have

$1! = 1$	$5! = 1 \cdot 2 \cdot 3 \cdot 4 \cdot 5$
$2! = 1 \cdot 2$	$\cdot$
$3! = 1 \cdot 2 \cdot 3$	$\cdot$
$4! = 1 \cdot 2 \cdot 3 \cdot 4$	$\cdot$
	$n! = 1 \cdot 2 \cdot 3 \cdots n$

The formula suggests that a computer would be very appropriate to calculate factorials because the task involves the sort of simple repetition for which the computer is so well adapted.

The working part of the computer routine will consist of a single step. If we use the abbreviation NFAC to represent factorial N, we may write

$$N \cdot NFAC \rightarrow NFAC$$

The statement shows how to calculate the new value of NFAC (for "factorial" and for "N") from the previous value, and also directs that the new value is to replace the old one in storage, as shown in Figure A7.1.

The next step is to type or punch the result and increase N so that it will be ready for the next calculation. The student should note that we have started with the working part of the routine. Now we go back to write the preparatory steps that lead up to the working part. This order of procedure contributes to efficient and logical thinking and prevents many errors. We shall start with a value of 1 for NFAC and a value

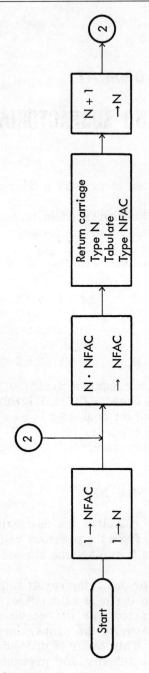

Figure A7.1. Calculation of factorials

of 1 for N.* It is convenient to use replacement statements for setting these initial values, even though NFAC and N might be said to have no earlier values to replace. We now have the complete plan shown in Figure A7.1.

The student may be tempted to omit the initialization step, relying upon values read in (that is, loaded) for N and NFAC. This would be poor programming practice. If the routine is interrupted, the operator will expect to start over without reloading the routine, but the values for N and NFAC are no longer the starting values. All routines should be initialized by programming.**

> EXERCISE 1. (a) Write a routine to carry out the plan shown in Figure A7.1. Allow a 20-digit field for NFAC, with a record mark following it, to stop typing during output. Use a 5-digit field for N and provide a record mark after it also. (b) Use the routine of part (a) to prepare a table of factorials. How far will the routine go without error?

The routine of Exercise 1 was limited to small numbers. If the student having access to a variable field length machine, such as the IBM 1620, wishes to extend the table further, he can capitalize on the machine's ability to handle large numbers directly. Provision must be made to deal with such numbers properly; for example, a large product area must be cleared to zero prior to each multiplication. In typing the results, it will be necessary to suppress the typing of high-order zeros, and so on.

> EXERCISE 2. (a) Modify the routine of Exercise 1 to allow for calculating and typing large factorials. (b) Consider what modifications would have to be made in the routine to include a restart procedure so that a long table could be prepared in several (interrupted) machine runs.

The preceding exercises have been designed to prepare a table of consecutive factorials. To calculate the value of an isolated factorial is something else again.

---

*The student should see that this is equivalent to using 1 as the value of factorial zero.

**Or, at the least, by positive action (such as reading in starting values) rather than being initialized by loading.

EXERCISE 3. (a) Modify the routine of Exercise 2 so as to read in, under switch control, the value m of the first N for which the result is to be printed. What value should be preset for m so that the routine will operate properly if this option is not exercised? (b) Improve the routine of part (a), if necessary, so that increasing values of m may be typed in, one at a time, without requiring the routine to start over with the calculations.

A subfactorial is formed in two steps from the previous subfactorial. Using !N for subfactorial N, we have as a recursion formula

$$!N = N \cdot !(N - 1) + (-1)^N$$

with subfactorial zero defined as unity. We would express the rule in words by saying that in order to obtain subfactorial N, you multiply the previous subfactorial by N, and then add or subtract 1 according to whether N is even or odd. Starting with 1, we would have

$$!1 = 1 \cdot 1 - 1 = 0 \qquad\qquad !4 = 4 \cdot 2 + 1 = 9$$
$$!2 = 2 \cdot 0 + 1 = 1 \qquad\qquad !5 = 5 \cdot 9 - 1 = 44$$
$$!3 = 3 \cdot 1 - 1 = 2$$

As you might guess from their name, the subfactorials remain less than the factorials, growing at a slightly smaller rate. Another expression for the subfactorial function shows its relation to factorials. Using the symbol $\Sigma_{r=0}^{N}$ to show the sum of the terms formed as r takes on all integral values from 0 to N, we can also write

$$!N = N! \sum_{r=0}^{N} \frac{(-1)^r}{r!}$$

where 0! is taken as equal to 1.

$$!N = N! \left[1 - \frac{1}{1!} + \frac{1}{2!} - \frac{1}{3!} + \frac{1}{4!} - \cdots + (-1)^N \cdot \frac{1}{N!} \right]$$

At this writing, no table of subfactorials beyond !20 has yet appeared in print. Their calculation consequently offers an

attractive project for a student who is looking for something
new.

The test for even or odd values of N, which is needed for
calculating subfactorials, is easy if the product N · 5 is formed
first. Another way to calculate successive terms is to multiply
the addend by (−1) after each calculation.

> EXERCISE 4. (a) Show by mathematical induction that
> the given series is equivalent to the previous def-
> inition of subfactorial N. (b) Write a routine for
> calculating large subfactorials.

The student should make careful provision for a restarting
procedure whenever the execution of the routine can be antic-
ipated to require large amounts of machine time. If he expects
to set new records in this problem, he should arrange to read
in the starting value for the subfactorials and the next value of
N. Then he can continue his production run at odd times whenever the machine is available. He will want to read in the
number of digits in the starting value so that he can set the
address correctly in a read instruction as well as in the output
instruction. He should also consider increasing the number of
digits allowable in the multiplier and the number of places cleared
for the product.

> EXERCISE 5. Make the necessary changes in the rou-
> tine of Exercise 4 to provide an effective restarting
> procedure.

> EXERCISE 6. (a) Modify the routine of Exercise 5
> so as to punch or print the results under switch
> control. (b) Extend the routine of part (a) so that
> it can be used, under switch control, to print or
> punch isolated values as in Exercise 3.

Problem A8

THE ANTIFREEZE PROBLEM

An automobile radiator holds 22 quarts. It is filled with a 60 per cent solution of antifreeze. How many quarts of the solution should be drained and replaced with pure antifreeze to bring the strength up to 70 per cent?

This is not a computer problem. For one thing, there is almost no computation to be done. For another, it is strictly a one-shot affair. And by the time the analysis of it is done, the problem is over. Let's analyze it anyway, in the traditional way of the freshman algebra class.* The situation is as pictured in Figure A8.1.

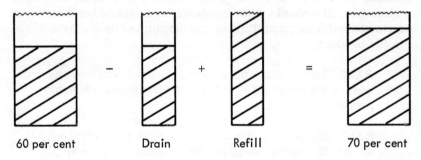

| 60 per cent | Drain | Refill | 70 per cent |

Figure A8.1. The antifreeze picture

We recall that the problem situation must be translated into an equation and that such an equation must have the same units in every term. We choose to write the equation in terms of quarts of antifreeze. Following Figure A8.1 directly, we have

$$0.60(22) - 0.60(x) + x = 0.70(22)$$

---

*Note that we are suggesting analysis, not programming. There is often strong pressure to "put it on the computer" when the problem is not a good computer problem at all. There is seldom any need to create work for a computer.

from which we can calculate the answer, 5 1/2 quarts.

The problem has three parameters: the size of the radiator, the starting concentration, and the ending concentration. If we call them A, B, and C respectively, the solution can be generalized

$$B \cdot A - Bx + x = C \cdot A$$

and solved for x in terms of the parameters:

$$x = \frac{A(C - B)}{100 - B}$$

It is clear that A is not an important parameter. Solutions can be calculated for a range of values of B and C and applied to any size radiator by one multiplication (in much the same way that compound-interest tables are all expressed in terms of one dollar).

Now we are beginning to see a computing problem. We can calculate a double-valued table in this form: To go from the concentration B (left scale of the table) to the concentration C (top scale), drain and replace by the amount indicated in the body of the table. The table will be triangular, since the problem is stated in terms of increasing the concentration only.

The resulting table would be of little practical value, since it would call for adding amounts such as 5.83 quarts. Antifreeze is usually sold only in whole quarts. The figures in the table must be adjusted up to the nearest integer. (If a final multiplication by A is to be made, then the rounding should be done on the final figure.) To do that in a system like Fortran can be a small problem by itself (see Problem J1).

With rounded figures, the table is of practical value; such tables are furnished by gasoline companies as an aid to motorists.

Problem A9

COMEDIES IN ERRORS

Most beginning programmers are delighted by the convenience of the Fortran programming system, which offers not only floating-point arithmetic but also the built-in functions, logarithms and antilogarithms (exponentials), sine, cosine, and arctangent. How good are the results produced by the various Fortran subroutines? Is the standard 8-place accuracy adequate for all practical calculations, so that the routines are foolproof, or must you avoid certain critical situations? Are the results actually accurate to 8 places? If not, are the values of one function, such as sine, equally accurate over the entire range of the function?

The student will find it entertaining as well as instructive to investigate these questions by actually using the computer. The following exercises are intended merely to whet the student's curiosity and to lead him into further explorations.

Since much of this investigation can be carried out with very simple routines, the IBM 1620 load-and-go version of Fortran known as GOTRAN may be appropriate.

In 1620 Fortran, the trigonometric functions are calculated for an argument (angle) expressed in radians. We know that the sine of 30 degrees is 0.50000000 exactly, but we cannot express 30 degrees in radians precisely. Is it possible to obtain the value of sin 30 correct to 8 digits with the 8-place Fortran subroutines?

> EXERCISE 1. (a) The value of $\pi/6$ is 0.523598775598, correct to 12 decimal places. Write a short Fortran routine to type out the values of sin x for x_1 = 0.52359877 and x_2 = 0.52359878. (b) Extend the routine of part (a) to interpolate, between the two values obtained, in an attempt to attain 0.50000000 with a Fortran routine. Explain the result. The sine of $13\pi/6$ (and all multiples of 2π more) should be the same (mathematically) as sine $\pi/6$. Are they?

40

EXERCISE 2. (a) Write a Fortran routine, as given in Exercise 1, to increase x_1 and x_2 by 2π repeatedly and type out the sines of the resulting angles. The value of 2π is 6.283185307179. (b) Improve the accuracy of the arguments by writing 2π as 6.2831 + 0.000085307179 and the other approximate numbers in the same style. Then have the routine add the least significant portions first and round off to 8 digits by adding 0.00000005 before combining (by addition) with the most significant portion. Finally, calculate the sines for $x_1 + 2n\pi$ and $x_2 + 2n\pi$ (n = 0, 1, 2, . . .), printing two angles and their sines on the same line.

The previous exercises involved errors in introducing the value of the angle. If we use an exact value, can we expect accuracy to 8 figures? For example, will $\sin^2 B + \cos^2 B$ turn out exactly 1.0000000 for random values of B?

EXERCISE 3. (a) Write a short Fortran routine to read in a value for B and to calculate and type the sum of $\sin^2 B$ and $\cos^2 B$. (b) As an alternative to reading in the values for B, rewrite the routine of part (a) so as to use the random number generator of Problem E7 to generate values at random and then to calculate $\sin^2 B + \cos^2 B$, typing the values of B, sin B, cos B, and $\sin^2 B + \cos^2 B$ on the same line.

The logarithms and antilogarithms furnished by Fortran are the natural logarithms and antilogarithms. The antilogarithm of y is therefore the same as e^y. This accounts for the symbol EXP(Y) used in Fortran. Will calculating $y = \log(x)$ and $x = \exp(y)$ always return to the original value of x? If not, is the error larger for larger values of x? If so, is the <u>percentage</u> error the same up to the largest values of x which can be used with your Fortran processor? Are the results the same if the Fortran statement is written $z = x^{1.0}$? Similarly, is $\log(e^x)$ equal to x up to the largest x for which e^x can be calculated by your Fortran processor?

EXERCISE 4. (a) Write a short Fortran routine to read in values of x and to calculate and type the value of $z = e^{(\log x)}$. Use the routine to investigate the questions suggested. (b) Write a short Fortran rou-

tine to read in values of x and to calculate and type
$z = x^{1 \cdot 0}$ Compare with the results of part (a), and
explain the outcome of the comparision in terms of the
methods used by your Fortran subroutines. What
would be the result of calculating $z = x^1$? (c) Write
a very short Fortran routine to calculate the largest
value of x for which e^x can be evaluated by your
Fortran processor. Then write a short routine to calculate $z = \log (e^x)$. Use the routine to investigate the
questions suggested above.

A spectacular demonstration of the power of the computer
and of the uncertainties in the results that can be obtained with
it may be based upon the simple formula for the sum of the
cubes of the first K positive integers:

$$s = \frac{K^2 (K + 1)^2}{4}$$

If we generate the successive integers by the replacement
equation

$$x = x + 1$$

we should get exactly the same result whether we actually calculate and sum the cubes or apply the formula, provided that
the intermediate and final results do not exceed 8 figures. Is
the statement true for larger values of K? Returning to smaller
values of K, suppose we calculate the successive integers by
some such elaborate method as

$x = \ln e^{x+1}$, or

$x = \tan^{-1} (\sin (x + 1)/\cos (x + 1))$, or

$x = \left(\ln e^{x+1} \cdot \tan^{-1} \frac{\sin(x + 1)}{\cos(x + 1)} \right)^{1/2}$, or

$x = \frac{1}{3} \tan^{-1} \left[\frac{3 \sin (x + 1) \cos^2 (x + 1) - \sin^3 (x + 1)}{\cos^3 (x + 1) - 3 \sin^2 (x + 1) \cos(x + 1)} \right]$

The true value of $1^3 + 2^3 + \cdots + 50^3$ is easily calculated by
the formula: It is 1,625,625. What result would be obtained if
you used one of the above methods to calculate each value of x?

Or if you used three different methods to find each value of x and multiplied the three results to obtain x^3 ?

Before you write any such routine, make a guess of the range within which you expect the calculated sum to lie, and write it down. Also obtain estimates from your classmates and from professional engineers and mathematicians whose judgment is highly respected in your community. Do not neglect to obtain an estimate from a programmer experienced with Fortran.

> EXERCISE 5. (a) Write a careful Fortran routine to calculate the values of x according to one or more of the given formulas. Then calculate the value of x^3 and the sum of 50 cubes. Arrange to type, under switch control, representative intermediate results. Design your output to demonstrate in the most spectacular way the tremendous amount of calculation being performed by the computer. Arrange to withhold the successive values of x, however, for a first demonstration, until the final sum has been printed and compared with the estimates made beforehand. (b) Vary the method used in part (a), letting your imagination run wild, but demonstrate clearly both the tremendous calculating power of the computer and the uncertainties introduced in the results when the methods become long and complicated.

When $x = \pi (162)^{1/2}$, exponentiating x produces the remarkable number $e^x = 262537412640768743.999999999999250$. Would you expect your Fortran processor to produce the first 8 digits of this result? Could you calculate the 33-digit number with your computer?

> EXERCISE 6. (a) Write a short Fortran routine to calculate $z = \exp (\pi (163)^{1/2})$. Compare the result with the number given. (b) Using fixed-point routines calculate the value of e^x for $x = \pi (163)^{1/2}$ correct to 35 decimal places. The value of π to 40 places is 3.1415926535897932384626433832795028841971.

Problem A10

THE BOUNCING BALL

A bouncing ball represents a physical situation that can be simulated approximately by a very simple mathematical model. Then we have a source of many interesting problems. The solution of these relatively simple problems introduces computing techniques that can be applied later to the complicated and specialized problems that arise in industry and engineering. Since the answers to some of the problems concerning a bouncing ball can be obtained by algebraic methods to any desired degree of accuracy, the student will also gain a valuable insight into the round-off errors involved in computer solutions, especially with the floating-point operations used in Fortran.

We replace the actual ball by a mathematical point (x, y) whose vertical acceleration is -32.16 feet per second per second, and whose horizontal acceleration is zero. That is to say, its velocity upward decreases 32.16 feet per second per second, or its velocity downward increases that much, while its horizontal velocity is constant. When the point reaches the x-axis, its vertical velocity is reversed in direction and reduced to 60 per cent of its previous value. This mathematical model will give us results which agree closely with the results of experiment, although many small effects have been disregarded.

Now we consider a ball that is dropped straight downward from a tower 102 feet high and rebounds each time to 36 per cent of its previous height.

> EXERCISE 1. (a) Write a Fortran routine to calculate the total distance traveled by the ball before coming to rest. (b) Use an analytic method to find the total distance as twice the sum of a geometric series, increased by the initial height. (c) Enumerate five or six small effects neglected in the mathematical model, in addition to the rotation of the earth, variations in the radius of the earth, influence of nearby mountain masses, and the like. (d) Show that the 36 per cent rebound agrees with the assumption

made in the problem about the loss in vertical velocity.

Next we add a touch of realism by tossing the ball straight outward with a speed of 5 feet per second so that it will clear the base of the tower.

EXERCISE 2 (a). Write a routine to calculate the total time until the ball reaches the ground for the fifth time and calculate how far it travels horizontally in that time. Solve the formula s = $\frac{1}{2}$gt^2 (g = 32.16 feet per second per second) algebraically for t before starting your flow chart. (b) Make a rough calculation by hand to determine the horizontal distance traveled, using h = 102 feet for the height of the tower and g = 32 feet per second per second. (c) Show algebraically that the graph of y = 102 − $\frac{1}{2}$g(x/5)^2 illustrates the path of the ball up to the first bounce. (d) Use a desk calculator to calculate the distance accurately to 8 significant figures, and compare with the computer solution. Explain the differences.

The student will recognize that the bouncing ball follows a series of parabolic arcs. We wish to write a routine to calculate points on that path. The technique we now illustrate is applicable to an enormous number of practical problems which do not appear to be geometric at all. We shall therefore adopt a useful abbreviation.

We plan to calculate the value of x and y for equally spaced intervals of the time t. We shall use the abbreviation d_x for the difference between successive values of x, and d_y for the difference between successive values of y. For simplicity, we shall write and type these as DX and DY. Similarly we shall write DT for the difference between successive values of the time t.

Since the horizontal velocity is constantly equal to 5 feet per second, DX = 5DT. If the horizontal velocity is H, we have DX = H · DT. The vertical velocity decreases from V to (V − 32.16DT) during any interval DT between points, so that the average vertical velocity during that interval is V − 16.08DT. The distance traveled upward during the interval is the average velocity times the time elapsed. Hence

$$DY = (V - 16.08DT)DT \quad \text{or} \quad DY = (V - 16.08DT)DT$$

Starting with any given values of X, Y, V, and T, we can calculate the changes by these three equations and then replace

$$X \text{ by } X + DX$$
$$Y \text{ by } Y + DY$$
$$T \text{ by } T + DT$$

to obtain the next point. In Fortran programming, replacement of one value of a variable with another is indicated by the equals sign, giving a so-called Fortran replacement equation. The working part of our routine is now:

$$DX = H*DT$$
$$DY = (V - 16.08*DT)*DT$$
$$X = X + DX$$
$$Y = Y + DY$$
$$V = V - 32.16*DT$$
$$T = T + DT$$

We shall need to initialize the variables and to make a test to determine when the ball strikes the ground. For the moment of impact we need to reverse the direction of V and reduce it by multiplying the negative of the rebound ratio R. A further test needs to be made at this time to determine when the five arcs have been completed. We use a variable, CNTR, for this purpose. Then we have a flow chart somewhat like Figure A10.1.

EXERCISE 3. Write a Fortran routine to calculate points on the path of the bouncing ball.

EXERCISE 4. Incorporate in your routine the Fortran subroutine to plot the path of the bouncing ball. Alternatively, incorporate the subroutine in your Fortran processor, and call upon it with your routine.

The bouncing ball problem can be displayed as an attractive demonstration with mildly competitive aspects. The object of a game is to choose a height so as to bounce the ball with a given number of bounces into a hole 2 feet across whose center is 40 feet from the base of the tower.

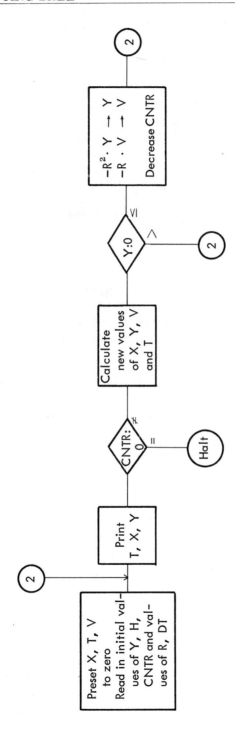

Figure A10.1. Flow chart for the bouncing ball problem

EXERCISE 5. Modify the bouncing ball routine so as to print out a message upon success or failure to bounce the ball into the hole. Messages can also be typed calling for the input data.

EXERCISE 6. Modify the bouncing ball routine so that the computer bounces the ball accurately into the middle of the hole under control of a console switch, after a miss or near miss by a player. Note that the initial height is directly proportional to the square of the horizontal distance.

The same technique can be employed to find the total distance traveled by the ball along the parabolic arcs. If the points are close together, the path between any two points, P and Q, approximates a straight line, as in Figure A10.2.

The length PQ is then given by $d_x^2 + d_y^2$.

Since the total length obtained in this way will depend upon the spacing of the points, it is desirable to make the computation two or more times with decreasing values of d_t. A comparison of results usually gives a good indication of the accuracy of the result accepted.

EXERCISE 7. (a) Write a Fortran routine to obtain the total distance traveled by the bouncing ball as measured along the parabolic arcs. Provide a special procedure for the broken arcs surrounding a bounce point. (b) Modify your routine to provide for at least two calculations with decreasing d_t.

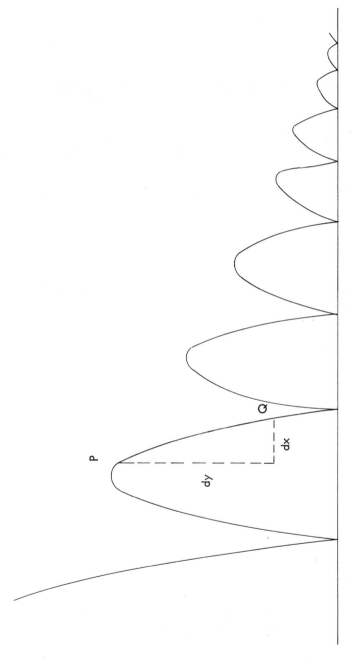

Figure A10.2. The bouncing ball.

Problem A11

SQUARE ROOT OF A NUMBER

How would you use a computer to find the square root of a number? There are many algorithms for extracting square root. Since most square roots are irrational, all methods involve successive approximations, a procedure for which the computer is ideally suited. Hence this problem is an excellent one to illustrate the essential characteristics of calculations made with computers.

We simplify the problem to begin with by assuming that the number whose square root we seek is between 0 and 1.* Then we make our first method depend upon the definition of square root. We start with the trial root x = 0.1. If $x^2 \leq N$, we increase the trial value by 0.1. If $x^2 > N$, we return to the previous value of x. This is the first digit of the root. Now we start advancing by 0.01. Continuing in the same way, we develop one digit of the root at a time until we reach the precision desired.

This first method is outlined in the flow chart of Figure A11.1. It is convenient to start with x = 0 but increase it at once by 0.1 before making the first test. We can describe this step briefly as

$$\text{Set } x = 0 \quad \text{or} \quad 0 \rightarrow x$$

The difference in successive values of x is represented by DX, which we may read as "the difference in x," "the x-difference," or simply "dee ex." Since its initial value is 0.1, we write

$$0.1 \rightarrow DX$$

The value for the radicand N is to be read in from the

---

*This assumption is not a serious restriction and is made for many square root algorithms. It implies merely that the algorithm will seek the square root sequence of digits corresponding to the given sequence. Thus, in terms of sequences alone, $(5)^{1/2} = (500)^{1/2} = (0.05)^{1/2} = (0.00005)^{1/2} = 22360679774997897$.

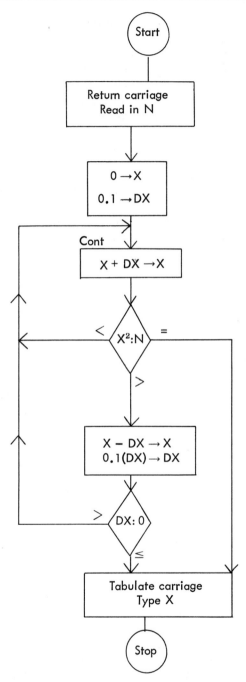

Figure A11.1. Simple routine for extracting square root

typewriter. A new line is started on the paper by returning the typewriter carriage.

The working part of the routine consists of two loops, one inside the other. The inner loop increases X by D X and then compares X^2 with N. The single statement $X^2 : N$ actually represents three instructions, as follows:

$$
\begin{array}{ll}
\text{M} & \text{X, X} \\
\text{C} & \text{PROD, N} \\
\text{BL} & \text{CONT}
\end{array}
$$

where PROD refers to the product area, with field address 00099. This program is repeated until X^2 is no longer less than N. If X^2 becomes equal to N, control is transferred to the output instructions. If X^2 becomes greater than N, X is restored to the next previous value. The value of DX is decreased to one-tenth of its current value. Then DX is compared with zero. If it is equal to zero (to the number of decimal places being carried), the routine advances to the output instructions. If DX is not yet zero, control returns to the box marked CONT (for continue). That box is therefore the beginning of the outer loop as well as the beginning of the inner loop.

> EXERCISE 1. (a) Write a routine to read in a 10-digit decimal fraction (with field mark) from the type-writer and to calculate a 5-digit square root according to the plan in Figure A11.1. (b) Modify the routine of part (a) so that a 6-digit square root is calculated and afterward rounded off to 5 digits by adding 5 to the 6th digit and then dropping that digit.

> EXERCISE 2. (a) Explain how the routine of Exercise 1(b) can be modified to extract the square root of any integer from 1 to 99. (b) Rewrite the routine of Exercise 1(b) so as to calculate to 4 decimal places the square roots of the integers from 1 to 99 and print each integer and its square root on the same line.

The routines already discussed apply the definition directly to calculate successive approximations to the square root of a number. The procedure was simple but highly inefficient in several ways. For example, each new trial required a complete new multiplication in order to calculate its square. As shown in Figure A11.2, the squares of consecutive integers can be calculated easily by adding. Since it requires less computer time to make two additions than to complete one multiplication, the execution of the routine would be speeded up by this improvement alone.

X	X^2	$D(X^2)$
0	0.00	0.01
0.1	0.01	0.03
0.2	0.04	0.05
0.3	0.09	0.07
0.4	0.16	0.09
0.5	0.25	0.11
0.6	0.36	0.13
0.7	0.49	0.15
0.8	0.64	0.17
0.9	0.81	

Figure A11.2. Plan for calculating a table of squares by addition

However, a little thought and experimentation will show that the calculation of the squares can be combined with the comparison test to shorten the routine greatly.

> EXERCISE 3. (a) Show that subtracting from N the successive odd numbers shown in the column headed $D(X^2)$ is equivalent to comparing N with the square of 0.1, 0.2, 0.3, . . . , 0.9 in turn. (b) Write a short code to determine the first figure of the square root of N by repeated addition and subtraction.

The method suggested in Exercise 3 is the machine equivalent of the first step in a common method for extracting square roots by hand. It can be found in manuals for desk calculators, where it is called the "1-3-5" or "odd number" method. In such a manual the student can find the rest of this method for extracting square roots with a desk calculator.

> EXERCISE 4. (a) Construct a careful flow chart for calculating the square root of a number by adapting the odd number method to machine calculation.
> (b) Complete the routine started in Exercise 3 to calculate the square root of a 10-digit decimal fraction by the odd number method.

The student has learned from Exercise 4 that the hand method for extracting the square root of a number is simplified when it is applied to a desk calculator or electronic computer. This simplification is attained at the cost of adding a considerable number of simple, repetitive steps. The remarkable ability of the computer to perform simple, repetitive steps at very high speed enables the root to be extracted in a very short time. The square root problem thus demonstrates an important difference between hand calculations and calculations for the computer: Simple, repetitive steps play a decisive role in most computer routines.

A still shorter routine for extracting the square root of a number can be designed by a special application of Newton's method* to the equation $X^2 = N$. If X_1 represents a trial root, we form the quotient $Y = N/X_1$. Then a better approximation, X_2, is obtained for the square root of N by averaging X and Y: $X_2 = (X_1 + Y)/2$. The new trial root X_2 can now be used to continue the process until X_2 and X_1 agree to the number of decimal places required.

> EXERCISE 5. (a) Using a division subroutine (if the special DIVIDE feature is not installed on the machine), write a routine to determine the square root of a 10-digit decimal fraction by Newton's method. Use 0.2 as a first trial root. (b) Adapt the routine of part (a) to extract the square root of any number from 1 to 99,999. Use $2 + (N/200)$ as a first trial root.

> EXERCISE 6. (a) Rewrite the routine of Exercise 5(a) as a subroutine. (b) Write a careful report documenting your subroutine, so that other persons at the computer installation can make use of it. Include:

> (1) Title
> (2) Programmer, date
> (3) Programming language used
> (4) Purpose
> (5) Calling sequence
> (6) Operating procedure, including other subroutines required
> (7) Description of method, including a reference to some textbook or magazine article (If an original method, give complete proof of its validity.)
> (8) Block diagram or flow chart
> (9) Program coding

---

*Explained in Problem A3.

(10) Sample case with machine results
(11) Card deck
(12) Estimate of execution, time, number of iterations required for various values of N, and the like
(13) Discussion of accuracy for various values of N

When floating-point arithmetic is used, as in Fortran, the square root of a number is extracted by using a subroutine that calls upon the logarithm and antilogarithm (exponential) subroutines of the system.

> EXERCISE 7. (a) Write a short Fortran routine to read in the area of a circle and to calculate the radius of the circle. (b) Elaborate the routine of part (a) to calculate the radius for areas 10(1)100; that is for each area from 10 to 100, increasing by 1 for each new circle.

A curious algorithm for extracting the square root of a number appears in mathematical and computing magazines from time to time. This method has been discovered and rediscovered several times in the past two decades. Although it is not an efficient method for extracting the square root of a number, it furnishes some interesting and informative exercises in the study of iterative processes.

The method depends upon the simple quadratic equation

$$X^2 - X + M = 0$$

We write the equation in the form

$$X = X^2 + M$$

That gives us a formula for X in terms of X itself. If X is less than 1, so that X^2 is smaller than X, we may use a trial value X_1 for X on the right-hand side and sometimes obtain a closer value X_2 to one root of the equation. That is, $X_2 = (X_1)^2 + M$. We can continue the process, obtaining

$$X_2 = (X_1)^2 + M$$
$$X_3 = (X_2)^2 + M$$
$$X_4 = (X_3)^2 + M$$

$$X_5 = (X_4)^2 + M$$
$$\vdots$$

In general, we write: $X_{n+1} = (X_n)^2 + M$. This is called a recurrence relation or recursion. We have used such relations in earlier methods of this problem and shall use them in other problems.

The roots of the equation $X^2 - X + M = 0$ are

$$X = \frac{1 \pm \sqrt{1 - 4M}}{2}$$

If we let $N = 1 - 4M$, then

$$X = \frac{1 - \sqrt{N}}{2}$$

and $(N)^{1/2} = 1 - 2X$. Solving for M, we have $M = (1 - N)/4$. Now we have the algorithm:

To find N, calculate $M = (1 - N)/4$. Then solve $X_{n+1} = (X_n)^2 + M$, starting with a suitable value X_0 and continuing until $X_{n+1} = X_n$ approximately to the required number of decimal places. Finally calculate N from $N = 1 - 2X$.

It is clear from reasoning or experiment that the process will not converge (lead toward a definite value) unless $X < 1$. Hence N must also be less than 1, as in some of the preceding methods. The student will be challenged in the exercise to investigate other conditions for convergence and the number of iterations (repetitions) required. Suppose we take $N = 0.17$ as an example and choose $X_0 = 0$. Then we get the results shown in Figure A11.3.

$$M = \frac{1 - 0.17}{4} = 0.2075$$

$X_{n+1} = X_n^2 + M$	$N \cong 1 - 2X$
$X_1 = 0.2075$	0.5850
$X_2 = 0.2505$	0.4990
$X_3 = 0.2703$	0.4594
$X_4 = 0.2862$	0.4276

$X_5 = 0.2894$	0.4212
$X_6 = 0.2913$	0.4174
$X_7 = 0.2924$	0.4152
$X_8 = 0.2930$	0.4140
$X_9 = 0.2934$	0.4132
$X_{10} = 0.2936$	0.4128

Figure A11.3. Square root of 0.17 by the
"squaring" algorithm

After ten iterations, the square root still differs from the true value of 0.4123 by 0.0005.

The very fact that the "squaring" algorithm for extracting a square root is one of the least efficient known makes it especially suitable for investigating the speed of convergence and its influence on round-off errors. The algorithm is very simple, and is easily coded using either fixed-point or floating-point arithmetic.

EXERCISE 8 (a) Write a routine to extract square roots by using the "squaring" algorithm. Make the starting value a parameter, to be read in from the typewriter. Provide for typing out intermediate results under switch control. (b) Use the routine of part (a) to study the speed of convergence and the accuracy of the "squaring" algorithm. Include the following considerations in your report:

1. What is the safest starting value?

2. Does the largest starting value for which the procedure converges depend upon N? If so, in what way?

3. How many iterations are required to converge to 4-digit accuracy from the safest starting value for various values of N?

4. How many correct digits can be expected in the root if eight digits are used throughout? Explain any apparent paradox which you encounter.

5. How can the correct answer in the example be bracketed (located in a definite interval)?

Problem B1

CURVE PLOTTING

If we wish to draw by hand the graph for an equation like

$$y = 5.142x^3 - 0.897x^2 + 3.145x - 7.250 \qquad (1)$$

we need to evaluate y for a number of values of x, thus giving us the coordinates of some points on the graph. This is easily done with a Fortran routine. (See also Problem A1.)

> EXERCISE 1. (a) Write a subroutine as described in Problem A1 to evaluate the polynomial over the interval from $x = -5$ to $x = +5$, with increments of 1 for x from one point to the next. Arrange to type in the limits and the increment so that they can be varied as may later appear desirable. (b) Plot the graph of the equation by hand.

How does one know that the range in which to plot is from $x = -5$ to $x = +5$? There are two basic assumptions being made in such a choice. First, we assume that the interesting part of the curve is the one involving its changes of direction; in crude terms, the region involving the bumps on the curve. Second, since the coefficients of the cubic are small (whatever that means), the interesting portion of the curve (whatever that means) will be near the origin. This is all highly subjective. It all boils down to experience and intuition, and the choice of range is really just a first approximation, to "get the feel" of the curve. Since we have arranged to enter both the limits and the increment on x as parameters in the plotting routine, we are free to change them as circumstances dictate. (It could develop that we are really interested in the behavior of the curve at $x = 100$, in increments of 0.003.)

For a slightly more complicated equation such as

$$4y - 12x = x^2y \qquad (2)$$

we would first solve algebraically for one variable (if we can)
to produce

$$y = \frac{12x}{4 - x^2} \tag{3}$$

In this case we would want to evaluate y for many more values
of x, to bring out the characteristics of the curve more clearly.
A computer routine will make it easy to calculate 100 or 200
points, so that we sweep over the interval from $x = -10$, say,
to $x = +10$, avoiding $x = +2$.

> EXERCISE 2. (a) Write a short Fortran routine to
> evaluate y as given in Equation (3) for values of x
> from -10 to $+10$ by increments of 0.1. (b) Plot the
> graph of the equation by hand.

The exercises have shown how the computer can be used to
calculate the points for plotting a curve by hand.

The student may wish to consider going a step further to
write a routine that will type out a crude graph on the console
typewriter. It will be convenient to plot the curve with the independent variable x running down the page, so that values of y
for consecutive values of x can be plotted on successive lines
by typing an asterisk at various positions across the page. If
the value of x is typed in the first five positions, about 81 positions are left for plotting y. Hence y must be scaled so that it
falls between -40 and $+40$.

> EXERCISE 3. (a) Write a routine to read in values
> of x and y from cards or tape, and also read in a
> scaling factor to multiply y so that it will not ex-
> ceed 40 in absolute value. Have the routine type the
> values of x at the left margin, and space according
> to the values of y, typing an asterisk to show the
> approximate location of the plotted point. (b) Use
> the routine of part (a) to type a graph of the curve
> in Exercises 1 and 2.

The student should be aware that this process of mechanical
plotting, although neat and pretty, is not efficient. For one thing
it consumes a great deal of computer time, since the typewriter
is a slow device. For another, it is capable of plotting only dis-
crete points for a smooth (that is, continuous) curve.

An equation such as

$$y^2 - 4y = x^3 \qquad (4)$$

can be solved for y to give <u>two</u> values of y for each value of x. To type out these two branches and also to plot far more complicated curves later, it is worth while to convert the plotting routine of Exercise 3 to a Fortran subroutine.

> EXERCISE 4. (a) Speed up the plotting portion of the routine in Exercise 3 by tabulating the typewriter 10 spaces at a time until the value of y is approached. (b) Then convert the plotting portion to a Fortran subroutine similar to the trigonometric function subroutines.

> EXERCISE 5. Write a Fortran routine to plot the semicubical parabola of Equation (4), utilizing your new Fortran PLOT (Y,*) function.

When we come to more complicated curves, the values of x and y are often given by separate equations involving a third variable, or parameter. For example

$$\left. \begin{aligned} x &= t(4 - t) \\ y &= 1/8 \ t^2(9 - t^2) \end{aligned} \right\} \qquad (5)$$

We can think of t as representing time. Then the parametric Equations (5) describe the path of a point which traces out the curve. Curves of this kind demand careful preliminary analysis before the points to be plotted are calculated with a computer. In the case of a single equation giving the relation between y and x, we are guided by simple notions in choosing our values for x.

    1. If the equation is "simple" and the coefficients are "small," then the significant portions (showing the principal characteristics of the curve) will be close to the origin. This relieves us of the duty of using abnormally large values for x.

    2. If we use a fine interval (say 0.1 for x), we can display all the peculiarities of the curve without taking any special care.

When a curve is described parametrically, on the other hand, these comfortable notions cannot be relied on. To show possible zeros, cusps, loops, asymptotes, and other peculiarities, we clearly need to choose values for t carefully. We will usually find that equally spaced values of t do not give equal intervals for x, so that simple plotting by machine becomes impractical.

One approach is to plot x and y against t on the same graph. Since we choose a constant difference for t and the separate equations are simple with small coefficients, we can use the previous comfortable notions for plotting these preliminary curves. Then by observing these separate curves we can decide upon the proper limits for t to show the characteristics of the curve. Of course the actual plotting must yet be done by hand.

> EXERCISE 6. (a) Modify your Fortran plotting function, if necessary, so that different characters can be used for plotting. (b) Write a short Fortran routine to plot x and y against t on the same graph, for Equations (5), using separate characters for x and y. (c) Plot the curve for Equations (5) by hand, from the results of part (b).

Other very interesting curves are given by the following parametric equations:

$$\left. \begin{array}{l} x = t(4 - t^2) \\ y = t^2(4 - t^2) \end{array} \right\} \tag{6}$$

$$\left. \begin{array}{l} x = a(t - \tanh\ t) \\ y = a/\cosh\ t \end{array} \right\} \tag{7}$$

where

$$\cosh t = \frac{e^t + e^{-t}}{2}$$

and

$$\tanh t = \frac{e^t - e^{-t}}{e^t + e^{-t}}$$

Equations (7) represent Schiele's antifriction curve,* about which a great deal has been written. It is one of the curves of pursuit, and is a favorite in puzzle problems. The hyperbolic

---

*Sometimes called the tractrix. An example of a problem that involves the tractrix is the following. A dog is 100 feet due south of a cat. The cat starts running due east at 20 feet per second. The dog runs 30 feet per second, always heading directly toward the cat. At what point will the dog overtake the cat?

cosine and the hyperbolic tangent, as defined above, are easily calculated using Fortran functions.

$$\left. \begin{array}{c} x = \dfrac{4t^2 - 1}{1 - t^3} \\[3mm] y = \dfrac{4t^3 - 1}{1 - t^3} \end{array} \right\} \tag{8}$$

The intriguing curves defined in Equations (6), (7), and (8), and many other curves to be invented and investigated by the student, suggest (as a longer project) a routine to type out the graphs of curves given by parametric equations. In this longer project, it is clear that we will need to obtain equally spaced values of x by interpolating in the table of x against t. Then we can easily calculate the values of y. The student has already discovered from Exercise 6, however, that these more elaborate and interesting curves may have three or four values of y for some values of x. He will therefore find it expedient to prepare a separate table of x against t whenever the successive values of t cause a reversal of the direction in which x is changing. By interpolating in each such table he can find the various values of t (and therefore of y) corresponding to a single value of x. His routine can, of course, be made to type them all on the same line.

EXERCISE 7. (Group project) (a) Write a routine to type a graph for Equation (6). (b) Modify the routine of part (a) to type a graph for Equations (8). (c) Modify the routine of part (a) to type a graph for other parametric equations invented by the members of the group after joint discussion of various proposals.

Problem B2

THE CROSSED LADDERS

Two ladders, one 25 feet long and the other 35 feet long, lean against buildings on opposite sides of an alley, as shown in Figure B2.1. The point at which the ladders cross is 12 feet above the ground. How wide is the alley?

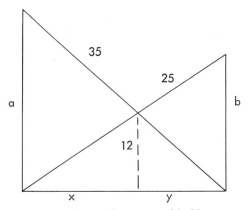

Figure B2.1. The crossed ladders

This is an old problem.* By using similar triangles twice, we can get

$$\frac{12}{a} + \frac{12}{b} = 1 \tag{1}$$

By applying the Pythagorean theorem twice, we obtain

$$a^2 - b^2 = 600 \tag{2}$$

*See, for example, Problem No. 25 in Ingenious Mathematical Problems and Methods by L. A. Graham (Dover Publications, New York, 1959), p. 18. This problem also appears as Exercise 37, Chapter 5, in Numerical Methods and FORTRAN Programming by D. D. McCracken and W. S. Dorn (John Wiley & Sons, New York, 1964), p. 159.

If we can solve these equations, we can find the width z of the alley as

$$z = \sqrt{(35)^2 - a^2}$$

By eliminating b, we obtain the fourth-degree equation

$$a^4 - 24a^3 - 600a^2 + 14400a - 86400 = 0 \qquad (3)$$

which can be solved by the methods of Problem A1.

> EXERCISE 1. (a) Solve Equation (3) by using one of the routines of Problem A1. (b) Use the result of part (a) to calculate the width of the alley.

The traditional approach, already illustrated, is to make the problem depend upon the solution of an equation of fourth degree. A more direct method for numerical solution is suggested by Figure B2.2 in which the graphs of Equations (1) and (2) are drawn on the same axes.

The required values of a and b are given by the intersection of the two lines. By taking advantage of the ease with which formulas are evaluated in Fortran, we simply calculate b for increasing values of a, say in steps of 1.0, according to both Equations (1) and (2); that is,

$$b_1 = \frac{12a}{a - 12}$$

$$b_2 = \sqrt{600 - a^2}$$

When b_1 falls below b_2, we reduce the step to increases of 0.1 in a and obtain a closer approximation. We continue this method of successive approximations until the result is exact, up to the 8-figure accuracy of Fortran arithmetic. It is not necessary to construct the graphs.

> EXERCISE 2. Write a Fortran routine to solve the crossed ladders problem by successive approximations.

The student will find that when problems arise in practical work, a numerical answer is usually required, rather than a formal algebraic solution. He should accustom himself to con-

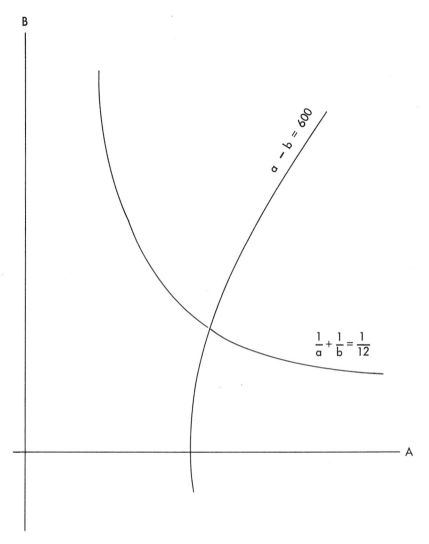

Figure B2.2. The numerical approach

sidering how a computer could be used to get a quick numerical result for problems he encounters in his theoretical subjects. In this way, he is preparing himself to make effective use of his developing programming skills.

Let us show still another approach to the problem which avoids the quartic equation in an ingenious way. We will relabel the drawing as in Figure B2.3.

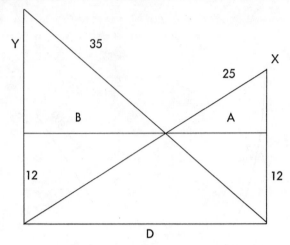

Figure B2.3. Another approach to the Crossed Ladders

We have

$$\frac{x}{12} = \frac{A}{B} = \frac{12}{y}$$

from which $x \cdot y = 144$. Also $(35)^2 - (y + 12)^2 = (25)^2 - (x + 12)^2 = D^2$. Suppose we guess at a value for x and evaluate both sides of the above equation separately.

Try

$$x = 7$$

$$y = \frac{144}{7} = 20.5$$

$$(35)^2 - (y + 12)^2 = 169 \text{ (nearly)}$$

$$(25)^2 - (x + 12)^2 = 264$$

Our guess for x was too small, the guess for y too big. For $x = 7.465$ and $y = 19.29$, the new figures are 245.9 and 246.1. We can continue the cut-and-try process as far as we please, and thus bracket the desired solution to as many decimal places as we want.

EXERCISE 3. Write a routine to solve the crossed ladders problem by the iterative scheme suggested above.

EXERCISE 4. Write a Fortran routine to determine

the longest ladder that can be carried in a horizontal position around the corner made when a 12-foot alley meets one 8 feet wide, as shown in Figure B2.4. Note that similar triangles give the relation

$$\frac{y}{12} = \frac{x}{\sqrt{x^2 - 64}}$$

and that the length L to be maximized is therefore

$$L = x + \frac{12x}{\sqrt{x^2 - 64}}$$

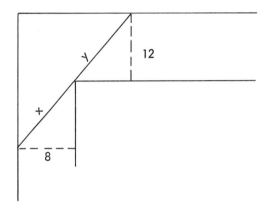

Figure B2.4. The alley corner

NESTING OF TRIANGLES

In analytic geometry, a triangle can be specified by giving the x and y coordinates of each of its three vertexes. In this problem two triangles are specified. Can one triangle fit inside the other?

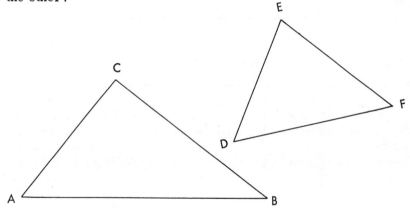

Figure B3.1

This is a long and also a difficult problem. We therefore apply the abstraction principle to cut it down to size. Later we will restore the original problem.

We suppose at first that the two triangles have each been moved so that the vertex of the smallest angle is at the origin and the longest side falls along the positive x-axis. Then they might appear as in Figure B3.2. Since our method involves mathematical formulas, it is appropriate to choose Fortran as the programming language.

We assume as a further simplification that the larger triangle is obtuse. Then we consider three possibilities as shown in Figure B3.3, with two vertexes coinciding and the longest sides falling in the same direction. It is clear from the diagrams in Figure B3.3 that for one triangle to fit inside the other in one of these positions the following conditions must hold:

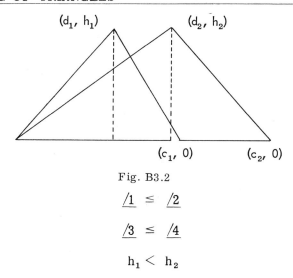

(d_1, h_1) (d_2, h_2)

$(c_1, 0)$ $(c_2, 0)$

Fig. B3.2

$$\underline{/1} \leq \underline{/2}$$

$$\underline{/3} \leq \underline{/4}$$

and

$$h_1 < h_2$$

It is also clear that if the base angles of the smaller triangle are both larger than the corresponding angle of the larger triangle, then the third angle must be smaller than the corresponding angle, and we have the third possibility, where the fit depends upon the altitudes. We do not need to consider solutions with reference to either of the other sides as a base, since the obtuse angle in this simplified case permits us to rotate any possible solution so that the long sides are parallel. Accordingly we arrive at the flow chart of Figure B3.4 for a routine that will give the coordinates of the smaller triangle for some position where it fits inside the larger triangle.

EXERCISE 1. Write a Fortran routine to solve the nesting problem for obtuse triangles.

Now we return to the original statement of the problem in which neither triangle is limited to obtuse triangles, and the triangles are not oriented. We are given (x_1, y_1), (x_2, y_2), (x_3, y_3) for each triangle. We can calculate the length of the sides by the distance formula, which is an application of the right triangle rule.

$$a = \sqrt{(x_1 - x_2)^2 + (y_1 - y_2)^2}$$

$$b = \sqrt{(x_1 - x_3)^2 + (y_1 - y_3)^2}$$

$$c = \sqrt{(x_2 - x_3)^2 + (y_2 - y_3)^2}$$

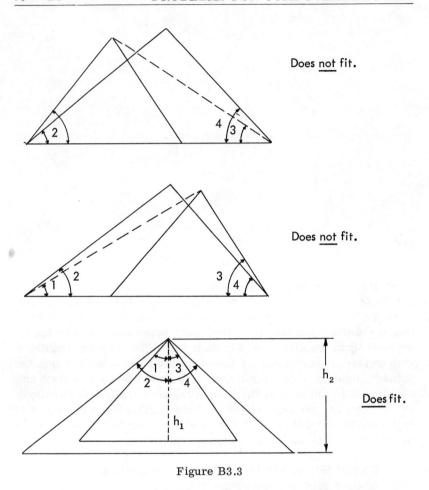

Figure B3.3

We rearrange the sides in order of size, so that (a) is the smallest, (b) is the next largest, and (c) the largest. Then by using Hero's formula and then the Pythagorean formula again we obtain the altitude

$$h_1 = \frac{2 \sqrt{S(S - a)(S - b)(S - c)}}{c}$$

where

$$S = \frac{1}{2}(a + b + c)$$

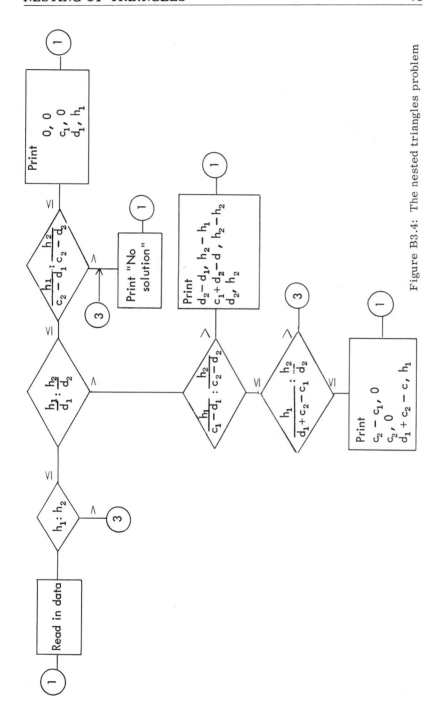

Figure B3.4: The nested triangles problem

and

$$d_1 = \sqrt{b^2 - h_1^2}$$

We shall also need $c_1 - d_1$.

Similarly we calculate h_2, d_2; also $c_2 - d_2$, $c_2 - d_1$, and $c - (c - d)$ or d   c − c . We now apply the method of the simplified problem to determine whether there is a solution with the long sides parallel. If not, we rotate the smaller triangle by the replacements

and try again, this time to see if there is a solution with the middle sides parallel. If not, we rotate the triangle once more and determine whether there is a solution with the short sides parallel. If not, then there is no solution at all.

EXERCISE 2. Write a Fortran routine to solve the nesting problems for any two given triangles.

EXERCISE 3. Extend the nesting problem to five triangles determining how many triangles will fit one inside another, and that one inside a third, and so on. If a triangle must be rejected, make sure that it is the one that leaves the maximum number nested.

Problem B4

THE OBTUSE TRIANGLE

What fraction of all the triangles that can be drawn in a rectangle one inch wide and two inches long are obtuse triangles? Suppose we are told that the exact answer to this problem is not known*, but an approximate answer, at least, is required.

In problems of this kind, where the mathematical analysis of all possible cases seems unfeasible but an approximate answer will suffice, we choose a random sample from the total number of cases and study that sample. This is called the Monte Carlo method because we are in effect playing a game of chance in order to solve a mathematical problem.

The high speed of a computer makes it possible to choose a sample of many thousands of cases. The Monte Carlo method is therefore essentially a computer method. It has been applied successfully in scientific and business problems which seemed too complicated for complete mathematical analysis. The mathematical methods that were applied to study games of chance have thus led to a new method that can be applied to other problems whose solutions have made great advances possible in science and engineering.

As we have done frequently in previous problems, we start by cutting the problem down to size. We choose a point at random on the base and on each vertical side of the rectangle in Figure B4.1 by generating three random numbers. Then we determine whether the triangle having these three vertexes is obtuse by applying the theorem of Pythagoras. We actually simplify the original problem in two ways. First, we restrict the triangles to the set of inscribed triangles, and second, we require that every triangle touch three given sides. Moreover, we are tacitly defining the probability distributions that are involved.

We may select a by generating a 3-digit random number with a random number generator, such as RNG described in Problem E7. Then we prefix a decimal point and round off to 2

---

*This is true. That is, a solution to the problem in analytic terms, leading to a precise value to the fraction, is not known at present.

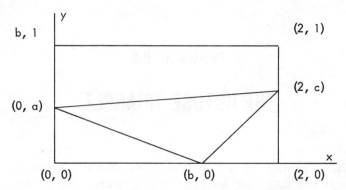

Figure B4.1. And inscribed obtuse triangle

decimal places. We select c in a similar way. For b we double the number before rounding off. Now we calculate the square of each side by the right triangle rule. If the largest square is greater than the sum of the other two squares, the triangle is obtuse.

Since a great many triangles are to be selected and tested, the student is well advised to consider ways to improve the method so as to speed up the process. For example, he may note that calling the random number subroutine once will furnish three 3-digit numbers. He may further consider whether it is easier to determine which square is the largest in order to make the test, or whether it is simpler to compare each square with half the sum of the squares.

> EXERCISE 1 (a) Draw a flow chart for the simplified obtuse triangle problem. Count the number of obtuse triangles and the total number of triangles sampled. Print under switch control the cumulative results and their ratio for every hundred additional samples. (b) Use the routine of part (a) to obtain a number of approximations to the required ratio. Observe whether the values so obtained seem to be approaching some definite value. (c) Mathematical analysis of this simple case gives a ratio of 0.874, including a few obtuse triangles with the vertex of the obtuse angle on one of the vertical sides of the rectangle. Estimate the size of sample required to obtain a ratio correct to two decimal places.

The student who has completed Exercise 1 is in a fair

position to judge how much work is involved to solve the original problem. He will need an abscissa and ordinate for each vertex, all of which can be obtained from two 9-digit random numbers.

EXERCISE 2. Rewrite the routine of Exercise 1 to calculate the ratio of the number of obtuse triangles to the total number of triangles which can be drawn with their vertexes inside or on the perimeter of a rectangle one inch wide by two inches long.

EXERCISE 3. Modify the routine of Exercise 2 to find the ratio of the number of obtuse triangles to the total number of triangles that can be drawn in a square.

Problem B5

INTERSECTING LINES*

In analytic geometry we think of a linear equation in two variables as representing a line. The problem of solving a system of two linear equations involving two variables is equivalent to finding the intersection of two straight lines. This geometric point of view clarifies many difficult problems, and is especially valuable in computing.

Let us consider the two equations

$$Ax + By = C$$
$$Dx + Ey = F$$

The values of the coefficients and the constants are to be punched in cards, with one card for each equation. When we consider a computer solution for this simple problem, we are immediately confronted with a question that did not arise in connection with hand computation.

1. Do the two sets of three numbers actually represent equations? If the two coefficients in either set are both zero, that set does not represent an equation.

> EXERCISE 1. (a) Write a short Fortran routine to read in the data from two cards and test whether the numbers actually represent equations. If not, type "CASE 1. NONSENSE." If so, type the data on two lines. (b) If you tested A and B separately, improve the routine in part (a) by testing both A and B at the same time. (c) If you tested the two sets of numbers with separate instructions, modify your routine to use a loop.

If the two sets of numbers do indeed represent equations, then they can also be regarded as representing straight lines in

---

*Suggested by Alexandra Forsythe, Cubberly High School, Palo Alto, California.

a plane. Before we proceed to find their intersection, we ask
  2. Do the lines intersect at all?
  3. Are there really two different lines?
  4. Can we find the intersection?
The first question is answered "No" in a hand calculation when an attempt to eliminate one variable results in the elimination of both. The second question is answered "No" if the elimination of both variables leads to an identity. We ask how the answers can be determined with the computer.

EXERCISE 2. (a) Extend the Fortran routine of Exercise 1 to find the intersection from the formulas

$$x = \frac{C \cdot E - B \cdot F}{A \cdot E - B \cdot D}$$

$$y = \frac{A \cdot F - C \cdot D}{A \cdot E - B \cdot D}$$

(b) Modify the routine of part (a) to test whether any intersection exists, and thus prevent a DIVIDE error. Test also whether the lines are the same in an equally simple way. Print the x and y values for the intersection if there is one; otherwise print the message

CASE 2.   SAME LINE   or
CASE 3.   PARALLEL LINES

The fourth question is made necessary by the round-off errors that may be introduced by machine calculation. It is possible for two straight lines to be so nearly parallel that round-off errors make the values found for their intersection extremely uncertain unless a sufficient number of figures are carried.
   Since the Fortran processor provides eight significant figures, round-off errors in this calculation do not usually affect the results appreciably. It is more likely that errors of measurement in the original data destroy the reliability of the results.
   Assuming that the input data is precise, there is still the possibility that the (real) point of intersection has coordinates that cannot be expressed in the range of our floating-point arithmetic. In computing terms, this would mean that the de-

nominator in the equations of Exercise 2 (a) is very small, but not zero.

EXERCISE 3. (a) Use your Fortran routine to show that the two lines

$$x + 5y = -17$$
$$1.5x + 7.501y = -25.503$$

intersect at the point (x = -2, y = -3). (b) Round off the data of part (a) to four significant digits and show that the values obtained for the intersection are (x = -17, y = 0). The error in x thus amounts to over 900 per cent.

EXERCISE 4. (a) Use your Fortran routine to find the intersection of the lines

$$2361.452x + 1427.527y = 19873.16$$
$$5917.389x + 3607.342y = 50222.00$$

(b) Find the intersection of exactly the same lines when the equations are multiplied by 8, and thus show the exaggerated effect of round-off errors when nearly equal numbers are subtracted.

Problem B6

THE RULED LINES

A sheet of paper 1 foot wide is divided into 101 equal parts by 100 equally spaced rules lines; these lines are colored red. The 1-foot width is also divided into 103 equal parts by 102 blue ruled lines. What is the shortest distance between any red and blue lines? (Since 101 and 103 are relatively prime numbers, no two lines coincide.)

This is not a good computer problem at all (according to the criteria outlined in the Introduction). You should be able to devise an analytic solution to solve the problem for any pair of rulings. However, attack this problem as though it _were_ a computer problem; there is much to be learned from it.

We shall use S1 for the position of the red lines and S2 for the position of the blue lines. Then the distance D between the lines is the absolute value of the difference between S1 and S2. We will store as SM the least value found for D. The working part of our program (in Fortran) is then as shown in Figure B6.1.

```
      D = S1 - S2
      IF (D) 50, 51, 51
   50 D = -D
   51 IF (D - SM) 52, 53, 53
   52 SM = D
   53
```

Figure B6.1

If S2 is less than S1, it should be increased by 1/103; but if S1 is less, it should be increased by 1/101. S1, S2, and S must be initialized to zero, SM initialized to 1, and a test should be made to determine when S1 reaches 0.5. It is clear from the symmetry of the problem that the pattern of ruled lines will repeat in reverse order for the other half of the page.

EXERCISE 1. (a) Write a Fortran routine to deter-

79

mine the least distance between any red and blue lines. (b) Calculate the difference between the width of the space between red lines and the space between blue lines, using common fractions. Calculate the accumulating difference between successive pairs of one red line and one blue line, attempting to make it equal to the width of the spacing between blue lines. Compare the least distance as calculated with the result of the routine in part (a).

EXERCISE 2. (a) Write a Fortran function subroutine to obtain the absolute value of a floating-point number. (b) Rewrite the routine of Exercise 1 to use the absolute value function. Make the numbers of lines parameters to be read in from the typewriter.

EXERCISE 3. (a) Modify the Fortran routine of Exercise 1 to use common fractions for m red lines and n blue lines. (b) By using Euclid's algorithm for finding the greatest common divisor of two numbers,* show that the least distance is the greatest common divisor of m and n divided by their product. Express this distance in terms of the lowest common multiple of m and n.

---

*Refer to J. V. Uspensky and M. A. Heaslet, Elementary Number Theory, McGraw-Hill Book Company, Inc., New York, 1939, p. 54.

THE HEIGHT OF THE ARC

A chord of a circle is 1/2 mile long and the arc it subtends is 1 foot longer. What is the height of the arc?

The problem is pictured in Figure C1.1. It is a problem in trigonometry, but of a type not covered in most texts. The scale is greatly distorted in Figure C1.1.

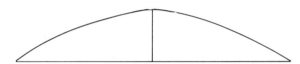

Figure C1.1. The height of the arc problem

The problem is pictured a different way in Figure C1.2, with half the central angle involved given as B. We then have the following relations

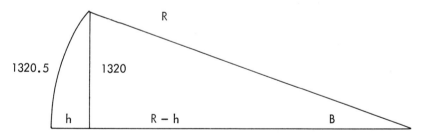

Figure C1.2. The problem repictured.

$$\frac{1320}{R} = \sin B$$

$$\frac{1320.5}{2\pi R} = \frac{B}{360}$$

from which we deduce that

$$\frac{\sin B}{B} = \frac{1320\pi}{(1320.5)(180)} = 0.01744668393$$

B is the (half) central angle, in degrees. If the constant (0.017446 . . .) is called k, we are to solve the equation

$$\sin B - kB = 0 \qquad\qquad (1)$$

for B. B is an angle of the order of 2° 44′. The height of the arc is around 31 feet. Or is it? These figures were arrived at by using a 7-place log trig table. What sort of result will you get using Fortran-calculated functions and, say, the Newton method on Equation (1)? (See Problem A3.)

Would it be easier to treat B in radians and use a series evaluation on

$$\frac{\sin x}{x} = 1 - \frac{x^2}{6} + \frac{x^4}{120} - \frac{x^6}{5040} + \cdots$$

The essential feature of this problem (besides being an interesting old puzzle) is to demonstrate the weakness in functions that are limited to 8-digit accuracy at best. In this problem, to get even 4 digits of accuracy in k, many more than 8 digits must be used along the way.

Problem C2

THE MOVIE SCREEN

A moving picture screen 20 feet high has its lower edge 10 feet above eyelevel. The angle y at the observer's eye which is subtended by the screen varies with the distance x of the observer from the plane of the screen. At what distance is the angle greatest?

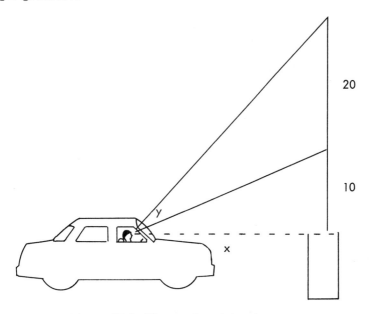

Figure C2.1. The moving picture screen

The tremendous calculating speed of a computer allows us to determine the optimum design or operating conditions in even complex situations by varying the parameters and making a new calculation. Let us apply that "cut and try" method to this elementary problem.

The Fortran system provides a subroutine that makes it easy to calculate the angle when the tangent of the angle is known.

We can therefore assume some small value for x, say 1 foot, and determine the angle of elevation of the top and the angle of elevation of the lower edge of the screen. Then y is the difference between these angles. We increase x 1 foot at a time, testing each new value of y against its predecessor. When the new value is less, we reverse our direction and refine our test by making the change in x equal to −0.1 instead of 1.0. If we write DX for the successive changes in x, we can describe this procedure concisely as −0.1DX → DX. We may continue in this way until two successive values of y are equal, up to the 8 figures allowed in Fortran floating-point arithmetic.

EXERCISE 1. (a) Construct a flow chart to solve the problem of the movie screen. (b) Write a Fortran routine to implement your flow chart.

EXERCISE 2. (a) Modify the routine of Exercise 1 (a) so that the height a of a screen and the elevation b of its lower edge are parameters to be read in from cards. (b) Use the modified routine to test the formula

$$x = \sqrt{b^2 + ab}$$

(derived by using the calculus) for the position where the angle y is a maximum, by choosing various values for a and b.

The "cut and try" method is known in mathematics as the method of successive approximations. It can be applied in a very wide range of circumstances. For example, in solving the equation

$$x^3 - 2x - 5 = 0$$

we can increase x from x = 1 by changes of DX = 1 until the value of the polynomial becomes positive.* Then we can reduce and reverse DX by the procedure −0.1DX → DX and continue changing x until the value of the polynomial becomes negative.

---

*The equation used here is Wallis' equation, used to demonstrate Newton's method when it was first published. The positive root of this equation is known to 1000 decimal places (see Communications of the Association for Computing Machinery, April 1962, p. 221).

Thus we obtain an approximate value in units first, then tenths, hundredths, and so on to any desired accuracy up to the 8-figure limit of Fortran arithmetic.

EXERCISE 3. (a) Write a Fortran routine to find the positive root of

$$x^3 - 2x - 5 = 0$$

(b) Elaborate the routine of part (a) to find the first root above any given value of x for any equation of fifth degree or less. (c) Use the routine of part (b) to find a negative root of

$$2.164x^5 - 0.866x^4 + 8.122x + 142.16 = 0$$

correct to 3 decimal places.

Problem D1

PERMUTATIONS

In many combinatorial problems we need to be able to generate systematically all the permutations of N symbols.* If N is less than 10, these symbols can be the decimal digits; for larger N, other symbols can be used, such as the letters of the English alphabet. We will illustrate a method with letters.

For N = 3, there are just six arrangements, readily displayed as in Figure D1.1.

Suppose we wish to generate all the permutations for N = 4, and we have at hand a subroutine that will produce on demand one of the six permutations of three things. For example, the N = 3 subroutine most recently gave us BCA when called; it will next produce BAC (as indicated by the arrow) when called, and after that CAB, and so on. After ABC it goes back to CBA.

The subroutine for N = 4 will act as follows. It takes the current output of the N = 3 routine and slides the fourth symbol D

---

*An example is the puzzle problem of the eight squares, arranged as in the figure below. The object is to insert the digits from 1 to 8 in the squares in such a way that no two adjacent squares (horizontally,

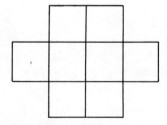

vertically, or diagonally) contain consecutive digits. The puzzle is easily solved by heuristic methods; a computer solution might call for trying all 40,320 permutations of 8 digits to find the four permutations that fit properly.

CBA
BCA
BAC ←———
CAB
ACB
ABC

Figure D1.1. The six permutations of three things

along the four possible interstices as illustrated in Figure D1.2. At some stage the permutation BAC is fresh; the D is then to be inserted at position 1, to produce DBAC.

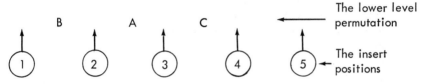

Figure D1.2. The scheme for N = 4

The next call produces BDAC (the D is now in position 2). When the position for D is 5 (that is, off scale, so to speak), it is time to restore its position back to 1 and call the N = 3 subroutine again.

The N = 4 subroutine will, in this manner, systematically output the 24 permutations of the four symbols. (Actually, the same principle could have been applied at the lower levels, but for N = 3 it is simpler just to store the six results.)

So we now have a subroutine that will deliver, on demand, the next of the 24 permutations for N = 4. Using that, we can readily program a subroutine for N = 5, which calls on the N = 4 subroutine as needed, which calls, in turn on the N = 3 routine as needed.*

You should write both of these subroutines, and test them out, before proceeding further. It might even help you to go further and write the complete subroutine for N = 6 also.

This process could be cascaded to any level; that is, separate subroutines could be written for N   7, 8, 9 . . . as high

*The method used here is due to Selmer M. Johnson. The original paper "Generations of Permutations by Adjacent Transposition," is found in Mathematics of Computation, Vol. XVII, No. 83, July 1963, p. 282. Besides ease of programming, Johnson's algorithm has the interesting feature that the only change between successive permutations involves the interchange of two adjacent symbols.

as one pleased. We discover, though, that the subroutines <u>are all alike</u>. Everything in them is a function of the N involved; but all the instructions are essentially the same. We would be violating a fundamental principle of computing; namely, that repetitive work is for computers, not humans. We should be able to write one routine for all levels.

Such a subroutine would be recursive, in that it would have to call on itself many times. There would have to be, in storage, two lists; for each N, there would have to be stored the position of the arrow for that N, as in Figure D1.2. The most important list would be the one to keep track of the internal N. Let us consider an example.

Suppose we set N = 6 and call the master subroutine, and the state of affairs is as follows:

For level 6, the arrow is at position 3.
For level 5, position 5.
For level 5, position 2.
For level 3, position 6.

Working backwards, this means that N3 (if we may use this notation) will next output ABC.

N4 stands now at

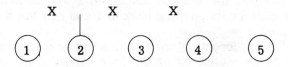

and the X's are ACB from the last call of N3.

Similarly, N5 stands at

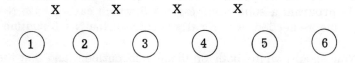

and the X's are the last output from N4. And so on. What are the letters in storage for N5 and N6? Where is the arrow for N6?

This all seems to be getting inordinately complicated, which is why we wanted you to write out in detail independent subroutines for N = 4, 5, and 6. If the goal is to get to N = 14, it will pay to keep track of all details in one grand routine, rather than to write eleven routines whose instructions are largely identical.

Your first attempt at the recursive subroutine is apt to be

messy, with many little lists stored here and there. Basically, you need only a few lists:

1. A list of the arrow positions for each level (these positions can be addresses, of course).

2. A list of the off-scale positions for each arrow.

3. A list of symbols. If we are manipulating letters, we need to keep a list of what letter goes with what N. Thus, for N = 13, this list might show M, but in the form of the digits 54 on the IBM 1620. (If the internal representation of letters proceeded smoothly, this list would not be necessary.)

4. A list of the running N. Let us say we call the subroutine with N = 10. It finds that it needs to call on the next lower level. We must keep track of the running N for the routine (it would be 9 next, and then possibly 8, and so on) as the subroutine moves itself from level to level.

Some of these lists could well be push down lists. This is a special form of stored list.* Suppose we have a list in storage as follows: 0̄00060̄0005̄00004. We wish to add an item to the list. First, the list must be pushed down; that is, each entry must be moved to the right in storage as follows: 0̄00060̄00060̄0005̄00004. Then, the new item, 0̄0007, can be stored (in the usual way) at the top. Similarly, when we read out the list just formed, we get the item 0̄0007, and the list must be pushed up; that is, each entry must be moved to the left. We are illustrating a last-in, first-out (LIFO) list. A whole body of computing techniques has sprung up around the ability to do list processing. At least two computer languages, LISP and IPL-V, have been created to facilitate list processing, and we are about to see list processing instructions incorporated into computer hardware.

We have suggested that the subroutine (to generate permutations at any level) be built up slowly. It is highly instructive to write independent subroutines for a few levels to get the feel of the problem. The step from many independent subroutines to one generalized subroutine is a big one, and a powerful concept. It exploits to the fullest the idea of nonrepetitive work.

---

*Whose name and concept came by analogy to the devices in restaurants that hold a stack of plates in a column supported by a spring.

Problem D2

LATIN SQUARES

Figure D2.1 shows two so-called Latin squares of order 5. Each row and each column of both contain the digits from 1 to 5 once and only once.

```
5 1 2 3 4          5 1 2 3 4
2 3 4 5 1          4 5 1 2 3
4 5 1 2 3          3 4 5 1 2
1 2 3 4 5          2 3 4 5 1
3 4 5 1 2          1 2 3 4 5
```

Figure D2.1. Two 5 X 5 Latin squares

Such patterns are of great use in the field of experimental design; in fact, tables of Latin squares of various orders are available to biometrists.

A 5×5 Latin square might be used, for example, in testing the growth effects of five types of fertilizers. By applying the fertilizers to groups of plants arranged in one of these patterns, the effects of other variables (type of soil, weather conditions, and so on) are minimized, and more information can be obtained than would be possible with an unstructured experiment.

The Latin squares shown in Figure D2.1 are rather simple; the reader can readily deduce the cyclic pattern that was used. More complex patterns (and of a higher order than 5) might be calculated by other schemes, such as the following one, described in terms of a 6×6 square, but applicable to any size.

1. Select all the elements of the top row by choosing a random permutation of the numbers from 1 to 6 (see Problem E6).

2. Suppose that permutation was 631425. This series provides the first row of the Latin square. It can also provide the directions for fitting (in this case) all the 5's in the square as shown in Figure D2.2 on the left. That is, the digit 5 appears in successive rows in positions 6, 3, 1, 4, 2, and 5. The next cyclic

6	3	1	4	2	5
		5			
5					
			5		
	5				
				5	

6	3	1	4	2	5
1	4	5	6	3	2
5	6	2	1	4	3
2	1	3	5	6	4
3	5	4	2	1	6
4	2	6	3	5	1

2	6	5	4	1	3
4	5	2	1	3	6
1	2	4	3	6	5
3	4	1	6	5	2
6	1	3	5	2	4
5	3	6	2	4	1

Figure D2.2. A 6 X 6 Latin square

arrangement of the permutation is 314256, which describes the
location of the digit 1, and so on. We are using the first line not
only to supply the digits but also to specify the order in which to
fit the digits. The middle square of Figure D2.2 is the completed
square. A second such square is shown at the right in Figure
D2.2.

Let us write a routine to generate a Latin square of seventh
order.

We consider first, as the working part of our routine a cyclic
permutation of the 7-digit number stored in addresses A+1 to
A+7, with a record mark in A+8. This can be accomplished as
indicated in Figure D2.3.

A	A+1	A+2	A+3	A+4	A+5	A+6	A+7	A+8
x	1	2	3	4	5	6	7	‡

Move the record one place to the left.

| 1 | 2 | 3 | 4 | 5 | 6 | 7 | ‡ | ‡ |

Move the first digit to the end.

| 1 | 2 | 3 | 4 | 5 | 6 | 7 | 1 | ‡ |

Figure D2.3. Cyclic permuting

EXERCISE 1. Write a short routine (of a dozen instructions) to read in a 7-digit number and type a
Latin square according to the scheme used in the
second square of Figure D2.1.

The more elaborate generation scheme of Figure D2.2 requires working with individual digits. A random permutation must first be generated (as in Problem E6) and then applied to the N × N cells of the square.

> EXERCISE 2. Write a routine to generate a Latin square according to the scheme of Figure D2.2.

Refer again to Figure D2.1. If the two 5 × 5 squares shown there are superimposed, then (reading down through the squares) it is seen that all possible 2-digit combinations (11, 12, 13, 14, 15, 21, 22, 23, 24, 25, 31, ... , 54, 55) occur just once. Such a combination is called orthogonal. It is fairly easy to generate sets of orthogonal Latin squares of order 4 (there are 72 sets possible) or 5. It is not possible for order 6.

The problem of constructing orthogonal Latin squares was investigated extensively by the mathematician Leonhard Euler. For the 6 x 6 case, the problem was stated as a puzzle. Each of six different regiments has six officers, one belonging to each of six different ranks. Can these 36 officers be arranged in a square formation so that each row and column contains one officer of each rank and one of each regiment?

Euler showed that the problem is solvable if the order, N, is an odd number, or is an even number divisible by 4. Attention then focused on the 6 × 6 case. It was conjectured by Euler that there is no solution for N = 6, 10, 14, 18, and so on. The conjecture was confirmed for N = 6 in 1901 by direct enumeration; that is, by generating all the 6 × 6 Latin squares and comparing every one with every other one. There the matter rested until 1959, when it was shown (analytically, not by enumeration) that Euler's conjecture was wrong and that orthogonal Latin squares exist for all orders greater than 6.

The student may read more on this subject in Martin Gardner's department in the November 1959 issue of Scientific American.

> EXERCISE 3. Develop a routine to construct two orthogonal Latin squares of order 5 or greater according to the scheme of Figure D2.1.

> EXERCISE 4. (a) Develop a plan to test two given Latin squares of order 6 for orthogonality by clearing 36 positions and making a tally into it. (b) Write a routine to test all Latin squares of order 6 for

orthogonality in pairs. Since there are $(6!)(5!)$ squares of order 6, the program should be improved as far as possible before a production run.

Problem D3

PUSHBUTTON RADIO PROBLEM

The student's attention has often been drawn to the importance of computers in getting numerical results for important practical problems where no theoretical solution is known. Here we shall show with a very simple example how the great speed of the machine can be used to accumulate data from which generalized conclusions can be derived. That is to say, the computer gives tremendous aid to the student who delights in mathematical research.

An automobile radio usually has five or six pushbuttons, which are used to swing the indicator to the frequency of certain preassigned stations. The buttons are normally set so that the leftmost button corresponds to the station with the lowest frequency, and which is therefore at the left of the dial. The other buttons, in order, refer to increasing frequencies. Pushing the buttons in sequence will cause the indicator to start at the left and move to the right across the dial. All the given stations can be tuned in successively with the least motion of the indicator by pushing the buttons in sequence. If the buttons referred to the same stations in a different order, pushing all the buttons in sequence would cause the indicator to travel farther. Now, if n stations are equally spaced on the dial, what is the greatest amount of travel possible when the buttons are pushed in sequence? Also, how many different connections of the pushbutton to the stations will give this maximum travel to the indicator?

We are asking in this problem for a formula, expressed in letters. We can easily set up a mathematical model to represent the pushbuttons. We form permutations of the first n whole numbers. Each permutation represents a particular connection between the pushbuttons and the stations. We prefix a 1 to each permutation to show that the indicator is initially at the leftmost station. We simply seek those permutations for which the sum of the (numerical) differences between adjacent integers is the maximum. If y is the maximum travel for N pushbuttons, we are asked for a formula expressing y terms of N. We are also asked for a formula for n, the number of permutations having y for the sum of the differences between adjacent integers.

We start by writing down all the permutations for N = 3 or N = 4. Figure D3.1 shows the travel for each permutation when N = 4. A "1" is to be understood preceding each permutation, as already explained. Thus, case K is analyzed as if a 1 preceded it:

$$\text{Stations} \quad 1\ 2\ 4\ 1\ 3$$

$$\text{Travel} \quad 1+2+3+2 = 8$$

Cases N and T are seen to have the greatest travel possible for four pushbuttons, which is a travel of 9.

> EXERCISE 1. Show by writing out all possible permutations that the greatest travel for three buttons is 5, and that only one case exhibits this maximum.

We could study the problem by hand in the same way for N = 5 and N = 6, but since the number of permutations of N things is N! (i.e., factorial N), there will be 120 and 720 cases, respectively. For successive values of N, the number of permutations increases by a factor of N; we therefore need the computer. With a modest amount of time and effort, we can obtain with the computer the data required to extend the table of Figure D3.2.

> EXERCISE 2. (a) Write a routine using the permutation subroutine of Problem D1 to calculate the maximum travel y for a radio with N pushbuttons, and the number n of cases that exhibit this maximum.
> (b) Use the routine of part (a) to extend the table in Figure D3.2.

We would not have much confidence in any formula for y or n that did not rest upon greater amounts of data than shown in Figure D3.2. The additional data obtained in Exercise 2 is therefore needed to test any tentative conclusions that we may draw from Figure D3.2. In even that figure, we notice that y is increasing, but that the differences are not constant, as would be the case if y were given by a first-degree expression involving N. The differences are themselves increasing, however, at a constant rate. We may therefore suspect that y is given by a second-degree expression, such as $y = ax^2 + bx + c$.

Case	Order of Stations	Total Travel
A	1234	3
B	1243	4
C	1324	5
D	1342	5
E	1423	6
F	1432	5
G	2134	5
H	2143	6
I	2314	7
J	2341	7
K	2413	8
L	2431	6
M	3124	7
N	3142	9
O	3214	7
P	3241	8
Q	3412	7
R	3421	6
S	4123	8
T	4132	9
U	4213	8
V	4231	8
W	4312	7
X	4321	6

Figure D3.1. The pushbutton radio problem for N = 4

EXERCISE 3. (a) Determine a tentative formula for y in terms of N by substituting N for X and the corresponding value of y from the table. (b) Test the formula for y, using values obtained in Exercise 2.

The differences in n show no such regularity as the differences in y.

EXERCISE 4. Use the results of Exercise 2 to discover the regularities, if any, in the quotients of successive values of (N!/n).

The pushbutton radio problem can be altered slightly to

Number of buttons N	Number of Possibilities N!	Maximum Travel Y	Number of Maximum Cases n	Ratio N!/n
3	6	5	1	6
4	24	9	2	12
5	120	14	4	30
6	720	20	12	60
7	5,040	27	36	140
8	40,320	35	144	280
9	362,880	44	576	630
10	3,628,800	54	3,360	1,080
11				
12				
13				

Figure D3.2. Tabulation of results for pushbutton radio problem

produce a fresh problem, which the student may use to test his skill in drawing conclusions from data produced by the computer. We ask: What is the maximum travel of the indicator if the buttons are pushed in cyclic sequence, starting and ending with the first button?

EXERCISE 5. Carry out the complete investigation of the pushbutton radio problem for the new condition that the buttons are pushed in cyclic order.

Problem D4

THE EIGHT QUEENS

Eight queens can be arranged on a chessboard so that none is under attack from any of the others; in other words, so that no row or column or diagonal contains more than one queen. Figure D4.1 shows one solution. How many others are possible?

	Column							
	1	2	3	4	5	6	7	8
1			0					
2						0		
3								0
4	0							
5				0				
6							0	
7					0			
8		0						

Figure D4.1. One arrangement of the eight queens

We must first adopt some notation to represent the position. One notation is simply to list the number of the column containing the queen for successive rows. The position in the figure would be recorded as 36814752.

A different solution is represented by 24683175. The solution 51842736 is not considered distinct from the first; it represents the position of Figure D4.1 when looked at from the right-hand side.

98

EXERCISE 1. (a) Show that each distinct solution is one of eight related solutions if the board can be inspected from either above or below. (b) Write out the set of eight related solutions which include the position in Figure D4.1. Suggest ways to generate the whole set of related solutions by starting with one solution.

To solve the eight queens problem completely, we might at first consider generating with the computer all the possible permutations of eight symbols and testing them for the conditions of the chessboard problem. Since there are factorial eight (i.e., 40,320) permutations, we prefer to start with less pretentious goals. Let us rather attempt to simulate the thought processes used by a human being in finding solutions. Then we will obtain a good many solutions, even without developing a systematic approach to the larger problem. After obtaining these solutions we may be able to see how to exhuast the problem. A human would probably proceed somewhat as follows:

1. Pick a column at random and place a queen in that column for row 1. Go on to the next row.

2. Pick a column at random for the row.

3. Test for attack in column or diagonal by the previous queen or queens.

4. If the newly placed queen is under attack, go back to step 2.

5. If there is no attack, go on to the next row, unless this is the eighth row.

The student should test this procedure by hand and write a routine to follow it with the computer. He will need to set aside a portion of storage to represent the chessboard, perhaps as in Figure D4.2.

If column 3 is chosen by the random number generator for the first row, ones should be stored in column 3 of all rows, and also in columns corresponding to the forward and backward diagonals, presuming they were set to zero.

If the number 13 stands for "row 1, column 3," then the numbers of the squares for the forward diagonal can be calculated by successively adding 11; that is, to deduce squares (in this case) 24, 35, 46, 57, and 68. In similar fashion, the squares for the northeast-southwest diagonal can be deduced by subtraction.

EXERCISE 2. (a) Write a routine using the random

Adress 04010	0	0	0	1	0	0	0	0	0	0	
04020	0	0	1	1	1	0	0	0	0	0	
04030	0	1	0	1	0	1	0	0	0	0	
04040	0	0	0	1	0	0	1	0	0	0	
04050	0	0	0	1	0	0	0	1	0	0	
04060	0	0	0	1	0	0	0	0	1	0	
04070	0	0	0	1	0	0	0	0	0	0	
04080	0	0	0	1	0	0	0	0	0	0	04089
04090	0	0	0	0	0	0	0	0	0	0	04099

Figure D4.2. Chessboard in storage

number generator RNG (Problem E7) to select columns at random and test for the chessboard conditions of the eight queens problem. (b) Provide for a halt in the routine of part (a) when a reasonable number of trials, say 20, fails to find any satisfactory column in some particular row.

The routine to simulate the procedure followed by a human being in finding solutions for the eight queens problem often fails to find _any_ solution because all columns of some row are under attack. The human being would soon learn to go back and change the location of one or more queens which had already been placed upon the board. In order to simulate a human player more closely, we must elaborate the routine to include this retreat.

EXERCISE 3. Modify the routine of Exercise 2 to reduce the row number when a satisfactory column cannot be found in some row. Take care to erase the column and diagonals emanating from the trial location before choosing a new column. The student

may wish to place this new method under switch
control, retaining the old method.

The student will notice that he has allowed the computer
routine to try the same column several times, just as a human
player would at first do. After some time, the player would learn
to mark unsuccessful tries in some way so that he can eliminate
repetition. Then he will know when it is time to change the position of a queen which was placed in an earlier row. In this
gradual way, the player makes a transition from random trials
in each row toward a systematic procedure. The programmer
may now wish to change the routine to reflect this change in at-
titude on the part of the player.

EXERCISE 4. Change the method of selecting trial
locations in each row so that the first acceptable
position is chosen. If no column is satisfactory in a
given row, reduce the row number. After a solution
has been obtained, type or punch it out. Then reduce
the row and seek for further solutions.

We have described a computer routine that could generate
all possible solutions for the eight queens problem. Many of these
are related solutions. Exercise 1 has shown that each distinct
solution gives rise to seven other related solutions. We now ask
how a human player determines whether two solutions are related. One way has been suggested: He imagines himself at a
different side of the chessboard. Another way is for him to imagine the chessboard rotated. We wish to simulate these imagi-
native procedures with the computer. We accomplish this simulation by generating the set of related positions from any given
position. Then we choose the position whose representation has
the least numerical value as the standard position for the whole
set. To compare two solutions, we determine the standard position for each and compare the two standard positions. In this
way we simulate the thought process of a player who has found
that it is easier to compare two solutions by noting the location
of the queen closest to a corner.
We start our investigation of related positions by inter-
changing rows and columns. We return to the position of Figure
D4.1 and write the row key and column key one under the other:

```
Row      1 2 3 4 5 6 7 8
Column   3 6 8 1 4 7 5 2
```

We interchange rows and columns, obtaining

```
Row      3 6 8 1 4 7 5 2
Column   1 2 3 4 5 6 7 8
```

Then we arrange the rows in order:

```
Row      1 2 3 4 5 6 7 8
Column   4 8 1 5 7 2 6 3
```

The result corresponds to listing rows for successive columns. Or we can imagine looking at the board from the right-hand side and from below the board. Still another way to arrive at the position is to imagine the board rotated about the principal diagonal which runs from the upper left corner to the lower right.

We now consider the working part of a routine to interchange rows and columns. For convenience we can use 8-digit numbers for the row key and the column key. Thus, to use the previous example, the row and column designations can be the numbers 12345678 and 36814752. To interchange rows and columns, we need only interchange these two numbers in storage. The new row and column designations can be ordered on rows by sorting the 2-digit pairs.*

EXERCISE 5. Write a routine to read in a position
and interchange rows and columns.

We can now arrange the rows in reverse order by complementing each digit in the row key:

```
Row      8 7 6 5 4 3 2 1
Column   4 8 1 5 7 2 6 3
```

and then arranging the rows in order:

```
Row      1 2 3 4 5 6 7 8
Column   3 6 2 7 5 1 8 4
```

---

*We have casually thrown in a subproblem of some difficulty here. See Problem L3 for reference to the topic of sorting by keys. Notice that in actual computer implementation there need not be pairs of numbers stored. If this step is to be programmed, it should be in the form of a subroutine.

The result is equivalent to rotating the board about a horizontal axis, or merely looking at it from below. The result of the two rotations, D about the diagonal axis and H about the horizontal axis, is a rotation of 90 degrees counterclockwise in the plane of the original position.

We can rotate the board about a vertical axis by complementing each digit in the column key. This rotation, V, is equivalent to counting the columns from the right side of the board:

$$\text{Row} \quad 1\ 2\ 3\ 4\ 5\ 6\ 7\ 8$$
$$\text{Column} \quad 6\ 3\ 7\ 2\ 4\ 8\ 1\ 5$$

By a judicious combination of these three rotations, we can obtain all the related positions corresponding to a given position. We must take care only to see that we do not repeat any one position before the set of eight positions is complete. We do not need to retain all eight positions. We choose the one with the smallest numerical value as the standard position to represent the complete set

EXERCISE 6 (a) Show that the successive rotations D, H, V, H, D, V, H will generate all the positions related to a given position. (b) Convert the routine of Exercise 5 to a subroutine to interchange rows and columns. Then write a routine to generate all the positions related to a given position.

The student is now ready to complete the eight queens problem by listing all the distinct solutions.* Each set of eight related solutions is to be represented by the standard position for that set.

EXERCISE 7. Write a routine to read in the solutions obtained in Exercise 4, convert each to its standard position, and store in a list while eliminating duplicate entries.

This problem has illustrated one method of attacking a problem: Simulate the procedure used in solving the problem by

---

*The student may wish to read a long account of the eight queens problem in W. W. Rouse Ball's classic Mathematical Recreations and Essays, The Macmillan Company, New York, 1962, pp. 165-170. Ball discusses the number of fundamental solutions to the problem.

hand. The student has observed during the development of the final method that a good machine procedure differs in important respects from the hand method. The simulation of human thought processes as in this problem is, however, an interesting and profitable investigation in itself.

The cover design of this book shows all the known solutions to the eight queens problem on one chessboard. The twelve patterns, represented by the digits from one to six in each of two colors, are arranged in a way that minimizes crowding on any one square.

Problem D5

THE PROBLEM OF COINCIDENCES

When children grow weary and restless on an extended automobile trip, they may sometimes be induced to play a game involving the license numbers of passing cars. The object is to find two licenses that agree in the last two digits. How many cars must pass, on the average, for some two of the licenses to agree in the last two figures?

As usual, we cut the problem down to size for a first investigation. We ask how many cars must pass, on the average, for two cars to have the same last digit. So we generate, at random, numbers from 0 to 9, counting how many must be produced before the last one agrees with some earlier one. We simulate many hundreds of subgames in this way, counting the number of subgames and the total score. The result enables us to calculate the required average by simple division.

> EXERCISE 1. (a) Write a routine to use the random number selector RNS (or its Fortran counterpart, RNS(T)) to simulate the license number game. Print the score for each subgame under switch control. (b) Extend the routine of part (a) to count the number of subgames and the total score. Print the results for each additional 100 subgames from 100 to 1,000. Calculate the required average.

> EXERCISE 2. Rewrite the routine of Exercise 1 to calculate the average number of cars for the last two digits to agree.

The simplicity of most games of chance makes them easy applications for the laws of probability. The notion of probability however, pervades our ordinary thought processes. There can be no question that most of our thinking is based upon incomplete information, so that we frequently reach conclusions that are strongly influenced by our notions of what is probably true. The common prevalence of superstitions demonstrates that our intuitive notions of probability are sometimes unreliable. The computer enables us to test some of those notions and in this way to clarify our thinking.

Let us phrase the question about license numbers so that the notion of probability is brought into sharper focus. Suppose someone offers you a bet. On the next 20 cars that pass, he offers to bet even money that some two of them will have the same last two digits on their license plates. Is this a fair bet? If the bet were based upon a different number of cars, how many cars <u>would</u> make it fair? Your answer will depend upon your judgment of the probability that the same number will be chosen twice if 20 numbers are selected at random from the numbers 00 to 99.

One way to investigate this new question would be to simulate the situation, as we did before. Instead, we shall apply the laws of probability to the problem.

It is clear that the probability will be the same if we pose the problem in the following way: What is the probability of drawing the same card twice in 20 draws from a deck of 100 cards, if the card is replaced after each draw? The problem is similar to the questions concerning the coincidence of calamities in Problem E4; only the parameters and the setting are changed. In all three cases, we are dealing with random numbers.

We shall calculate the probability in an indirect way. We find it more convenient to calculate the probability p_k that of k numbers chosen at random from a set of N numbers <u>no two</u> will be the same. Then the required probability is simply $1 - p_k$.

We use a "recursion" formula for calculating p_k in terms of p_{k-1} :

$$p_k = p_k \cdot \frac{N - k}{N}$$

That is, the probability for k numbers is expressed in terms of the probability for one less number. The probability for k = 1 is p_1 = 1, or certainty. We increase k by 1 at a time until the probability falls to 0.5. This is the "break-even" point, at which the betting game is fair to both players.

EXERCISE 3. (a) Write a Fortran routine to calculate the probability that of k numbers selected at random from a set of N numbers, no two will be the same. Arrange to read in the value of N from the typewriter. Print k and p_k for k = 2 to k = N. (b) Use the routine of part (a) to calculate the probabilities for the license plate problem. (c) Obtain, by a simple summation of the results in part (b), the average number of cars for the license number game.

EXERCISE 4. (a) Use the routine of Exercise 3 to calculate the probabilities for the coincidence of calamities, discussed in Problem E4. That is, N = 52. (b) Apply the program of Exercise 3 to the birthday problem: What is the probability that some two persons in a certain club will have their birthdays fall together? Here N = 365. The number of persons k in the club can vary from 2 to 365. For a larger club, the probability is, of course, equal to 1.

In the study of the superstition concerning the coincidence of calamities (Problem E4) we find that common judgment about coincidences is usually faulty when it concerns the clustering of events occurring at random. The same mistaken judgment applies to the license plate problem. It is clear that some two license plates must have the same number if 100 cars are included after the first car. In this case the probability is 100 per cent. Also, for only one car after the first, the probability of matching the last two digits is 1 per cent. Therefore, reasoning falsely, many persons estimate that it will take about 50 cars to make the probability 50 per cent. They suppose that numbers chosen at random from a uniform distribution will be scattered evenly over the range. On this supposition, they conclude that the break-even point is one-half the total number N of possibilities. We shall use the computer to find a better basis for reasoning.

EXERCISE 5. (a) Rewrite the routine of Exercise 3 to calculate the probability p_k for successive values of k until p_k becomes equal to or less than 0.5. Call this value of k the break-even point b for that particular value of N, the latter being read in a card or from the typewriter. Print N and b. Read the value of N from a card or from the typewriter. (b) Use the routine of part (a) to calculate the break-even point b for various values of N: 2, 10, 50,

100, 200, 300, 500, 800, 1,000, 2,000.

Mathematical facts are more easily utilized in general reasoning when they are simply expressed. We are now in a position to prepare a graph to show whether there is some simple relationship between the break-even point b and the total number N of possibilities. Then we will need a simple rule in words. Let us consider some simple ways in which people have become accustomed to thinking mathematically. For example, the distance traveled during a trip is proportional to the rate of travel, and also to the time required. Braking distance required to bring a car to a stop is proportional to the <u>square</u> of the distance. Gravitational attraction between two bodies is <u>inversely</u> proportional to the <u>square</u> of the distance between them.

> EXERCISE 6. (a) Plot a graph by hand for b against N, using ordinary coordinate paper. Also make graphs on logarithmic and semilogarithmic graph paper. (b) Having determined a suitable formula for b in terms of N, write a short Fortran routine to calculate the probabilities by formula corresponding to points already plotted on the graphs. (c) Plot these estimated points on the same graphs as before to show how well the formula approximates the true probabilities.

> EXERCISE 7. (a) Formulate in words a simple rule which is reasonably accurate for the break-even point. (b) Write a short report concerning the clustering of random numbers. Include the simple rule and the results obtained in the previous exercises. Suggest an appropriate name for the rule.

Problem D6

THE BUBBLEGUM PROBLEM

The makers of a certain brand of gum wrap a comic strip around each piece of gum. There are 100 different numbered strips. If they are packed at random, or if the customers buy them at random (or both), how many pieces of gum, on the average, will a customer have to buy to receive a complete set?

It is a curious but significant fact that most people cannot make a reasonable estimate of the answer to this problem. It is clear that at least 100 purchases are necessary to obtain a complete set. It is also possible that a customer might make thousands of purchases before obtaining a complete set, even if the comic strips are truly distributed at random. To guess where the average lies between these extremes requires an understanding of random choices which is far beyond common experience.* The computer offers the student an unusual opportunity to study such questions by using large amounts of random data generated by the machine.

One method of selecting a random permutation of a set of 100 elements is to choose elements at random from the set, rejecting any element which has already been chosen, as explained in Problem E6. We can adapt that procedure to this problem. We need to count the total number of elements that are chosen before completing the permutation, including those rejected.

Before rushing into a production run on a problem such as this, however, the student should consider the sixth fundamental principle of the introductory chapter: Cut the problem down to size. Accordingly, he might undertake to count the number of purchases required to complete a set when there are only fifteen different strips, instead of 100, and to tabulate the results for 1,000 trials, as shown in the flow chart of Figure D6.1.

---

*The student will find it informative, as well as entertaining, to obtain and record as many estimates as possible (including his own) before proceeding.

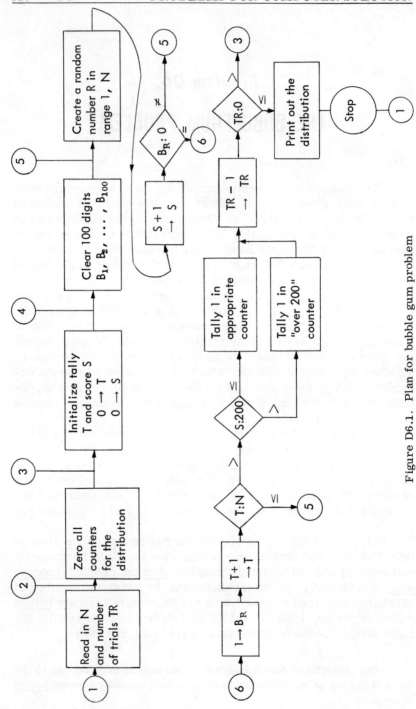

Figure D6.1. Plan for bubble gum problem

EXERCISE 1. (a) Write a routine to implement the
flow chart. Or modify the routine in Problem E6
so as to provide for counting the total number of
random numbers generated and to tabulate the results in 187 counters, one for each total from 15 to
200, and one for any total over 200. (b) Calculate
the mean (average) number of choices for 1,000 or
more trials by hand or with the aid of a routine from
Problem M6. (c) Compare the actual result with the
estimates made beforehand by yourself, your classmates, and business or professional people whose
judgment on nonmathematical matters is generally
regarded as highly reliable. Can you explain any
wide divergence you may find?

The results obtained in Exercise 1 illustrate in a striking
way how unreliable common judgment can be when a large
number of factors are involved. This is one reason why computers are being applied in numerous ways to aid in designing
aircraft, industrial plants, and scientific experiments; in planning production schedules; in studying transportation and storage
problems; and in simulating in various ways the effect of proposed changes upon the conduct of large business.

It often happens that a problem arising in one setting has
other, more important, applications. We therefore seek a general solution to the bubblegum problem. Our mathematical
model is a set of n elements, numbered consecutively from 1
to n. If we choose at random from the numbers 1 to n, how
many choices are required, on the average, to select each element at least once?

EXERCISE 2.(a) Use or modify the routines of Exercise 1 so as to calculate the average number of
random choices required to select each element of
a set of n elements at least once, starting with
n = 2. (b) Tabulate the results of part (a) by hand
or with the computer, up to n = 10.

The regularity in the results obtained in such an experiment as Exercise 2 suggests that some simple formula might
apply.

EXERCISE 3. (a) Represent by the symbol $_nE_p$ the
number of choices expected in order to complete the

permutation of a set of n elements when there are only p elements left to be chosen. Then show that $n^E p = 1 + (p/n) \cdot (n^E p - 1) + [(n - p)/n] \cdot (n^E p)$ and simplify. Now derive a series formula for $n^E n$ by starting with $n^E o = 0$. (b) Write a short Fortran routine to evaluate the formula of part (a) for values of n from 2 to 100. (c) Estimate the time required for the computer to complete 1,000 trials with n = 100.

Problem E1

ROULETTE

Figure E1.1 shows the layout of a roulette wheel. Roulette is played by betting against a bank. The bank offers odds on any bet, based generally on the proper calculation for a wheel with 36 sectors. Since the wheel has 38 sectors (counting the zero and double zero) designed to be all equally likely to receive the little ball, the bank pays slightly less than the true odds. At a rough calculation, the bank will pay out 94.74 cents for every dollar that is bet. Thus, there is a bias in favor of the house. (Special bets may be made on the zero and double zero sectors themselves.)

Since roulette wheels in well-run casinos are properly built and maintained, the 38 possible results occur with equal frequency in the long run; the wheel is, in fact, a fine mechanical random number generator modulo 38. There is no need to rig the wheel; played honestly, it will return that average of 5.26 cents per dollar played. The trick for the house, is to see to it that large numbers of dollars are played.* The secret lies in the phrase "in the long run." There can be short runs during which a player (through luck alone) can win. Those who win will talk; those who lose will be helpfully silent, and the word (of winning) spreads. The best proof that the casino wins a percentage of the total money played is this: the wheel is still there. It is expensive, housed in plush surroundings, and maintains a highly paid banker—and all this money (plus profit) comes from the players. The casinos are not established as philanthropies. Despite these obvious truths, men devote years to devising what they hope will turn out to be winning systems. The casinos are very happy to encourage this sport.

One betting system—the Martingale—applies to any game of chance that offers even money bets. There are three possible

---

*The percentage applies to the total amount played, and may be many times the total amount brought into the casinos. If the same $1,000 is played ten times, the casino collects its percentage on $10,000.

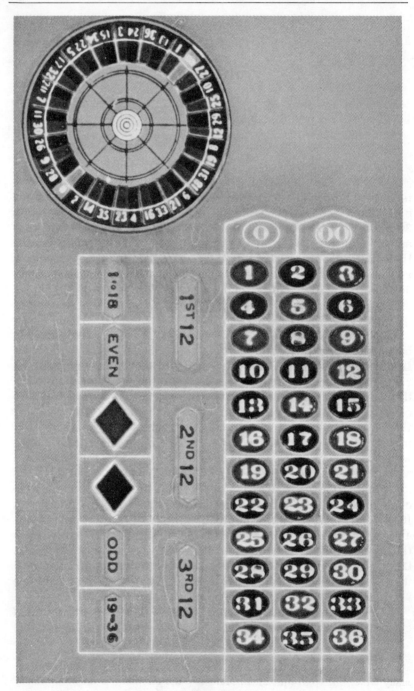

Figure E1.1.

even money bets in roulette: odd-even; red-black; and first
18-last 18. The two zero sectors make these bets slightly less
than even, as far as the correct odds are concerned (by 5.26
per cent, to be exact), but the principle applies. The Martingale
—or doubling—system is quite simple. Bet one unit of money.
If you lose, double the bet. When you win, go back to a one-unit
bet. If this process could continue unchecked, you would be
guaranteed one unit of winnings for each complete round; that
is, each time the bet returns to one unit. Two checks interrupt the
system, and they are both in favor of the house:

1. The house has more money than you have. The house
can stand a run of losses of great length. You can only stand
losses proportionate to powers of 2. That is, if you have at any
moment a bankroll of $1,024, you can stand only nine losses in
a row (starting with a $1 bet) and your bankroll is then gone.

2. The house will not allow you to double your bets without
limit. Generally, you are allowed no more than eight doublings
(the number varies from place to place). Thus, if your smallest
bet is $1, the house will not permit you to bet more than, say,
$200 on any one spin. There may even be a tighter ceiling; a
given table may be restricted to bets under $100 no matter what
your own minimum is.

Nevertheless, the Martingale betting system appears attractive. It will seem to operate to the player's advantage in a
small range. We can demonstrate with our computer that the
fundamental principle still holds: In the long run, the house takes
5.26 per cent of the total amount played. (No betting "system"
can alter the mathematical expectation of the game, of course.)

Since the roulette wheel is a random number generator, it
can be simulated with our computer random number generator,
given in Problem E7. If we generate a 9-digit random number
and reduce it modulo 38, the result represents a spin of a
roulette wheel (letting 37 stand for double zero).

We can, in fact, simulate the entire Martingale betting system. Let us set the player's stake at $20, the player's unit bet
at 50 cents, the house limit at $100, and the limit per game at
$50. Thus, a game can end one of two ways: either by going
broke (i.e., the system calls for a bet larger than the current
stake) or by winning $30. When either occurs, a new game will
be started with the same conditions. When a game ends, we will
type out the number of plays, the state of the player's stake, the
last bet made or attempted, and the maximum size the player's
stake reached during the game. The latter is the amusing figure,
since it shows how much you would have won if you could select
the best position from each game. Of course, this cannot be

determined until the game is over.

The flow chart (in broad brush style) is shown in Figure E1.2. There can be many things added, and parts of the broad flow chart will have to be developed into whole flow charts of their own before coding.

S is the stake initialized to 2,000 (cents). B is the unit bet of 50 cents. C is the counter for the number of wheel spins. M is the field for the maximum value attained by S.

The type of bet (odd-even, red-black, or first-last) is chosen by a random number from 1 to 3.

The subroutine for the wheel spin should set triggers for each type of bet. Let these triggers be numbers, as follows:

T_1 = 1 if wheel is odd, 0 if even. We are betting on odd; therefore both 0 and 37 count as losses.

T_2 = 1 if wheel result is 01 through 18, 0 if 19 through 36, or 00, or 37.

T_3 = 1 if red; 0 if black, or 00, or 37. A table of the red values must be searched.

A manual switch can be coded at Reference 6 to enable us to type after every play, showing C, S, B, type of bet, wheel result, and the win or lose trigger.

Another switch can be coded at Reference 1 to allow for reading in different values of S and B.

The entire program runs about one game per minute. Five minutes of computer time corresponds to about four hours of actual play.

EXERCISE 1. Code the Martingale betting system for playing roulette as described.

Results of such a routine in actual use are shown in Figure E1.3. The initial stake was $15, the minimum bet was 50 cents, and the upper limit to the stake was $30.

Column A shows the number of wheel spins during the game. Column B shows the largest stake that existed during the game. Column C shows the stake when the game ended. Column D shows the bet that the system was calling for when the game ended.

For example, the fourth game was a winner; after 65 spins of the wheel, the stake had doubled.

On the other hand, the second game lost. There must have been five losses in a row, so that the system called for a bet of $16. Since the stake was only $2 at that time, the game ended.

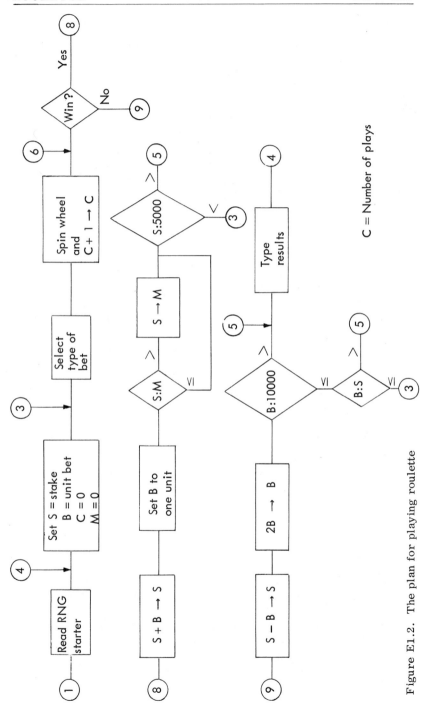

Figure E1.2. The plan for playing roulette

	A	B	C	D
(1)	55	28.50	13.00	16.00
(2)	15	17.50	2.00	16.00
(3)	17	17.50	2.00	16.00
(4)	65	30.00	30.00	0.50
(5)	45	27.50	12.00	16.00
(6)	61	30.00	30.00	0.50
(7)	20	18.50	3.00	16.00
(8)	57	30.00	30.00	0.50
(9)	10	16.50	1.00	16.00
(10)	28	22.50	7.00	16.00
(11)	61	30.00	30.00	.50

Figure E1.3 Some results from the roulette routine

You might make some observations from Figure E1.3. There are a total of 434 wheel spins, representing close to eight hours of play with a physical wheel. The total amount in to the bank is $165 (11 × 15). The total amount out is $160, which is slightly better than one might expect from the odds. The sum of column B is $268.50, from which fact we can draw no conclusions.

Would you expect the sum of column C (for the same number of games), as compared to the total input, to change if the conditions of the system were changed? For example, would the net result differ if the initial stake were $15 but the cutoff point were set at $20 instead of $30?

> EXERCISE 2. Modify your routine to show (either after every game or on demand under switch control) the total amount played and the net amount won or lost. You might also wish to type the ratio of these two numbers.

There are countless other betting systems that have been tried by hopeful players. You can exercise your ingenuity to show with the computer that no system can have the slightest effect on the mathematical expectation of the game. You can thus confirm, by simulating a vast number of trials on the computer, a principle that many persons have been unable to reach in a whole lifetime of gambling experience. The gambler believes (fervently) that it should be possible to find some arrangement or order of his bets that will alter the expectation in his favor. The casinos are delighted to foster this idea. Two simple truths should demolish the concept:

1. Every bet is independent and can have no bearing on any other bet.

2. As was pointed out earlier, the casinos are still in business.

Consider another "winning system." It is noticed that the bet on black on the roulette wheel is nearly an even money bet. But the bet on the third column (i.e., the numbers 3, 6, 9, . . . , 36), which pays two to one, seems to offer different odds on black, since the column contains eight reds and four blacks.

Now, it is a well-known principle that when you can get different odds (on opposite sides) on the same event, you can guarantee a win (not just increase the expectation). It seems that here we have differing odds on the same event. The system specifies continued betting of one unit on each of these bets: black, and third column. The analysis offered is this. Out of 38 plays (giving each sector in the wheel an equal chance to appear), there will be two losses due to the zero and double zero; that makes (−4) from the (+76) units invested.

Of the red results, the 10 that lie in the first two columns are all losses; we have (−20) since they lose also on the bet on black. But the right-hand eight reds pay off at 2 to 1, for a net of (+16).

Of the black results, the 14 in the first two columns both win and lose each time. The four blacks in the third column win on both bets for a net of (+12).

It seems that we can put 76 units in and get 80 units out. This is nonsense, of course. If the flaw isn't glaringly obvious. then do

EXERCISE 3. Program the betting scheme described above and run it for 1,000 spins of the wheel, keeping track of the net amount won or lost and the total amount played (and perhaps the ratio of these).

Problem E2

THE GAME OF DICE

In the game of dice, a player bets even money on his chance of winning when he throws the two dice. If he throws 7 or 11, he wins immediately. If he throws 2, 3, or 12, he loses immediately. For all other numbers (i.e., 4, 5, 6, 8, 9, 10) he must continue to throw until either that number, called the point, appears again (and he wins) or the number 7 intervenes (and he loses).

As in roulette (see Problem E1), the true odds are slightly less than 0.50 for the dice thrower to win.* In the long run, then, he must lose. But it is those short (winning) runs that intrigue the players, plus the ever-present delusion that a system can be devised to alter somehow the mathematical expectations. Numerous systems have been invented and reinvented countless times. We shall describe a system that was probably used by Caesar's legionaries, who doubtless supposed that they had invented a new and wonderful mathematical principle. We suggest that the system (and the whole game of dice) be programmed and run on the computer. This will enable the student to compress a great deal of experience into a few minutes or hours in a meaningful way, so that he can demonstrate the true principle that betting systems do not change the mathematical expectation set by the laws of probability.

Write down a series of numbers, say the integers from 1 to 10. Bet the sum of the first and last numbers (that is, 11 units to start). After a win, cross out the first and last numbers of the series. After a loss, add the amount lost as a new number at the end of the series. The "theory" is this: There will be about as many wins as losses, so eventually the entire list will be crossed off, at which point the player will be ahead by the sum of the original series. The system described above is called the "progressive" system, since the amounts that are won are the successive entries on the list. (The name "progressive" also has an attractive sound to it.)

The same checks operate on the progressive system as on

---

*The odds are 244 to 251; see Exercise 3(b) of this problem.

the Martingale (described in Problem E1 on roulette), so that the system cannot be followed indefinitely.

The student should see that there is little to be gained in writing a routine merely to play a game of dice. The computer is a very expensive piece of equipment to substitute for two small cubes of plastic. But manufacturing and marketing in a competitive business field often have many of the aspects of a game. In testing the plan devised for this simple game, the student is taking a first step toward understanding how computers can be used in modern business to replace guesswork in important decisions of management.

We will need the dice toss subroutine described in Problem E7. This subroutine will be shown as a single block in the flow chart. First we outline the working part for the game of dice, as shown in Figure E2.1. Here again we have an example of one subroutine calling upon another.

EXERCISE 1. (a) Write a routine to play the dice game. (b) Initialize the random number generator RNG and type the output of the dice-tossing routine for 50 tosses. (c) Play several games of dice by hand according to the results of part (b). Check the routine in part (a) to see that it exactly recreates those games when RNG is initialized to the same values, thus testing the routine carefully. (d) Convert the routine to a subroutine.

Next, we outline the betting system. The routine is initialized by reading in the date, the stake S of money available for the game, and the series required by the system. Each game continues until either the stake S reaches the goal (i.e., the list is exhausted), or the system demands a bet B larger than the stake S at that time, or larger than the house limit L of, say, $100. The date and time of use of the computer is used to initialize the random number generator. The output at the end of each game should include:

1. The value of the current stake S when the game ends.
2. The value of the next attempted bet B.
3. The number N of plays.
4. The greatest value M attained by the stake during the game.

The flow chart for simulating the "progressive" system will then resemble Figure E2.2. The student should add to the flow chart in order to print, under switch control, the number cast

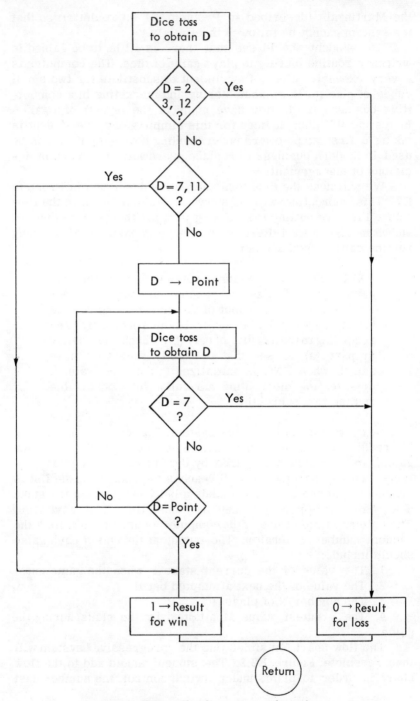

Figure E2.1. The dice game subroutine

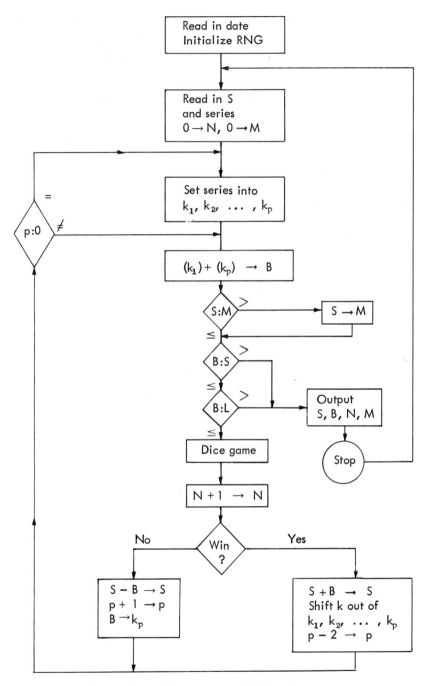

Figure E2.2. The "progressive" betting system

each time. Also under switch control, the routine should print
S, B, M, and the result at the end of each dice game. These outputs will be helpful for debugging the routine, and can also be used
to illustrate the procedure for demonstration purposes.

The series may be terminated with a record mark (on the
IBM 1620) when it is read in from the typewriter. Another way
to convert it into a record is to preset record marks in the series
area as part of the initialization. The series can then be transferred to another area to serve as k_1, k_2, $\cdots$, k_p. A scan of
k_1, k_2, $\cdots$, k_p can be made with operation 45 (BRANCH NO
RECORD MARK) to locate k_{p+1} for use after a loss. After a win
the whole series can be shifted left one word length with operation 31 (TRANSMIT RECORD) in order to eliminate the current
value of k_1. The current value of k_p can be eliminated by setting
a record mark in it. Then k_{p-1} becomes k_p, and the series is
shortened by two numbers.

This fact is indicated in the flow chart by the line $p -
2 \rightarrow p$, but it is only the <u>address</u> of k_p that is actually altered as
there is no need to keep a tally for p. In a similar way, the line
$p + 1 \rightarrow p$ indicates that the address of k_p is changed after a loss,
but no address is actually assigned to p. The series is therefore
adjusted by two instructions after a win, or by two other instructions after a loss. When the address of k_{p+1} is the same as
the address of k_1, the series has been marked out, and the routine returns to set the same series anew.

> EXERCISE 2. (a) Modify the flow chart of Figure
> E2.2 so that additional output can be obtained under
> switch control. (b) Write a routine to simulate the
> "progressive" betting system for the game of dice.
> (c) Modify the routine of part (b) to print messages
> for input and also labels for the output columns.

> EXERCISE 3. (a) Modify the routine of Exercise 2
> to obtain the cumulative results for a great many
> complete games. Use switch control to suppress
> printing for individual games. Calculate the total
> amount bet, the number of dice games played, the
> total won, the total lost, and the probability of win-
> ning a single game of dice as shown by this experi-
> ment. (b) By using the laws of probability show that
> after the first cast the player has a 1/3 chance of
> winning if his point was 4 or 10, 2/5 change of a
> win if the point was 5 or 9, and 5/11 chance for a

point of 6 or 8. Hence calculate the probability of winning a single game of dice from the laws of probability. Compare with the result of Exercise 2 (a), and thus verify the fundamental principle that the betting system does not alter the mathematical expectation.

The student who has performed Exercise 3 will realize that he is acquiring a powerful tool for analyzing proposed financial policies. He will also understand that application of the tool may require the accumulation of large amounts of statistics to establish the fundamental probabilities involved. He should be prepared to find the "betting system" fallacy involved in many business decisions. He will understand further that delusions are not given up readily, so that mathematical results must often be presented with great tact as well as with simple clarity. It may be his task to show in a particular application that large sums may profitably be invested to make the fundamental mathematical probabilities more favorable (or to select favorable probabilities) because it is these which determine the mathematical expectation, and not the particular scheme for distributing the risks.

Problem E3

THE 13 DICE

What is the probability, when 13 dice are cast together, that all the numbers (1, 2, 3, 4, 5, and 6) appear at least once? Such a problem can be attacked analytically; that is, we can express the required probability in exact form for perfect dice. For the problem stated above, the task is not difficult. Suppose the problem increases in complexity a bit: What is the probability, when thirteen dice are cast together, that the number 3 appears at least three times, the number 5 does not appear, and the numbers 1, 2, 4, and 6 appear at least once?

We can obtain an approximation to any such probability we seek by simulating the specified situation on the computer and playing the game many times.

> EXERCISE 1. (a) Using methods presented in Problem E2, write a routine to simulate the tossing of a die 13 times. (b) Under switch control, arrange to type the number of such sets of tosses, and the number of them that display each of the six possible numbers at least once.

There is a closed-form solution to this latter problem; namely,

$$p = 1 - \frac{6 \cdot 5^d - 15 \cdot 4^d + 20 \cdot 3^d - 15 \cdot 2^d + 6}{6^d}$$

where the superscript d is the number of dice. As usual, the formula calculates the probability of the six numbers not appearing, and then subtracts from one for the desired probability. For the situation given at the start of this problem, d = 13. A subproblem of some interest is the evaluation of the formula for d = 6(1)50.*

---

*This notation means that d takes on all values from 6 to 50, increasing by ones.

Problem E4

SIMULATION OF A SUPERSTITION

Someone once said, "The birth of science was the death of superstition." There is less truth than wishful thinking in this assertion. It overlooks two facts: Modern science provides many new things to be superstitious about, and simultaneously provides rapid communication to aid their spread. And few, if any, of the old superstitions seem to have died.

However, the point is that science provides a way to discriminate between truth and superstition. Consider a very common belief: Troubles come in threes. They do indeed, but not for the reason implied in the folklore saying. Random events usually appear in bunches or clusters, but they do so in accordance with the laws of probability. We can demonstrate this truth (about the real world) by a simulation program on a computer. In a sense, nearly every computer routine is a simulation; the exceptions are those routines that explore a number situation directly (such as the problems in this book that explore the properties of the 2^X series).

We can simulate occurrences in the real world in the particular situation of this problem by generating random numbers with the computer. Thus, we substitute a mathematical model for the slow passing of time, so that we can speed up our experimentation by large factors as compared to the real world.

We may start by generating random numbers in the range from 1 to 52. Each random number thus generated represents the week of the year during which an event occurs. We easily calculate that the probability two given events will occur in the same week is 1/52, or nearly 2 per cent, if only two events occur in a year. We can easily write a simple computer routine to test whether the probability that two events will occur in the same week is 10 per cent when <u>ten</u> events occur in a year.

> EXERCISE 1. (a) Write a routine to generate 10 random numbers in the range 1 to 52, using RNG, the random number generator described in Problem E7, and to print a line showing the weeks during the year

when the 10 events occurred. (b) Print results for 100 years (100 lines) using the routine of part (a), and calculate (very roughly) the probability that two events in a given year will occur in the same week.

EXERCISE 2. (a) Elaborate the routine of Exercise 1 in the following ways: Arrange to suppress printing of results for individual years under switch control. Test whether the same number occurs twice in the same year, thus indicating two events in one week. Count the number of these "double events." Print the cumulative number of years after each 100 years, the number of double events, and the percentage. (b) Use or modify the routine of part (a) to obtain percentages for 5, 15, and 20 events per year. (c) Calculate the probability for 5, 10, 15, and 20 events in the same year by applying the laws of probability. According to those laws, the probability that two events do <u>not</u> fall in the same week is $(52/52) \cdot (51/52)$; that three events do not fall in the same week is $(52/52) \cdot (51/52) \cdot (50/52)$; and so on. Compare the results obtained in parts (a) and (b). (d) It is possible for 52 (but not 53) events to occur in different weeks of the same year of 364 days. Calculate the probability for 52 events occurring at random to fall in different weeks of the same year.

Our first approach was to test whether two events occurring at random times could be observed to fall often in the same calendar week. Although it is possible for 52 events to occur in different weeks of the same year, we found that this distribution is extremely unlikely. Contrary to ordinary opinion, if even so few as 10 events are counted in a year, the odds are better than even that two will occur in the same week as the result of chance alone. This result is strikingly different from common belief, which supposes that 10 events occurring at random during the 52 weeks of the year will occur at widely spaced intervals. It is not surprising that such an erroneous belief might lead superstitious people to fear that the occurrence of two extraordinary events in the same week has some dire significance. And if three calamities occur within a week of each other, even though not necessarily in the same calendar week, superstitious awe has been aroused in persons who were otherwise completely reasonable.

We can simulate this new condition very conveniently by representing a year as a line of unit length. An event taking place in that year can be represented in time as a point on the line whose distance from the zero end can be selected by a random number generator.

For example, if the random number generator produces the number 63108, this number can be taken as 0.63108 and can represent an event that occurs 230 days, 8.3 hours after the start of a common year of 365 days. One week is about 0.01918 year. We wish to explore with a computer program the probability (for events which occur at random times) of a cluster within this time span.

We start by having our routine generate three random times. These are arranged in order, and a test is made to determine whether the difference between the earliest and latest events is less than or equal to 0.019178. If so, the result to be typed is the number 3.

If not, a fourth time is chosen and sorted properly in its sequence within the first three. The test now is: Do any three of the four events occur within the space of one week? If so, the result we seek is the number 4.

The process is continued until success is achieved, which must occur by the time 105 events are located, since this would amount to more than two per week, but will in most cases occur long before, as shown by the simpler examples in Exercises 1 and 2. Time magazine lists from five to ten deaths of prominent people per week, which amounts to 300 or so per year. It is obvious that selections can easily be made which appear to support the "calamity" superstition.

For example, suppose that eight times have been selected, as shown on the left side of Figure E4.1. On the right side of the figure the times have been ordered. There is no set of three that occurs within the "distance" 0.019178. Yet it should be evident that it gets increasingly difficult to fit more events into the series spaced far enough apart to avoid the clustering we seek. If we continue to select times at random, the sought-for clustering must eventually appear. It is already evident that random numbers do not have to be evenly spaced. The operation of the laws of probability makes it probable that a cluster of three events in one week will occur long before we run out of room to space further events in the line. In this particular example, one more event located among the last three would almost (but not quite) satisfy the requirement.

0.21594	0.02624
0.87615	0.09779
0.02624	0.21594
0.43972	0.43972
0.85279	0.67264
0.67264	0.85279
0.89902	0.87615
0.09779	0.89902

Figure E4.1.   Eight times chosen at random

EXAMPLE 3. (a) Construct a flow chart for the routine to test the clustering of events that occur at random times. Include the random number generator from Problem E7 and the sorting subroutine from Problem L3.* (b) Write a routine according to the flow chart of part (a). (c) Modify the routine to suppress the printing of results for individual years under switch control, but to tally the results.

Let's turn the problem around the other way. How many random events can we have at most in a year so that there is still space between any two of them of at least R in width (R being an arbitrary choice; say, 0.019178)? Or, for 100 events occurring at random, what is the probability that there exists in the year a space of width R?

These latter forms of the problem have a practical application. Suppose the events being considered are the positions of man-made objects circling the earth. The space R is the portion of the sky that can be observed from a given observation station. The probability we seek is then the probability that at any given moment there is no satellite to observe.

---

*For efficiency, consider two facts. Once a series of numbers is in sort, an additional number need only be inserted in the right place; that is, it is not necessary to go through a complete sorting process. Secondly, the possibility of success can only be in the region of the inserted number; it is not necessary to test the entire sorted series for the cluster that is being sought.

Problem E5

THE RHINE TEST

Experimenters in the field of extrasensory perception (ESP) have for many years used an experiment involving a deck of cards. There are 25 cards in the deck, with five identical cards in each of the five suits. The deck is shuffled, and the subject is asked to name the suit of each card in turn without seeing it. The card is then shown. Some subjects make much higher scores than others and are judged to have ESP.

Experimenters with ESP often reason that if the guesses were completely random, then a match should occur, on the average, once in five tries, or the expected number of matches is five for the entire deck. When a given subject scores higher than five, this is taken as contributory evidence of some type of thought transmission (or other form of ESP).

The student should first perform at least one ESP experiment with a deck of cards. Then he may wish to write a routine to calculate the empirical (experimental) distribution of scores on the basis of chance alone. That is, he can simulate the experiment a very large number of times, using one of the random number generators described in Problem E7.

The deck is represented in storage by 25 symbols in an area labeled S (for source):

$$(S) \qquad 1111122222333334444455555$$

To shuffle the deck, we scramble the symbols and place them in an area called A, perhaps as follows:

$$(A) \qquad 3142552153412134235143254$$

To simulate the test, we scramble the symbols independently into an area called B:

$$(B) \qquad 3523142534154235142341512$$

To find the score, we count the number of matches in the cor-

131

responding positions of A and B; it is 4 in our example. A tally of <u>one</u> is added to a counter that is to hold the number of scores of 4. The expected score for any one game is 5, but it is possible to have any score from 0 to 25. We also wish to count the total number of scores. We therefore provide 27 counters. After each additional thousand such games, we type the total number for each score. When 10,000 games have been tabulated, we expect the distribution of scores to be fairly representative, and we can read the percentage occurrence of each score almost directly from the table, by placing a decimal point to mark off two decimal places. A typical set of results for 100 games is shown in Figure E5.1.

Number of Matches	Times Occurred
0	0
1	0
2	4
3	18
4	12
5	24
6	17
7	14
8	5
9	2
10	3
11	0
12	1
13-25	0

Figure E5.1. Typical results for 100 games

First we need a subroutine to simulate the shuffling of a deck of 25 cards, as suggested in the flow chart of Figure E5.2. We have already established three storage areas, S, A, and B, each 25 digits long. The subroutine sets up two more: W (for work area) and D (for deck). The subroutine first moves the symbols from area S to area D. This is abbreviated in the flow chart by writing $c(S) \rightarrow D$, where the symbol $c(S)$ means the contents of the area S. We use S_1 to indicate the address of the first digit in area S, and W_1 to indicate the first digit in area W. Each time the subroutine is called, area W will be filled with a new scrambled version of the symbols in area S. A neat check

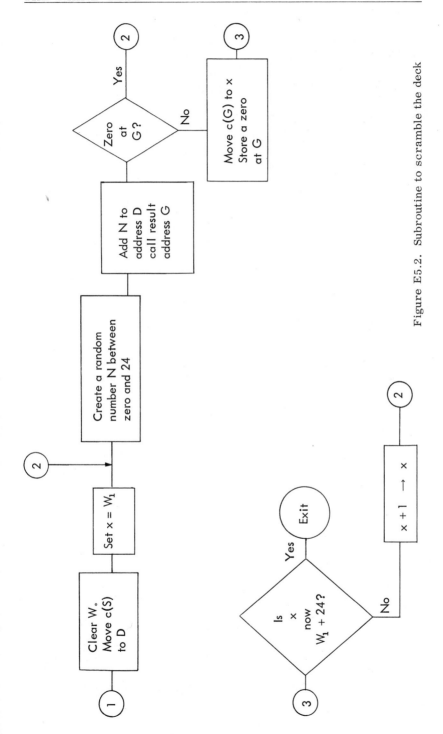

Figure E5.2. Subroutine to scramble the deck

can be programmed for the action of the subroutine; namely, that the contents of W should sum to 75. The main routine will use the subroutine for simulating the shuffle of the card deck, moving c(W) to A. It will use the subroutine again to simulate the answers given by a subject, this time moving c(W) to B.

> EXERCISE 1. (a) Write a routine in accordance with the flow chart of Figure E5.2 to simulate the shuffling of a deck of 25 cards by scrambling 25 symbols. (b) After checking out the routine of part (a), convert it to a subroutine.

A second subroutine is needed to make the comparisons between areas A and B. The flow chart of Figure E5.3 applies.

A tally is made in the appropriate counter by creating a new address from the address of the first counter, somewhat as G is formed in Figure E5.2, but adding a multiple of c(M).

> EXERCISE 2. Write a routine to compare areas A and B, following the flow chart in Figure E5.3.

With the subroutines at hand, the main routine can be coded to play any number of games. The flow chart of Figure E5.4 now applies. L is the limit of the number of games to be played before typing the distribution of scores. For debugging purposes, L is set to some low number (say, 1); for production, L would be set to 100, or 1,000.

> EXERCISE 3. (a) Write a main routine to play 1,000 games and type the cumulative results after each additional 100 games. Assemble the routine with the three subroutines. (b) Change the routine of part (a) to type only nonzero results in the case of more than 12 matches, and type the number of matches. (c) Modify the routine of part (b) so that 10,000 games can be played.

The exercises have given reliable estimates of the distribution of scores if answers are given by shuffling an answer deck. It remains to investigate some chance factors which may produce scores that are consistently low or consistently high. In the actual conduct of the Rhine test, the subject does not have an answer deck, but is instructed to try to visualize the card which is face down on the deck in front of him. Under these

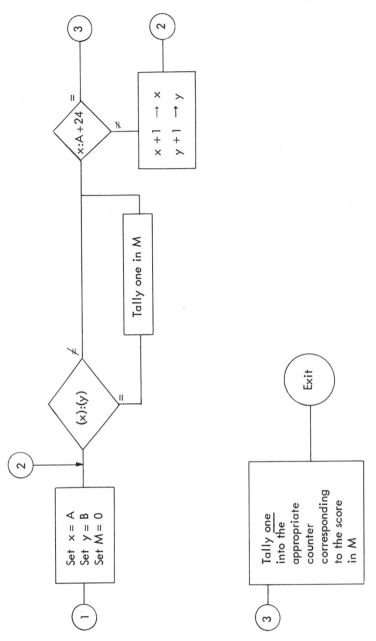

Figure E5.3. Subroutine to compare areas A and B

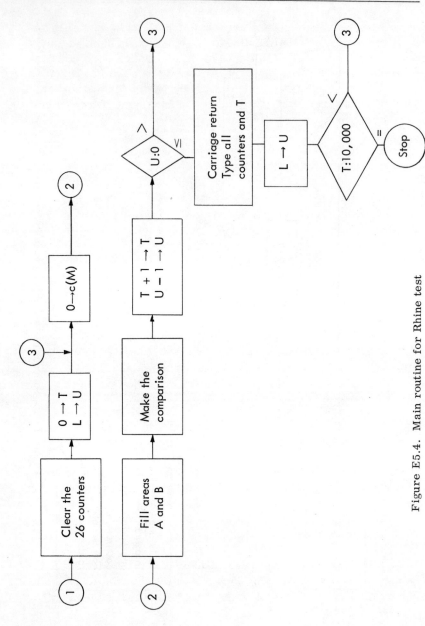

Figure E5.4. Main routine for Rhine test

circumstances, he does not (or should not) make any effort to recall what guesses he has already made. Consequently he may guess a suit more or less than five times, which does not correspond to the shuffling method that has been used in exercises to simulate the test. The student may now wish to investigate the effect of choosing a suit at random, without trying to recall how many times that suit has already been called.

> EXERCISE 4. (a) Write a routine to choose suits at random and compare immediately with a given deck.
> (b) Extend the routine to play 1,000 to 10,000 games and tabulate results as in Exercise 3.

Exercise 4 has shown whether remembering the previous guesses (in order to even up the suits) has a significant effect upon the results of the Rhine test. The student will see that remembering the suits that have already been shown (rather than the suits that have been called as guesses) might have a pronounced effect upon the results.

> EXERCISE 5. (a) Show by applying the laws of probability that five matches can be expected if the subject chooses suits at random. (b) Show that there must be in the deck five cards of at least one suit until five cards have been shown. Hence, if this suit is called, the probability of a match increases steadily for five calls. Show similarly that there must be at least four cards of some suit left in the deck until ten cards have been shown, and so on. Calculate the expected number of matches if the subject chooses in this favorable way. (c) Write a routine to choose at random from suits with the largest number of outstanding cards, playing 10,000 games and typing results as in Exercise 3.

> EXERCISE 6. Modify the routine of Exercise 5 (c) so as to choose at random from the suits with the least number of outstanding cards, and play 10,000 games, typing the results as before.

Problem E6

RANDOM PERMUTATIONS

Counting the number of ways a set of N things can be ordered or arranged is important in many problems involving combinations, chance, and the principles of statistics. The number of ways N different things can be arranged in a single line (permutations) is factorial N (written N!). In some combinatorial problems, we need to generate all the permutations systematically, as described in Problem D1. For other problems, related to probability and statistics (especially when the number N is much over 10, and N! becomes enormous), it suffices to sample the N! permutations (provided that we are careful in our sampling plan to avoid bias). We can think of the task of selecting a random sample from a set of N things, for illustration, as the beginning of a procedure in which the whole set is placed in random order.

A simple and obvious way to scramble the order of N things is to number them consecutively, and then to choose those numbers at random with a random number generator, such as RNG described in Problem E7. If a number obtained from the random number generator has already appeared, it is disregarded, and more numbers are generated until a sample of required size is obtained, or until the whole set has been placed in random order, whichever is required.

The flow chart of Figure E6.1 suggests an effective way to carry out the procedure. It is assumed that a sample of size S from all the (N!) permutations is desired. If a complete permutation of all the N things is required, S is made equal to N.

EXERCISE 1. (a) Write a routine in accordance with the flow chart of Figure E6.1 to select a sample of 10 permutations for $N \geq 10$. (b) Change the routine of part (a) so that the sample is placed in storage. Place the typing under switch control. (c) Change the routine to a subroutine with N and S as parameters specified in the calling sequence.

138

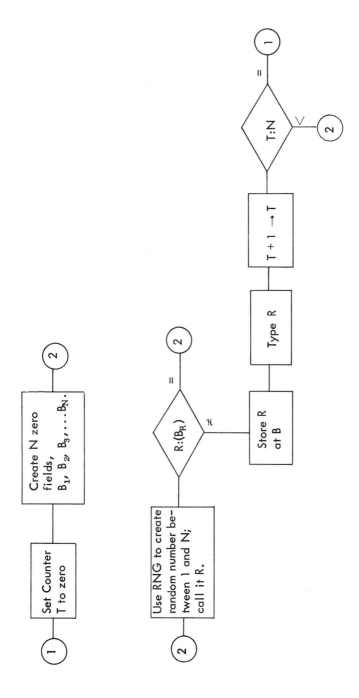

Figure E6.1. Random permutation routine

The procedure described for selecting random permutations can be used also for generating complete permutations of the whole set if the number N of things in the set is not too large. If N is around 15, the program starts out faster than the typewriter, but the student can observe a slowing down, so that the last number takes a noticeable amount of time, during which successive random numbers are generated and discarded until the right one is found. With larger values of N, this effect will be exaggerated, so that a better method is needed. Obviously, the last number should be the easiest to find, since there is only one possibility left.

Instead of numbering the set of N things consecutively from 1 to N, we may number them with large random numbers (say, of 9 digits) supplied by a random number generator. Then we may sort them by using the random numbers as a key. This gives us a random permutation of the whole set of N things, even for large sets. Sorting with a key is explained in Problem L3.

> EXERCISE 2. Write a routine to simulate the shuffle of a deck of playing cards by generating 52 large random numbers and sorting the symbols representing the cards by using the random numbers as a key.

Testing the results of a routine intended to produce perfectly random permutations is difficult. Figure E6.2 shows some typical results for N = 11 from the generator described first. Each line appears to be a properly randomized arrangement of the numbers from 1 to 11. How can we tell? One way is to count the number of permutations in which the kth element of the permutation is the number k itself. The probability for this to happen by chance can be calculated from the laws of probability. For the sample permutations shown in Figure E6.2, four of the eight results exhibit this characteristic, as shown by the circled numbers. (The second line counts only as a single permutation, even though it contains two circled numbers.)

> EXERCISE 3. (a) Show by actually enumerating all the permutations of N things for N = 2, 3, and 4 that the probability for the coincidence test is

$$\frac{1}{1!} - \frac{1}{2!} + \frac{1}{3!} - \cdots \frac{1}{N!}$$

6	8	10	9	1	5	4	11	3	2	7
7	3	4	11	8	(6)	9	1	2	(10)	5
11	7	4	6	2	10	1	3	5	8	9
9	10	1	(4)	6	8	11	5	2	7	3
3	8	4	5	6	7	11	1	2	9	10
4	1	7	2	10	11	6	3	(9)	8	5
7	9	11	8	10	2	5	6	1	4	3
10	5	4	3	6	7	11	(8)	1	2	9

Figure E6.2. Random permutations for N = 11

(For large values of N, say 10 or more, this probability approaches $1 - (1/e)$, where e is the base of
natural logarithms. It is therefore approximately
equal to $1 - 1/2.71828$, or 0.63212.) (b) Write a
routine to generate 1,000 permutations with N = 15
and count how many of them have their kth element
equal to k.

The coincidence test applies equally well if the permutations
are rotated cyclically. This furnishes a basis for further
checking.

RANDOM NUMBERS

In the conduct of any business, when decisions must be made upon a basis of incomplete information, reliance is often placed upon "good judgment." For important decisions, perhaps involving millions of dollars, it is becoming increasingly common to supplement the intuitive ideas of probability which underlie good judgment with mathematical calculations based upon carefully collected statistics. The concept of random choice plays a central role in these calculations. We shall explain this concept in terms of a simple game.

When a perfectly symmetrical die is rolled out of a cup on to a level surface, we suppose that in the long run no particular face will be uppermost oftener than any other face. That is, in a very large number of trials, we expect each of the six numbers from 1 to 6 to occur about one-sixth of the time. The casting of a die represents our notion of a random distribution of the numbers from 1 to 6. In a similar way, we would define a random distribution of the numbers from 1 to 999,999,999 as a selection in which each number under one billion has the same probability of appearing, but is otherwise unrestricted.

We can simulate a random distribution of the numbers from 1 to 6 by imagining a sequence of one billion digits. In this sequence the numbers 1 to 6 occur an equal number of times. We plan to select from them in an apparently irregular order according to a rule which will not repeat until an extremely large number of choices has been made. This plan requires us to generate numbers between zero and one billion. We divide such a number by 6, discarding the quotient but retaining the remainder. That is, we reduce the number <u>modulo</u> 6. Then we add 1, making a nearly random choice of one of the numbers from 1 to 6.

We generate the 9-digit numbers (i.e., between zero and one billion) by using a property of certain prime numbers. If any number less than p is multiplied repeatedly by two and reduced modulo p after each multiplication, where p is a prime of the form (8n + 3) or (8n + 5), all the numbers less than p will be obtained in scrambled order once and only once before the results start repeating, as explained in Problem F6 on primitive roots. We use a prime number P of the proper form, which is very near one billion, say 999,999,893, so that we obtain almost a billion different numbers exactly once before repeating any one of them. The probability for selecting one of the numbers from 1 to 6 is therefore almost exactly equal to the probability for each of the other numbers.

> EXERCISE 1. Write a routine to simulate the casting of a die. Generate 9-digit numbers by doubling the previous result and reducing modulo 999,999,893 (which can be done in this case by subtraction, rather than division). Store the result. Then select a number as described, by dividing the result by 6 and adding 1 to the remainder. Describe and implement a procedure to test this routine thoroughly.

The scrambling effect in Exercise 1 can be increased in various ways. One simple way is to use a larger multiplier. Another way is to scramble two different numbers and add them, after reducing each with a different prime. The second way is used in the flow chart of Figure E7.1. The prime number Q, which is used to reduce the second product, is 999,999,883. In that flow chart the scrambling is increased still more by adding the sum to the previous result, S, and discarding any overflow beyond 9 digits. A subroutine* to implement the flow chart on the IBM 1620 computer is shown in Figure E7.2. It will be called RNG, for "random number generator." The calling sequence is 17 19000 x̄xxxx where xxxxx represents the location of the calling instruction. The output of the generator is a 9-digit random number addressed at 19927, embedded in a 10-digit field whose high-order digit is always zero.

> EXERCISE 2. Write a routine to use the RNG subroutine of Figure E7.2 to simulate 1,000 throws of a die and tabulate the results, showing how many falls were obtained for each number from 1 to 6.

The numbers generated by RNG are satisfactory for many applications of random distributions of numbers, but they are

---

*Taken from F. J. Gruenberger and D. D. McCracken, Introduction to Electronic Computers, John Wiley & Sons, Inc., New York, 1963, p. 59, with slight modifications.

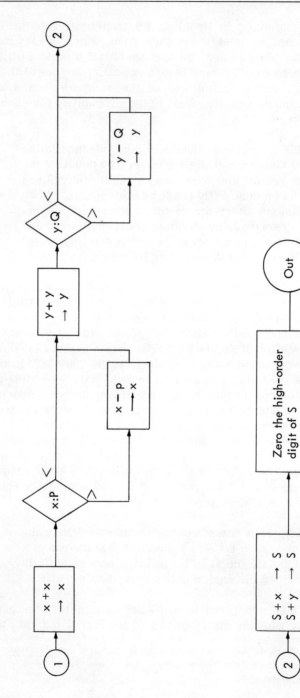

Figure E7.1. A random number generator

Location	Op	P	Q	Remarks
19000	11	18999	$\bar{0}0012$	Create exit
12	26	19162	18999	
24	21	19179	19179	$x + x \rightarrow x$
36	24	19179	19191	x:P
48	47	19072	01100	
60	22	19179	19191	$x - P \rightarrow x$
72	21	19203	19203	$y + y \rightarrow y$
84	24	19203	19215	y:Q
96	47	19120	01100	
19108	22	19203	19215	$y - Q \rightarrow y$
20	21	19227	19179	$S + x \rightarrow S$
32	21	19227	19203	$S + y \rightarrow S$
44	15	19218	$0000\bar{0}$	Zero to S
56	49	$\bar{0}0000$	00000	Exit
68	00	$\bar{0}3141$	59265	x
80	00	$\bar{0}9999$	99893	P
92	00	$\bar{0}2718$	28183	y
19204	00	$\bar{0}9999$	99883	Q
16	00	$\bar{0}0000$	00000	S

Figure E7.2. A random number generator (RNG) for the IBM 1620 computer.

obviously not selected at random, because they can be generated again in precisely the same order by using the same starting values of x, y, and S. This is true of all numbers generated with the computer; numbers such as those produced by RNG are therefore called pseudo-random numbers.* The ability to repeat the numbers in the same order is useful for checking out a routine. At other times the point of entry into the vast stream of numbers is chosen at random by changing one or more of the starting values. For example, x might be chosen as the date and hour of execution of the routine. Provision should always be made in the main routine for reading the value of x into the subroutine from the typewriter. Another way to vary the starting point is to provide at the beginning of a routine for calling

---

*When we use the expression "random number," we really mean a number selected at random from a prescribed set of numbers. In the random number generator, "random" may be regarded as modifying "generator" rather than "number."

upon the subroutine repeatedly under switch control without using the output. About a hundred numbers per second will be generated with the Model I IBM 1620. The switch setting can be changed after a random time varying up to two or three seconds, thus making the output unpredictable.

> EXERCISE 3. (a) Improve the routine of Exercise 2 by providing for reading in the starting value of x. (b) Use the routine of part (a) several times to tabulate the results of 1,000 throws of a die each time, using different starting values for x.

The results obtained in simulating the casting of a single die show the same probability for any number from 1 to 6. This simple situation no longer prevails when two dice are thrown.

> EXERCISE 4. (a) Show by using the laws of probability that when two dice are thrown, the probability for the occurrence of various numbers from 2 to 12 varies from 1/36 to 1/6. (b) Write a subroutine in accordance with the flow chart of Figure E7.3 to simulate 1,000 throws of two dice and tabulate the results.

The subroutine in part (b) of Exercise 3 is used to simulate the tossing of two dice in Problems E2 and E3.

> EXERCISE 5. (a) Calculate by hand, as before, the probabilities for a throw of three dice. (b) Write a routine to use the dice-casting subroutine three times to simulate the casting of three dice, and tabulate the results for 10,000 throws.

Simulation of the casting of dice requires selection at random from a set of six integers. Other problems involving probability may require selection at random from a set of different size. We may combine the random number generator with a subroutine to select a number from a set of any given size. The combined subroutine can be referred to as the random number selector (RNS). It is convenient to retain the original linkage when the new one is added so that RNG and RNS may be used as two independent subroutines, although in fact they form a single subroutine with two entries.

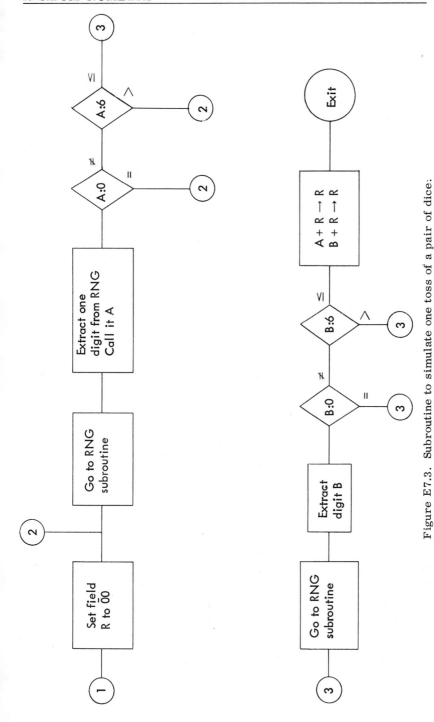

Figure E7.3. Subroutine to simulate one toss of a pair of dice:

EXERCISE 6. (a) Write a routine to select a number at random from the first N integers. (b) Convert the routine of part (a) into a subroutine. Provide two linkages so that the subroutine can function as RNG or RNS. (c) Write a routine to use the RNS subroutine to select 1,000 numbers at random from the integers from 1 to 38 and tabulate the results.

It is clear that the set of numbers x referred to in Figure E7.2, which contains exactly one of each number between zero and p, is not a random selection of numbers. It is merely a scrambled set of nearly a billion numbers, which were used at first instead of the numbers S for choosing numbers at random from the first six integers. The set of numbers S is of far greater size. If the right-hand digit is disregarded, the set has been found by extensive tests of many kinds to represent a very good approximation to a random selection from the first 100 million integers. Some of these tests are described in Problems E11, E8, E9, and E10.*

The cycle length of a random number generator is the number of fresh numbers that are produced before the same numbers begin to repeat in the same order. In RNG, it is the size of the set of numbers S. We can estimate the cycle length of RNG in the following way. The set of numbers x contains $P - 1$, or 999,999,892 numbers, while the set of numbers y contains $Q - 1$, or 999,999,892 numbers. If we merely add x and y, the same numbers would not repeat in the same order until the number of random numbers generated reached the least common multiple of $(P - 1)$ and $(Q - 1)$. This is the basic cycle length of RNG. Since $(P - 1)/2$ and $(Q - 1)/2$ are prime numbers, the least common multiple of $(P - 1)$ and $(P - 2)$ is $[(P - 1)(Q - 1)]/2$. The actual cycle of the generator is consiaerably longer, because of the way the output is progressively totaled in forming the numbers S. The actual cycle length for RNG is around 10^{27}.

The cycle length of RNG could be made as long as we please by means of simple modifications. For example, we could use larger numbers for P, Q, x, and y. Or, we could add another variable z, and reduce it with a third prime R, and so on. However, although RNG operates in a very simple way, its cycle length is adequate. It is difficult to sense the size of a number like 10^{27}. If there were a computer fast enough to generate

---

*It has been pointed out, however, that the generator given in Figure E7.2 exhibits a high degree of correlation between successive numbers generated.

and use a billion random numbers per second, RNG would furnish fresh numbers for more than 31 billion years.

EXERCISE 7. (a) Modify the RNG subroutine slightly so that the cycle length is less than one million (for 3-digit numbers) by using the following values:

$$x = 1$$
$$P = 997$$
$$y = 1$$
$$Q = 971$$

and resetting S to zero for each random number. The last three digits of S will represent the random numbers. The first number will be 004; the cycle length should be the least common multiple of 996 and 970, which is 483,060. (b) Write a routine to test the cycle length of the 3-digit random number generator of part (a) by calling the subroutine repeatedly. Regarding the first results as 9-digit numbers (000000004, 000000008, 000000016, 000000032), test for the next occurrence of this sequence. When it happens, stop and print the number of calls.

EXERCISE 8. (a) Modify the RNG subroutine so that the result is converted to a floating-point number between 0 and 1 and stored in the format used by your Fortran processor. Also modify the RNS subroutine so that N is replaced by a floating-point argument T. (b) Convert the subroutines of part (a) to Fortran functions RNG(T) and RNS(T), where T is a dummy argument for RNG(T). Insert the subroutines in your processor.

EXERCISE 9. (a) Write a Fortran routine to draw a card at random five times from a deck of 52 playing cards, if the card is replaced after each draw. (b) Change the routine of part (a) so that five different cards are drawn.

Problem E8

THE GAP TEST FOR RANDOM DIGITS

Suppose that we have 1,000 digits stored in consecutive addresses and that we intend to use them to make random choices for a computer problem. How can we test the sequence of digits to ascertain whether the digits are distributed at random? The gap test is one of six standard tests that are used for this purpose.

If each digit has the same probability of occurring, we would expect a particular digit to occur at intervals of 10 digits on the average. In the gap test, we select some digit and count from that digit to the next appearance of the same digit, and from there to the next appearance, and so on. For example, if we examine the first 250 digits of the number e* (that is, the base of the system of natural logarithms), we find zeros occurring at the following intervals, starting from the decimal point: 13, 8, 22, 24, 5, 40, 1, 2, 18, 7, 1, 9, 6, 18, 12, 10, 3, 14, 2, 5, 16, 10, and 4. The average interval for this small sample is 250/23, or 10.87, which is close to the expected average of 10.

We can make a further comparison with the results to be expected if the digits were selected at random. We calculate the variance of the distribution, using the method described in Problem M6. The variance for random digits is calculated as 90 by using the laws of probability. The variance for this small sample is 85.03, which is reasonably close to the expected value.

To complete the gap test, the intervals should be counted for all the other digits separately, as well as for zero.

> EXERCISE 1. (a) Write a routine to read in from cards the first 1,003 digits after the decimal point of e, as found in Figure E9.3. (b) Write a routine to count the intervals between zeros for the fractional part of e up to 1,000 decimal places, and to type the results.

---

*They can be found in Figure E9.3.

We can determine whether the mean and variance differ to a significant extent from the expected values by applying the statistical methods described in Problem M6. The variance of the mean (average) is expected to be M/N; for the sample, this is 90/23, since M refers to the expected average for the intervals, and N refers to the number of intervals (not to the original number of digits, of course). The expected standard deviation of the mean is about 2, i.e., the square root of the variance. The actual mean value of 10.87 is well within the 95 per cent range of expectation, since it differs from the expected mean by far less than twice the expected standard deviation.

The variance is also within the fluctuation limits for 95 per cent expectation. The cutoff value of chi square for $N - 1$ degrees of freedom is obtained from the table in Problem M4; it is 33.9. The variance of the variance is $(N - 1)V$ or $22(85.03) = 1,870$. It is less than χ^2 times the expected variance, which is 33.9(90) or 3,051, so that the variance passes the test. To complete the gap test, these determinations must be made for every digit (0 through 9).

EXERCISE 2. (a) Use the routines of Exercise 1, as well as routines for the mean, variance, and standard deviation from Problem M6, to carry out the gap test for zeros in the fraction part of e. (b) Modify Exercise 1 (b) so as to suppress printing and to allow the counting for any digit. Combine the required routines so that the mean, variance, and standard deviation can be printed out for each digit from 0 through 9.

Problem E9

THE POKER TEST FOR RANDOM DIGITS

Of the various standard tests of randomness that are applied to a given set of digits, the poker test is one of the most stringent. At the same time it is one of the most difficult to apply, since it can lead to a long string of logical decisions to be carried out by the computer routine. This very useful test for randomness is an excellent illustration of decision making in computer programming.

In the poker test, we compare the repetition of digits in small groups of digits with the frequency to be expected according to the laws of probability. For convenience, we choose groups of 4 digits, and determine the frequency of occurrence for 4 digits of one kind, three of a kind, two pairs, one pair, or all different, as shown in Figure E9.1. We may form the groups by taking the first 4 digits, and then the next 4, and so on. A stricter test is to take each successive grouping of 4 digits, starting with the first digit, then the second digit, and so on, so that each digit (except the first 3 and the last 3 of the sequence being examined) is tested in four different groups. The expected frequencies are shown in relation to 1,000 sets of 4 digits, and should be checked by the student.

To program the test we start with the working section, part of which is suggested in Figure E9.2. We need only 14 comparisons to classify the group of digits according to the 15 patterns, because the last comparison will separate two patterns.

> EXERCISE 1. (a) Use the laws of probability to calculate the expected frequency for each type of repetition by extending the method applied to calculate the expected frequencies for two dice. (b) Finish the flow chart of Figure E9.2 and write a routine to type out, on one line, the frequency for each type of repetition in a sequence of 1,003 digits. (c) Use the routine of part (b) to test the first 1,003 digits of e, the base for natural logarithms, as given in Figure E9.3.

Pattern		Type	Expected Frequency	Examples
1	AAAA	4 of a kind	1	7777
2	AAAB			2226
3	AABA	3 of a kind	36	3303
4	ABAA			5055
5	ABBB			9111
6	AABB			6655
7	ABAB	2 pairs	27	3737
8	ABBA			0440
9	AABC			2234
10	ABAC			5658
11	ABCA	1 pair	432	9729
12	ABBC			1002
13	ABCB			5696
14	ABCC			8611
15	ABCD	none alike	504	1234

Total   1000

Figure E9.1. The pattern of repetition in the poker test of randomness.

The name of the test was suggested by the similarity of the patterns to the grouping of hands in the card game of poker. Yet in the card game, a hand has five cards. This test would become much more complex if the digits were to be analyzed five at a time. Before undertaking any such extension of the test, the student should consider whether any improvement can be made in the method for groups of 4 digits, thus applying the principle Look for a better way.

The student will see that there are only 6 basic comparisons to be made within each group of 4 digits, taking 2 at a time. The 14 comparisons required to complete the logic illustrated in Figure E9.2 include repetitions of these basic comparisons. How can we use these 6 basic comparisons, 2 at a time, to distinguish the 15 different patterns?

We can systematize our testing by making all six basic comparisons for each group of four digits; this can be done with a short loop. For each comparison that tests equal, a tally can be made in a counter. The start of this scheme is shown in Figure E9.4.

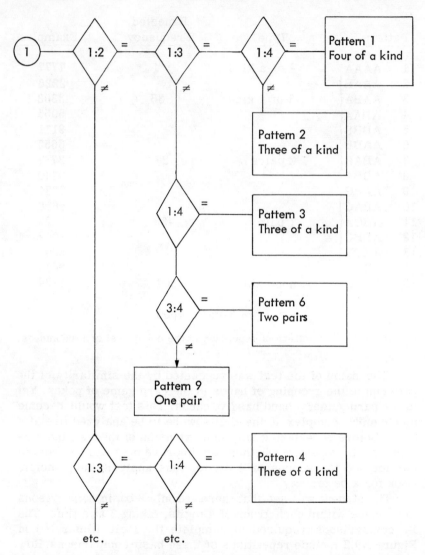

Figure E9.2. Partial flow chart for the poker test, illustrating the logical decisions

e - 2.71828	18284	59045	23536	02874	71352	66249	77572	47093	69995
95749	66967	62772	40766	30353	54759	45713	82178	52516	64274
27466	39193	20030	59921	81741	35966	29043	57290	03342	95260
59563	07381	32328	62794	34907	63233	82988	07531	95251	01901
15738	34187	93070	21540	89149	93488	41675	09244	76146	06680
82264	80016	84774	11853	74234	54424	37107	53907	77449	92069
55170	27618	38606	26133	13845	83000	75204	49338	26560	29760
67371	13200	70932	87091	27443	74704	72304	96977	20931	01416
92836	81902	55151	08657	46377	21112	52389	78442	50569	53696
77078	54499	69967	94686	44549	05987	93163	68892	30098	79312
77361	78215	42499	92295	76351	48220	82698	59193	66803	31825
28869	39849	64651	05820	93923	98294	88793	32036	25094	43117
30123	81970	68416	14039	70198	37679	32068	32823	76464	80429
53118	02328	78250	98194	55815	30175	67173	61332	06981	12509
96181	88159	30416	90351	59888	85193	45807	27386	67385	89422
87922	84998	92086	80582	57492	79610	48419	84443	63463	24496
84875	60233	62482	70419	78623	20900	21609	90235	30436	99418
49146	31409	34317	38143	64054	62531	52096	18369	08887	07016
76839	64243	78140	59271	45635	49061	30310	72085	10383	75051
01157	47704	17189	86106	87396	96552	12671	54688	95703	50354
021									

Figure E9.3. The first 1,003 digits in the decimal representation of e

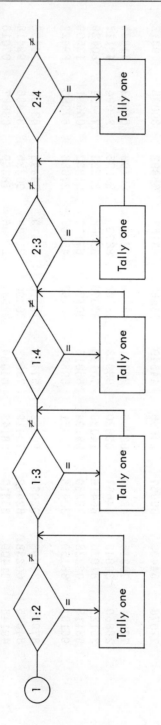

Figure E9.4. A simpler scheme for the poker test

The first comparison in Figure E9.4 indicates "compare the value of the first digit to the value of the second digit," and so on. If all six comparisons come out unequal (for a case like 2835), then the total tally will be zero. Examination of Figure E9.1 will show that all the cases of two pair will result in a tally of 2, and that each of the five types has a unique total.

EXERCISE 2. (a) Determine the totals to be expected from the schemes of Figure E9.4 for each of the types shown in Figure E9.1. (b) Write a routine to implement this shortened test. (c) Apply your routine to a known set of digits,   or a set generated by a RNG routine.

EXERCISE 3. (a) Write a routine in 25 instructions or less, plus input and output instructions, to perform the poker test on 1,003 digits. (b) Apply the routine of part (a) to the first 1,003 digits of π (as found, for example, in Mathematics of Computation, Vol. 16, No. 77, January 1962, p. 76). (c) Calculate by hand or by means of a routine of Problem M4 the value of chi squared for the results of part (b). Draw a conclusion about the randomness of the digits in the decimal representation of π.

The poker test was designed for hand computation, in which it was far more convenient to tabulate the 5 types of repetition than to tabulate the 15 different patterns. With the limited counts that are usually made by hand, the use of 5 classes instead of 15 also gave more reliable results. The student may use the computer to tabulate the frequencies for the 15 patterns and also to apply the chi squared test directly to the results.

EXERCISE 4. (a) Use a random number generator (see Problem E7) to store 10,003 (pseudo-random) digits. Then use, or modify, the routine of Exercise 1 to classify successive groups of 4 digits according to the 15 patterns. Finally, use your chi-squared routine to test the randomness of the digits. (b)

Follow the plan of part (a) to test the output of your random number generator in various ways: Is a sequence of the first digits of the output a random sequence? Does a sequence of the last digits qualify? Does a sequence of the interior digits meet the test?

EXERCISE 5. (a) Calculate how many different patterns can be formed when 5 digits are included in a group. (b) Modify the routine of Exercise 2 to read in and test 1,004 digits for randomness by applying the poker test to groups of 5 digits. Calculate the value of chi squared for each pattern. (c) Discuss the changes in the effectiveness of the poker test for about 1,000 digits when the group is increased from 4 to 5.

EXERCISE 6. (a) Devise a poker test that will include five of a kind, full house, and straights, as well as the other types of repetition. (b) Discuss the usefulness of such a test for random digits.

The poker test may be used to test the randomness of the output from a random number generator, the spins of a roulette wheel, the digits in the decimal representation of an irrational number, and so on. It is not so easy to construct test data of controlled nonrandomness. The following example is very good. If the 10 digits 1234431112 are repeated 101 times, the first 1,003 digits will show a distribution of 100 each of patterns 2, 3, 5, 7, 8, 9, 10, and 15, and 200 of type 14. The result will then be 100 of none alike, 200 of two pair, 300 of three of a kind, and 400 of one pair. This result can be used to test the routine thoroughly. The chi-squared value for such a regular distribution will be enormous; it is 6890.211.

The poker test of random digits is one of eight standard tests. Two of them are simple and are not discussed in this book. They are the frequency test (a count of the appearances of each digit from zero to nine) and the serial test (a count of the appearances of each combination of two digits, ranging from 00 to 99). In addition to the gap test, the poker test, and the d^2 test (covered here at some length), there are three other tests:

The maximum test. For three consecutive digits, a maximum is defined as the situation in which the situation in which the center digit is greater than either of the outside two digits (e.g., 387). In theory, this situation will occur 285 times out of each 1000 sets.

The correlation test. This test can take many forms. It is a test of the correlation between successive numbers produced by the generator.

The coupon collector's test. In this test, a count is made of the number of digits required to make up a complete set of the ten decimal digits (see also Problem D6).

Of these eight tests, six are concerned with random digits, rather than random numbers (the d^2 test and the correlation test deal with numbers), and moreover are intrinsically decimal in nature; they are therefore well suited to exploration on a decimal computer.

How many such tests does it take to establish that a given scheme of generation is completely satisfactory? There is no such limit; for any set of random digits (or random numbers) produced by an algorithm, a new test can probably be devised for which the set will fail. The generator given in Problem E7, for example, fails the correlation test, but passes the other seven tests nicely. It could be modified so that it would pass the correlation test, but it would then probably fail some other, more subtle, test.

These statements are readily demonstrated. Any random digit generator should produce the sequence 5555, with probability .0001 of appearing. Longer strings of 5's have corresponding probabilities; they are smaller, but non-zero. Using familiar algorithms (particularly congruential schemes, as in Figure E7.2), such strings cannot be extended indefinitely, and thus a new test has been proved to fail.

The interested reader is referred to the article "Random Number Generators" by T. E. Hull and A. R. Dobell in the SIAM Review, Vol. 4, No. 3, July, 1962, for a comprehensive survey of the subject, plus a bibliography of 148 other papers that encompass most of the work up to 1962. New articles appear in the literature about one per month.

Problem E10

THE D² TEST OF RANDOM NUMBERS

If two points are chosen at random within a unit square, what is the probability that they are more than one-half unit apart?

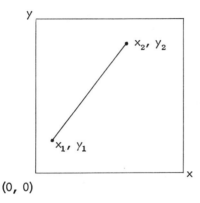

(0, 0)

Figure E10.1. Two points within the empty square

This little problem can be quickly attacked by a student who has access to a random number generator, such as described in Problem E7. Two numbers produced by the generator, each regarded as a decimal between zero and one, can be used to represent the coordinates of a point within the square. Two pairs of numbers will represent two points, say (x_1, y_1) and (x_2, y_2). The square of the distance between them is given by the theorem of Pythagoras:

$$d^2 = (x_2 - x_1)^2 + (y_2 - y_1)^2$$

We are asked for the probability that d is greater than 0.5, or that d^2 is greater than 0.25.

161

EXERCISE 1. Write a routine to call upon a random number generator, and calculate the squared distance for 1,000 pairs of points chosen at random within the square. Count the number of results greater than 0.25 and type it out. The problem can be elaborated in a natural and very useful way.

We may now ask: What is the (percentage) distribution of the squared distances for pairs of points chosen at random within the square?

EXERCISE 2. Rewrite the routine of Exercise 1 so as to tabulate the results in twenty classes: 0.0 up to (but not including) 0.1, 0.1-0.2, and so on, ending with 1.9-2.0.

The probability that the square of the distance between two points within or on the unit square is less than the value B^2 is given in Figure E10.2 for comparison with results of Exercise 2.

B^2	P	B^2	P
0.1	0.234832	1.1	0.985703
0.2	0.409805	1.2	0.992048
0.3	0.549300	1.3	0.995788
0.4	0.662018	1.4	0.997926
0.5	0.752987	1.5	0.999080
0.6	0.825601	1.6	0.999652
0.7	0.882349	1.7	0.999898
0.8	0.925163	1.8	0.999982
0.9	0.955593	1.9	0.999999
1.0	0.974926	2.0	1.000000

Figure E10.2. Selected values for B^2 and P

The values in Figure E10.2 were calculated from analytic formulas.*

The other standard tests of randomness (in Problems E8 and E9, for example) test individual digits; this d^2 test operates on random <u>numbers</u>. Most practical applications of random number generators involve numbers rather than digits, so the d^2 test is realistic.

> EXERCISE 3. Compare the results of Exercise 2 with the table of Figure E10.2, thus applying the d^2 test to the output from your random number generator.

The student may wonder whether the last 3 digits of the output from a random number generator might be as good a representation of a random choice as the first 3, or whether the middle 3 would be better than either. He can now investigate these questions for himself.

> EXERCISE 4. (a) Use or modify the routine of Exercise 1 to test a sequence of random numbers, each consisting of the last 3 digits of the output from your random number generator. (b) Following the same procedure, test numbers formed of the first 3 digits of the output from your random number generator. Also test separately numbers formed of the middle 3 digits. (c) Apply the same procedure to test a sequence formed by extracting <u>three</u> 3-digit numbers from each 9-digit number produced by the generator.

---

* For $B^2 < 1.0$ the probability is

$$P = \pi B^2 - \frac{8B^3}{3} + \frac{B^4}{2}$$

and for $B^2 \geq 1.0$, the probability is

$$P = \frac{1}{3} + (\pi - 2)B^2 + 4(B^2 - 1)^{1/2} + \frac{8}{3}(B^2 - 1)^{3/2}$$

$$- \frac{B^4}{2} - 4B^2 \operatorname{arcsec} B$$

The derivation of these formulas is given in <u>Integral Calculus</u>, Benjamin Wilson, London, 1891, p. 390.

Problem E11

OTHER RANDOM NUMBER GENERATORS

The random number generator (RNG) described in Problem E7 is based on a general recursion relation:

$$X_{n+1} = MX_n \text{ modulo } P$$

where the multiplier M is 2 and the modulus is a prime having a primitive root of 2. The use of 2 as a multiplier makes for easy programming (that is, using only additions). Since such a generator is not satisfactory by itself, two of them are operated independently and the results are added into a field called S.

On machines having a fixed word length, it is sometimes more efficient to use a larger value of M and reduce modulo P by truncation; that is, by letting P be essentially the word size of the machine and simply discarding everything in the product (of M times X) that exceeds one word in length. The trick then is to pick a suitable value of M. For example, the following recursion has been used on binary machines that have a 36-bit word:

$$X_{n+1} = 23X_n \text{ mod } (2^{35} + 1)$$

Again, on a decimal machine with a word length of 11 decimal digits, the following recursion has been used:

$$X_{n+1} = 7^{13} X_n \text{ mod } (10^{11})$$

For a decimal word length of any size, it has been suggested that M be chosen from this expression:

$$[1 + 10 (4L + 1)]^A \tag{1}$$

such that L is not a multiple of 5, and with L and A chosen to yield the largest number that fits the computer word.*

---

*These formulas are derived from considerations in number theory.

The point of this problem is the suggestion that the student select a recursion and explore it. Suppose, for example, that we consider a decimal machine with a word length of 10 digits. The modulus is then 10^{10}, and the multiplier, from Formula (1), might be chosen (with L = 2 and A = 5) as 6240321451 = M.

The first task, then, is to write a subroutine that will output random numbers according to this recursion:

$$X_{n+1} = 6240321451X_n \bmod (10^{10})$$

The initial value X_0 can be taken as any 10-digit number (nonzero, of course), such as 3141592653.

With such a generator operating, many questions need investigating. A few are listed here.

1. Are there peculiarities to the low-order digits of the output? Can you predict, for example, the cycle lengths of the units, tens, and hundreds digits?

2. Are there peculiarities to the whole numbers that are produced? For example, does each number have a common divisor?

3. What is the cycle length of the generator? (You would have to explore number theory to find out, but you can get a good clue by investigating cycle lengths of similar generators for which the word length is, say, 3 digits.)

4. How do the resulting numbers test for randomness? (See Problem E10, the d² test.)

5. How do the resulting digits test for randomness? (See Problems E8 and E9.)

6. If the new generator is used in dice tossing (see Problem E7), how do the results (of, say, 36,000 tosses) compare with those produced by the RNG described there?

Problem E12

COUNTING FISH

A game warden catches exactly 100 fish from different parts of a lake, using various methods. After marking their tails with dye, he carefully returns them to the lake. The next week he again catches 100 fish, observing that 9 of them have dyed tails. He dyes the tails of the remainder and returns them all to the lake. What is a careful estimate of the number of fish in the lake? How much could the warden improve the accuracy of his estimate by repeating the procedure in subsequent weeks?*

We have here a problem in sampling. We are asked to estimate the total size of some collection by counting a sample chosen in some particular way. The principle is used frequently in daily life. The collection is referred to in statistics as a "population," whether it refers to people or things. It is not unusual for people to misuse the principle, drawing an incorrect conclusion from too small a sample. We have an opportunity to simulate the situation with the computer and to gain a valuable understanding of the uncertainty which is introduced when some conclusion about a whole "population" (of any kind) is based upon observation of a sample of that population.

We simulate the lake by clearing 10,000 positions of storage in the computer. Then we simulate the fish by placing 1's at random in that area of storage. If two students work as a team on this important problem, one student can choose the number of fish to be simulated for the first trial, while the other member of the team attempts to estimate that number.** On subsequent trials, the members of the team exchange roles. We use a random number generator from Problem E7 to choose the positions for the fish. Now we are ready to "go fishing."

We select positions in the "lake" by generating 4-digit numbers at random and adding 10,000 to that number. If the

---

*It is assumed, of course, that a fish's chance of being caught remains constant.

*Alternatively, the routine may generate a random number between 100 and 10,000 to determine the number of fish, and punch that number for later reference.

position contains a "1," we have "caught a fish"; if not we cast
again. We continue until we have caught 100 different fish. Then
we simulate dyeing their tails by replacing the "1" with "−1."
We may as well write the routine to count how many of them
already have dyed tails; of course, the result is zero the first
time.

> EXERCISE 1. (a) Write a routine to clear (to zero)
> positions 10,000-19,999 and then to "stock the lake"
> with N fish where N is a parameter to be read in by
> the routine. Use the random number generator RNG
> to select positions where the ones are to be stored.
> (You must check each position to see whether it has
> been selected before.) Stop when N different positions
> have been selected. (b) Write a routine to "go fishing."
> Print the number, x, with dyed tails, for each week
> up to 9 weeks after the first. (c) Combine the rou-
> tines of parts (a) and (b).

> EXERCISE 2. (a) Show by applying the laws of prob-
> ability that we would expect to catch 10 fish with dyed
> tails out of 100 fish the first week if there were
> exactly 1,000 fish in the lake; show that the ratio
> the following week would have risen to 0.19. Cal-
> culate the expected ratio for the following seven
> weeks. (b) Use the routine of Exercise 1(c) to make
> 10 trials of 10 weeks each for a stock of exactly
> 1,000 fish in the lake. Compare the results with the
> expected ratios calculated in part (a).

Exercise 2 has shown that the actual results are different
from the expected results more often than they are the same.
The most we can hope for our prediction is that it will agree
with the actual result oftener than any other prediction would
have done. The considerable experience obtained with Exercise
2 demonstrates clearly that we cannot demand that our prediction be fulfilled even half the time. We note that the experience
is roughly equivalent to ten seasons of actual fishing.

The variation in the results obtained for any particular week,
after the first, is undoubtedly the result of many small, un-
identified causes. This is the situation that approximates a
normal distribution. We can therefore apply the methods of Problem M6 to estimate the variance for the expected results and
apply this to test our actual results.

EXERCISE 3. (a) Calculate the variance v for the expected ratios calculated in Exercise 2(a) and prepare a table showing a range for each ratio such that two-thirds of the actual values should fall within the range if the distribution is truly normal. Use the formula

$$v = np(1 - p)$$

where n = number of fish and p = expected ratio. (b) Compare the actual results with the ranges of part (a). Draw a conclusion concerning the type of distribution.

EXERCISE 4. (a) Repeat the experiment of Exercise 2 with a stock of 10,000 fish and samples of 1,000. (b) Calculate the comparatively smaller ranges expected for this experiment, and test the results as before.

We now have the capability of making a careful estimate of the number of fish in the lake, based upon a count of the samples taken. The estimate will include a range, within which the actual number may be expected to lie two-thirds of the time. As explained in Problem M6, the range can easily be extended, without further experiment, to include 95 per cent, or 99 per cent, or any specified part of the actual cases.

EXERCISE 5. (a) One member of a team is to stock the lake with fish, making the total number lie between 100 and 10,000 (preferably between 500 and 2,000 for a first trial). The other team member is to estimate the number of fish, within a stated probability range as explained above. (b) The team, alternating roles, is to carry out the experiment at least 10 times. Prepare a report giving the results and discussing the uncertainty always introduced when measurements on a sample are applied to the whole population. Distinguish between laws of physical science, which are often verified by a few cases, and relationships in biology, medicine, sociology, and economics.

For students interested in research, the field of sampling offers very attractive opportunities. The increasing number of applications of mathematics to many fields have made sampling techniques exceedingly important. The notable successes—and spectacular failures—of public opinion polls illustrate in the political field how far we have come* and how far we have to go in mastering the techniques of sampling.

Further investigation into this particular fish counting problem might involve altering all the parameters one at a time: the number of fish, the sample size, the number of samples. The student might consider the practical effect of returning the fish to the lake immediately, instead of at the end of the fishing period. Also, does the size have to be the same for all samples in one series? Could the results of three successive samples be averaged? If so, how should the average be calculated? There is a real challenge in the following questions:

1. If we can tolerate an error of 20 per cent in our estimate of the number of fish with a probability of two-thirds or better that the true total lies within our estimated range, how small a total sample can we get by with?

2. For a given total sample, what is the best number of individual samples, and how should the total be distributed among them? Is there a significant improvement in the estimate when the sampling is performed in this optimum way?

> EXERCISE 6. (Group Project) (a) If the fish are returned to the lake immediately, with their tails dyed, should any change be made in the routine to improve the simulation? (b) If the results of three samples are to be averaged, would the average be calculated for the number of fish or for some ratio? What ratio? Would the arithmetic mean be used or the geometric mean? (c) If the results of three samples are to be averaged, how would you take into account the fact that the later samples are more reliable than the first (that is, they have a smaller variance)? (d) Calculate the size of a single sample required to meet the 20 per cent tolerance requirement two times out of three.

---

*Since 1943 when the failure of a national magazine, The Literary Digest, was attributed to its sponsorship of a large opinion poll and the utter failure of polls to predict the re-election of President Truman in 1948.

KENO

The game of keno involves the integers from 1 to 80. A player selects 10 of the numbers and marks his choices on a slip of paper. The banks then selects 20 of the numbers from 1 to 80 at random. If 5 or more of the numbers selected by the player match those drawn by the bank, the bank pays according to the schedule shown in Figure E13.1. Each payoff is on the basis of a unit bet; that is, for six matches, the player has won 17 units for his bet of one unit.

The payoff table is heavily weighted in favor of the bank. For example, the probability of 10 matches is 0.00000011221; the true odds are therefore 8,911,860:1 for this case, but the bank pays 24999:1.

In commercial use, the 20 random numbers are drawn by the bank through a mechanical device consisting of 80 numbered pingpong balls circulating in an airstream. We can simulate the entire system by selecting random numbers (in the range 1 to 80) generated by a scheme given in Problem E7. Two subroutines can be written; one to create 10 random numbers, the other to create (independently) 20 random numbers. For each game, these subroutines are called and a count is made of the number of matches between these two sets of numbers. The result of each game should be entered into a table of values, ranging from 0 to 10. After a suitable number of games, the result of the distribution can be printed.

Number of Numbers that Match	Bank Pays
5	2 (on a bet of 1)
6	18
7	180
8	1,800
9	2,600
10	25,000

Figure E13.1. The payoff table for keno

At first glance, keno differs from other games of chance (for example, roulette) only in mechanical details. One important difference is that keno is a group game. The chance for a given player to win is small, but with many players the probability becomes large that someone will win after each game. The game is cleverly designed to capitalize on this phenomenon. For example, the expectation (i.e., the product of the probability of a given number of matches and the payoff for that number) is highest for 7 matches.

Problem E14

THE INNER PRODUCT METHOD OF RANDOM NUMBER GENERATION

Back in the Middle Ages of computing (that is, in the mid-1940's), it was suggested that a way of generating random numbers was as follows. Pick a number of, say, 8 digits. Square it. Of the 16 digits in the product, extract the middle 8 digits. Repeat.

The process is certainly simple, and seems to work. The output (under certain conditions) tests nicely for randomness, using the customary tests.

Let us illustrate the inner product method with 4-digit numbers, as shown in Figure E14.1.

Starting with 1234, the series develops as shown; the transition from 5227 to 3215 is spelled out in detail.

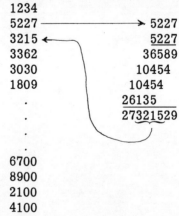

```
1234
5227 ─────────────────► 5227
3215 ◄                  5227
3362                   36589
3030                   10454
1809                   10454
  .                    26135
  .                  27321529
  .

6700
8900
2100
4100
```

Figure E14.1. The inner product method

In spite of its attractive simplicity, the inner product method has at least two weaknesses:

1. It can degenerate to zeros at any point. This is not too serious a weakness, since the appearance of all zeros in the output is easy to detect.

2. The process can degenerate to short cycles. That is, the process can produce, say, a thousand random numbers and then have the 1001st number identical to the 924th; from that point on, the series repeats with a cycle length of 77. This form of degeneration is hard to detect.

Both of these effects are unpredictable, which is to say that they depend on the starting value. The effects can be delayed, or suppressed (for example, by using longer numbers), but the danger is ever present. Since far better schemes for random number generation are available, the inner product method is no longer used.

You will gain understanding of the method and its weaknesses if you personally discredit it. Write a subroutine to generate random numbers with the inner product method, using 4- or 6-digit numbers.

Write a routine to call the subroutine a few thousand times to get started; if it degenerates to zero during this phase, note the cycle length of degeneration. If it does not degenerate to zero, store the current value and determine the cycle length from that point on, by repeated calls of the subroutine and comparison after every call with the stored value. Repeat the whole process with various starting values.

For a run in which the cycle length is longer, test the output as outlined in Problems E8, E9 and E10.

PRIME NUMBERS

The study of whole numbers (positive integers) is a wide and interesting field, rich in opportunities for the student to exercise imagination, reasoning, and his skill in programming. This subject has been called "higher arithmetic" or "theory of numbers," but its many branches are fascinating to students and professional mathematicians alike. Although it has a long history and has been extensively investigated by some of the greatest mathematicians of the past, it probably offers the greatest promise to the student who wishes to use a computer to make independent discoveries in mathematics. For these reasons the study of positive whole numbers is the most attractive field to many beginning programmers who would like to undertake original research.

A fundamental property of a whole number is its divisibility. It is clear that any two whole numbers can be added or multiplied and the result will always be a whole number. However, only certain pairs can be divided exactly, one by the other. Numbers* are therefore classified at once according to their divisibility. If a number can be divided by two other numbers, it is called "composite"; we can decompose it into the product of two other numbers. Any number (except the number <u>one</u>) that <u>cannot</u> be expressed as the product of two other numbers is called "prime." The number <u>one</u> can be divided only by itself; it is called "unity." A prime number can be divided only by itself and unity. The divisibility of numbers is at the root of many problems involving numbers.

The definition gives the basic method for determining whether a number is prime: We divide by all smaller integers down to 2, testing whether the remainder is zero for at least one of them. If not, the number is prime.

> EXERCISE 1. Consider writing a routine to determine by division whether a given number is prime.

---

*We shall use the term "number" to mean "positive integer" in this problem.

The number would be read in from the typewriter.
Print the smallest factor, if there is one; otherwise,
print PRIME.

Various improvements can be made upon this basic method.
It is obvious that the number is not prime if it is any even number greater than 2; hence only odd divisors need to be tried, and,
indeed, only odd numbers are eligible in the first place. Also,
it is not necessary to try divisors greater than the square root
of the number. If such a divisor is exact, the quotient would be
less than the square root, and would already have been discovered.

EXERCISE 2. Improve the routine of Exercise 1,
as suggested in the flow chart of Figure F1.1, so
that only odd divisors are tried, starting with 3 and
increasing by 2 until the square of the divisor exceeds the number N. After printout, increase N by
2 and continue.

Since the division method is inefficient for developing a
table of consecutive prime numbers, various schemes have been
devised to avoid division. The basic idea underlying all such
schemes is called the "sieve of Eratosthenes" (276 B.C.—
195 B.C.). Imagine a list of all odd numbers, from 3 up. Strike
out every third number after 3, every fifth number after 5, and
so on, leaving the prime numbers above 2.
We may apply the idea of Eratosthenes in a computer routine for the IBM 1620 to find all the prime numbers under 1,000
by actually generating all the odd numbers under 1,000 and storing them in consecutive 5-digit fields, as shown in Figure F1.2.
We may start, for example, with the address 10000-10004 and
end with 12495-12499. We change the first number from 1 to 2.
Then we find the next nonzero number, which is 3 and is stored
at address 10009. This is our first "base prime" to be used for
sifting out its multiples. We need a loop to blank out every third
number above 3 by storing zeros in its place. Hence we calculate
the product of the field length by 3, getting 15. We store a zero,
in the form 00000 at address 10024, 10039, and so on, each address being 15 greater than the preceding address. The loop
ends when we arrive at an address greater than 12499. We repeat the loop for the next (nonzero) integer, which is 5.
The loop is thus used to sift out multiples of the base

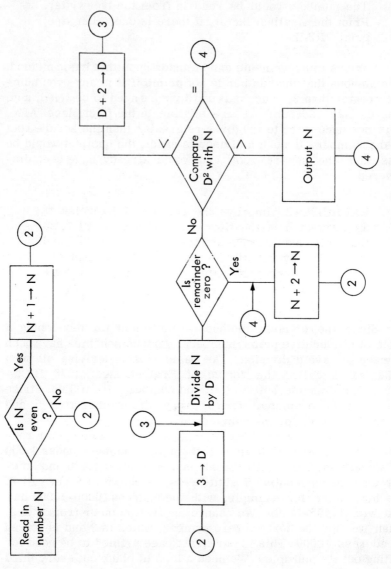

Figure F1.1. Consecutive prime numbers by division

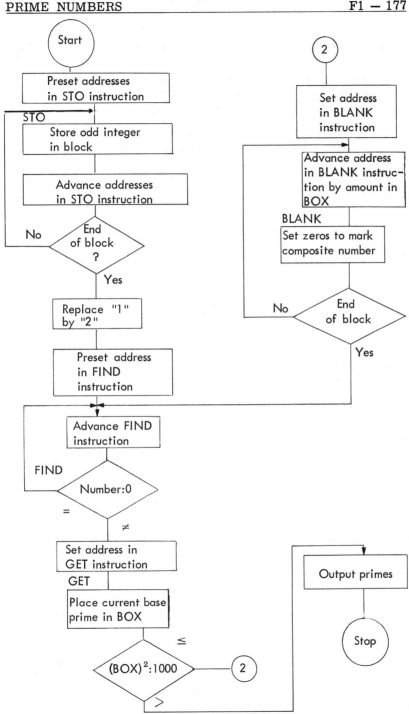

Figure F1.2. Sieve method for generating consecutive prime numbers

primes. When the square of the next base prime exceeds 1,000, the sifting is finished; all the remaining numbers must be prime.

> EXERCISE 3. Write a routine following the plan in Figure F1.2 to generate the primes less than 1,000 and to print or punch the prime numbers.

The preceding method is already fast and efficient, but it can be improved in many ways. For example, there is actually no need to store a table of odd numbers as a preliminary step. We can, instead, merely clear a number of positions, say 10,000 positions, and allow these to represent the odd numbers from 1 to 19,999. During the sifting process we store a digit, such as 1, in the positions corresponding to composite odd numbers, leaving the other positions zero. Then we generate and print or punch the prime numbers corresponding to the positions containing zero. The pattern of ones and zeros is called an array.

> EXERCISE 4. (a) Write a routine to sift out the composite numbers from 1 to 19,999 and to print or punch the consecutive primes, starting at any given number less than 20,000. (b) Devise a method for condensing the array so that all the primes under 20,000 can be stored in compact form on 30 to 40 cards.

The student may wish to consider how to apply the sieve of Eratosthenes to blocks of numbers above 20,000. To do this, he will need a base table of primes up to the square root of the largest number in the block. For numbers under 1,000,000, he will need a base table of primes under 1,000, as produced by Exercise 3. He will also need to know where to start in the sifting process for each of these primes. When he is sifting out multiples of 37 from the block 20,000 to 39,999, for example, he needs to know the first multiple of 37 over 20,000. A little thought or experimentation will show that this multiple can be found by dividing 20,000 by 37, and subtracting the remainder from 20,037. This multiple was available when multiples of 37 were being sifted from previous blocks and could have been stored at that time in an auxiliary table. This auxiliary table would make it unnecessary to perform the divisions.

> EXERCISE 5. (a) Write a routine to calculate the auxiliary table by division for each prime from L up to M, where L and M are given numbers. Store

the table or punch it in cards (or paper tape) under switch control. (b) Use the routine to prepare an auxiliary table for primes between 1 and $(20,000)^{1/2}$.

EXERCISE 6. (a) Write a routine to sift the numbers in a block from N to N + 19999 using an auxiliary table such as that prepared by the routine in Exercise 5. (b) Elaborate the routine of part (a) so that the auxiliary table is converted during its use to an auxiliary table for the next block. Provide for punching the table under switch control. (Note that the table must be extended to include the multiples for primes greater than the square root of the last number in the current block, but smaller than the square root of the last number in the next block. This can be done by using the routine of Exercise 5(b) or by storing the squares of the primes in the auxiliary table beforehand.)

The various other schemes that have been developed over the years (usually to create large tables of consecutive primes) have all been variations of the division method or the sieve method. The Alway process* is an ingenious scheme to calculate the remainders on division without actually having to divide. Similarly, the scheme of C. B. Poland† was devised to avoid division, which is a relatively costly process on most computers, especially on the particular computer (IBM 702) used. The Poland scheme was used again in 1957, with implementation and modifications by C. L. Baker, to calculate the first 6,000,000 primes on the IBM 704. The job took about 120 hours, in contrast to the years required to make the calculations by hand.

The importance of the principle Look for a better way is dramatically illustrated by the problem of calculating prime numbers. The simple division method would be hopelessly inefficient for calculating a large table. Avoiding division was a great improvement, but the search for a better method continued.

---

*Described in G. G. Alway, "A Method of Factorisation Using a High-speed Computer," Mathematical Tables and Other Aids to Computation, Vol. 6, No. 37, January 1952.

†Described in F. J. Gruenberger, The First Six Million Prime Numbers, The Microcard Foundation, Madison, Wisconsin, 1959.

The calculation of the first 6,000,000 primes was repeated in 1961, on an IBM 7090, in 21 minutes. Part of the improvement in speed came from the machine; perhaps this gave a factor of 5 or so. The remaining factor of 60 came from the use of a better algorithm, essentially the sieve of Eratosthenes.

It should be obvious that the sieve is efficient only when the number of numbers being sifted in a batch greatly exceeds the largest base prime needed; that is, the square root of the largest number in the batch. Suppose, for example, we were sifting 2,000 odd numbers in the range between 100,000,000 and 100,004,000. This would require base primes up to 10,001. For a given batch, we would not have any opportunity at all to use most of the base primes, since their multiples would not occur in that small batch. Thus, for use with large numbers, the series of odd numbers to be sifted should be very long. On a binary computer we can allow each bit in storage to represent an odd number, and thus the series to be sifted can be tremendously long.

> EXERCISE 7. (a) Suggest procedures for the IBM 1620 which allow a long series to be sifted even if storage is limited to 20,000 positions. Consider separately what saving in storage might be accomplished if the table of base primes is very long. (b) Write a routine to determine the primes between 100,000,000 and 100,020,000 in one block.

The sieve procedure is an obvious use of index registers. Each application of the innermost loop can be greatly speeded up by indexing; in fact, that loop is then just two instructions long for most indexed machines.

> EXERCISE 8. If a Model II IBM 1620 or some other machine with indexing is available, modify your prime number generator to make use of the indexing feature.

Problem F2

CHAINED PRIMES

A description has been given in Problem F1 of a method to generate many prime numbers at one time with the computer. The student may wonder whether he might be able to push back the boundaries of knowledge a bit by using such a routine. If so, he needs to know which directions are most promising.

New records in connection with prime numbers are indeed being set frequently, as mentioned in Problem F3, but they often require large amounts of machine time on very large computers. Extensive tables of prime numbers in consecutive order are already available. As of the time of writing, the largest printed table of consecutive primes is The First Six Million Prime Numbers.* Many more millions of prime numbers, however, are recorded on magnetic tape. Scattered tables exist of consecutive primes in high ranges. The most fruitful field for the student is the investigation of prime numbers with special properties. For example, he might prepare a modest table of twin primes, such as 11-13, 17-19, 29-31, etc., which are consecutive odd numbers.

> EXERCISE 1. Write a routine to select twin primes from an array representing 20,000 consecutive primes, stored by a routine of Problem F1. Type or punch the pairs under switch control.

The student might investigate primes of some special form, such as $8k \pm 3$, or primes which are the sum of two squares. A very interesting challenge is the discovery of "chained primes."

Two prime numbers form a chain if the larger is just one more than twice the smaller one. A chain of six prime numbers is shown in Figure F2.1.

At this writing, no table has yet been published of chains of six, and there is no assurance that any others exist until they have been found. No example is yet known of even a single chain of seven primes.

---

*Published by The Microcard Foundation, Madison, Wisconsin, 1959.

$$63,419$$
$$126,839$$
$$253,679$$
$$507,359$$
$$1,014,719$$
$$2,029,439$$

Figure F2.1.   A chain of six primes

To discover chains of two prime numbers we shall find it convenient to operate two sieves of the kind described in Problem F1. Then we shall have in storage two arrays representing consecutive prime numbers. One sequence will be twice as long as the other and will contain, scattered in it, all the primes that form chains with primes in the shorter sequence. For example, the array in positions 05000 to 09999 may represent the odd numbers 50,000 and 60,000, marked so as to show which are primes. Corresponding to this sequence, we have an array of double length in positions 10000 to 19999 that represents the odd numbers between 100,000 and 120,000, and this also is marked to show the primes in this range. We can now select all the chained primes whose smaller member is in the 50,000's. We print both members of each pair, under switch control, for checking out the routine. For a production run we punch the larger member only, ten primes to a card.

EXERCISE 2. Rewrite the routine of Exercise 6(a), Problem F1, so as to read in a starting value N and calculate two arrays: Array A is to represent the prime numbers between N and N + 10,000; array B is to represent primes between 2N and 2N + 20,000. Eliminate each prime in array A for which there is no chained prime in array B by storing a digit in the location representing that prime.

A routine like the one in Exercise 2 makes severe demands upon the storage capacity of a computer with only 20,000 storage positions. There are various ways to meet the storage problem. For example, array B may be condensed before array A is calculated, by eliminating the positions which correspond to odd numbers of the form 4a + 1; these numbers cannot possibly form chains with smaller numbers. Furthermore, the same section of routine can be used to calculate both arrays, and then it can be replaced by following parts of the routine.

EXERCISE 3. Write a routine to convert the un-
marked positions of array A into prime numbers.
Print, under switch control, each prime number and
its calculated chained prime. Punch the primes, also
under switch control, 10 at a time into cards.

We could program three sieves at once and select from the
output primes that form a chain of three. With six sieves operating in synchronization, we could produce a table of chains of
six primes. It is clear, however, that no prime can belong to a
chain of six without also belonging to six chains of two. We can
therefore pick out all chains, of whatever length, from our list of
chains of two.

EXERCISE 4. Write a routine to read in under
switch control the higher members of each chain
of two. Test each prime to see if its "double" (plus
one) is in the list. If so, print it, thus forming a list
of chains of three. Primes belonging to chains of four
or more will appear twice in this list and can be
selected by inspection.

"LARGEST" PRIMES

One list of special prime numbers has always been short, and promises to remain so. This is the list of "Mersenne primes," which are prime numbers of the form

$$M = 2^P - 1$$

where the exponent p is itself a prime. A number of this form is easily seen to be composite if the exponent is not prime. But for all prime values of p up to 19, except 11, the Mersenne number, M, is prime. In 1644 Father Marin Mersenne conjectured that M is prime for only four values of p above 19, i.e., for 31, 61, 127, and 257. It was discovered that $2^{257} - 1$ is composite; this has been known for a long time. The rest of the "history" on this subject is almost all recent, with developments occurring at the present time, so that it is especially important to give the date of any article that is quoted concerning Mersenne numbers (including this one)

The number $M_{127} = 2^{127} - 1$ held the record as the largest known prime for a long time, the longest time for any number to hold that distinction. As late as 1950, a serious attempt to find a larger prime than M_{127} ended in failure. The number $3 \cdot 2^{159} + 1$ had been suggested as a likely candidate, but it turned out to be composite (although its factors were not determined at that time, and have not yet been discovered). The report of this research concludes: "Thus another attempt to discover a larger prime than $2^{127} - 1$ ends in disappointment."

> EXERCISE 1. (a) Show how to factor any number of the form $2^{ab} - 1$ (which is not a Mersenne number), (b) Write a routine to calculate and to type or punch a Mersenne number of any order.

That was in 1950, just as the modern era of electronic computers opened. Since then, Mersenne primes for p = 521, 607, 1279, 2203, 2281, 3217, 4253, 4423, 9689, 9941, and 11213 have been discovered. The date for M_{4423} was September 1961; for the last three, the dates are 1963. By the time you read this the list will already be longer. These enormous primes cannot be tested directly by division: M_{11213} has 3,376 digits. However, there is a simple way to establish primeness for a Mersenne number, $M = 2^p - 1$. We calculate the sequence

$$A_n = [(A_{n-1})^2 - 2] \quad \text{modulo M}$$

starting with $A_1 = 4$. If $A_{p-1} = 0$, then the Mersenne number M is prime; otherwise not. The test is illustrated for $p = 13$ in Figure F3.1. The test is short for this comparatively small prime, but it should be noted that the calculation depends upon the size of p in two ways. First, there are $(p - 1)$ lines, each containing a multiplication, subtraction, and division. Thus, in order to test M_{11213}, 11,212 lines are required. Second, the divisor is $2^{11213} - 1$, which has about 0.3p decimal digits, or 3,376 digits in this latter case, used to calculate the modular value of A_n. The multiplicands can run up to this length, and the dividends can be twice as long. The test for M_{11213} took 135 minutes on the very large and fast ILLIAC II, at the University of Illinois. The same calculation on a Model I 1620 would take 25,000 hours (which is over 1,000 24-hour days). All eligible Mersenne numbers from M_{9941} up to M_{12143} have been tested on ILLIAC II. It is clear that you would need access to very large and very fast equipment to extend the table of Mersenne primes in this way.

EXERCISE 2. (a) Write a routine to test whether a given Mersenne number is prime. (b) Use the routine of part (a) to show that M_{257}, which was so long supposed to be a prime, is actually a composite number. (c) Use the routine of part (a) to show that no Mersenne number between M_{127} and M_{521} is prime, and thus partly explain why M_{127} was the "largest known prime" for so many years. (d) Discuss the prominence of Mersenne numbers in the search for large primes. Consider whether the word "discover" is appropriate in connection with Mersenne primes.

EXERCISE 3. Use the routine of Exercise 1 to make a display of the largest known primes from 1950 to the current date, showing each prime in both expo-

n	$(A_{n-1})^2 - 2$	$A_n = [(A_{n-1})] - 2 \mod M_{13}$
1		4
2	14	14
3	194	194
4	37634	4870
5	23716898	3953
6	15626207	5970
7	35640898	1857
8	3448447	36
9	1294	1294
10	1674434	3470
11	12040898	128
12	16382	0

Figure F3.1. Verification that Mersenne number $M_{13} = 2^{13} - 1 = 8191$ is prime

nential and expanded form. (Credit should be given to D. B. Gillies of the University of Illinois for M_{9689}, M_{9941}, and M_{11213}.)

Although M_{127} was the largest known Mersenne prime for a great many years, Euclid had already shown by reasoning that the sequence of prime numbers is unending, so that a "largest" prime does not exist and hence cannot ever be found. In Euclid's proof, we imagine forming the product of all possible primes, and then add one to the product. Since the result is not exactly divisible by any prime number smaller than itself it must itself be a new prime number, or else contain a prime factor larger than any of the known primes.* It follows that there cannot be a limited number of prime numbers.

While the student cannot be expected to produce a prime larger than M_{11213}, there are other areas involving prime numbers that might be fruitful. Figure F3.2 shows a table of consecutive primes. The first pair of these

---

* Notice that Euclid's proof does not provide an algorithm for creating large primes:

$$2 \cdot 3 \cdot 5 \cdot 7 \cdot 11 \cdot 13 + 1 = 30,031 = 59 \cdot 509$$

1000000009649
1000000009651

was, at one time, the largest known pair of twin primes (that is, primes differing by two). The last two entries in Figure F3.2 are also twins, and are slightly larger. This "record" could easily be broken.

10^{12} plus:

9649	10117
9651	10123
9691	10173
9703	10201
9769	10209
9829	10227
9891	10249
9909	10263
9913	10281
9919	10287
9963	10309
9973	10377
9991	10389
9999	10411
10021	10431
10033	10447
10039	10479
10047	10483
10069	10489
	10491

Figure F3.2. Some consecutive prime numbers greater than 10^{12}

Problem F4

POWER RESIDUES

In many kinds of counting, especially in telling time, we do not continue indefinitely using larger and larger numbers, but we return periodically to zero and "start over." Thus we count 60 seconds for a minute, or 60 minutes for an hour and then start over. We count seven days for a week and then count again from the beginning, giving the eighth day the same name as the first. An odometer registers up to 99,999 miles and then returns to zero. This idea is represented in mathematics as "congruence." Two numbers are said to be congruent with reference to a certain period, called a modulus, if they have the same remainder (residue) when divided by that modulus. A little experimentation will demonstrate that the definition shows the relation between ordinary counting and this special kind of periodic counting. Thus, $23 \equiv 2$ (modulo 7) means that 23 and 2 have the same remainder when divided by the modulus 7.* Congruence is thus a special kind of equality that allows us to replace all integers by integers less than the modulus. With respect to the modulus 7, every integer is equivalent (in the sense of being congruent) to one of the integers 0, 1, 2, 3, 4, 5, or 6. This special set is called "the least non-negative residues."

EXERCISE 1. (a) Write a subroutine to reduce any integer with respect to the modulus 7 to a non-negative integer less than 7 and replace the integer by its equivalent "residue." Provide for changing the sign of both dividend and divisor in the case of a negative number so that the residue will be positive or zero, but not negative. Alternatively, the modulus may be added to a negative residue in order to convert it to a positive residue. (b) Write a routine to read in two 5-digit numbers and then use the sub-

---

*It is more simply written as $23 \equiv 2$ mod 7; "modulo" is a form meaning "reduced by means of the modulus." A special application is given in Problem H2.

routine of part (a) to calculate their sum, difference, product, and the sum of their squares, all in "modulus 7" arithmetic.

Changing now to a larger modulus, we consider the powers of 2, reduced with respect to the modulus 37. As shown in Figure F4.1, the powers of 2 cover the set of positive residues for modulus 37, from 1 up to 36. Every number that is not divisible by 37 is therefore congruent (modulo 37) to some power of 2. The exponent of the power is called the index for that number with respect to the power base* 2. Power bases are of very wide use in studying problems dealing with whole numbers. The indexes of whole numbers are in some ways analogous to the logarithms used in connection with decimal fractions.

Tables of these residue indexes (sometimes called the least exponent of a prime number) are useful to number theorists but, at present, have no practical value to others. The calculation of such a table, however, offers a superb example of one way that a long and difficult problem can be cut down to size.

Notice that in Figure F4.1 in the residue column all the numbers between 1 and $(p - 1)$ appear once and only once within the first $(p - 1)$ powers. They appear in more or less scrambled order (the basis for the work done in Problem E7).

> EXERCISE 2. (a) Verify that the table of residues can be calculated completely in modular arithmetic by multiplying each residue by 2 and reducing modulo 37. (b) Write a routine following the plan in Figure F4.2 to calculate the residues of the powers of 2 with respect to the modulus 37.

Some other numbers (such as 5, 13, 15, 17, 18, 19, 22, 24, 32, and 35) can serve as a power base for modulus 37, but not all. If a number is to serve as a power base for a modulus p, the modulus must be a prime number, and the lowest power of the base to have a value of 1 must be the $(p - 1)$th power. Otherwise the power residues would start repeating before all numbers less than p were represented. The smallest power base is the most convenient to use.

> EXERCISE 3. (a) Rewrite the routine of Exercise 2

---

*A power base for a modulus is traditionally called a "primitive root" of that modulus.

Exponent	Power	Residue (mod 37)
1	2	2
2	4	4
3	8	8
4	16	16
5	32	32
6	64	27
7	128	17
8	256	34
9	512	31
10	1024	25
11	2048	13
12	4096	26
13	8192	15
14	16384	30
15	32768	23
16	65536	9
17	131072	18
18	262144	36
19	524288	35
20	1048576	31
21	2097152	29
22	4194304	21
23	8388608	5
24	16777216	10
25	33554432	20
26	67108864	3
27	134217728	6
28	268435456	12
29	536870912	24
30	1073741824	11
31	2147483648	22
32	4294967296	7
33	8589934592	14
34	17179869184	28
35	34359738368	19
36	68719476736	1
37	137438953472	2

Figure F4.1. Residues for powers of 2 modulo 37.

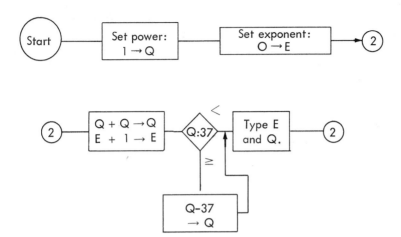

Figure F4.2. Flow chart for calculation of powers of 2 modulo 37

to determine the least exponent of a given number,
a, for which the power has a value of 1 when reduced
by a given prime modulus. (b) Use the routine to find
the smallest power base for the prime modulus $p = 23$.

The sequence of powers of any (whole) number, when reduced
by some modulus p greater than 1, must start repeating when
all the positive integers less than p have been represented, if
not before. It is easy to see that the power preceding the first
repetition must have the (reduced) value 1, and that this power
marks the end of a period of recurring values. If the modulus
is a prime number p, the (p − 1)th power is <u>always</u> 1, according
to a very famous theorem of Fermat. That is,

$$a^{p-1} \equiv 1 \bmod p$$

for any prime p, providing that a is not exactly divisible by p.
It is also easy to see that if any lower power of a has a value of
1, the exponent of that power must be a factor of p − 1.

EXERCISE 4. (a) Explain why the period of repetition
must divide p − 1 if it is less than p − 1. (b) Use the
routine of Exercise 3 to find the period for the powers
of 2 with respect to the modulus 227.

In the example of Exercise 4(b), the solution will take 226 excursions around the loop, although there are actually only two possible periods: 113 or 226. We are forced to develop a more efficient method for large values of p, since the brute force method is hopeless. With an IBM 1620, each trip around the loop takes about 3 milliseconds. If the period should turn out to be p − 1 when p is around a million, the calculation for just one value of p would take nearly an hour. To calculate a table of periods for a considerable number of values of p it is necessary to substitute brains for brute force.

Think of the complete calculation for one value of p as represented by the line in Figure F4.3. If the routine ever gets beyond the midpoint $(p - 1)/2$ without finding a power equal to 1,

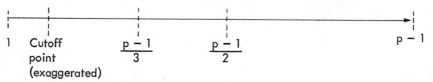

Figure F4.3. The plan for improving the calculation of periods of powers of 2.

there is no purpose in testing any further powers; the period is already known to be p − 1. Similarly, if the point $(p - 1)/3$ is passed, we can jump immediately to $(p - 1)/2$, and so on.

We shall outline an attack on this problem for large values of p, say around a million. A considerable amount of detail will be left for the student's planning.

Suppose we choose an arbitrary cutoff point of 2,000 where we will discontinue the brute force method. We calculate successive powers of 2 up to the 2,000th power (reducing modulo p as before) provided no power of 2 in this range has a residue of 1 when reduced by the modulus. Then we will start skipping, as indicated in Fig. F4.4 for the particular prime, p = 1,000,621.

Having passed the cutoff point with no success, we proceed to examine only eligible values as given in a table such as that of Figure F4.4. We reason that the next eligible value for the exponent must be 2,180, and we can jump directly to that value without having to proceed further through the values 2,001; 2,002; 2,003; and so on.

The next power to try is the one with exponent $(p - 1)/D$. We will surely have less than 500 additional exponents to try; actually there are less than 90.

D	1	2	3	4	...	7	...	459
(p − 1)/D	1000620	500310	333540	250155	...	x	...	2180

Figure F4.4 Calculating eligible exponents over 2000

Now we need a method to calculate isolated powers of 2, rather than the successive powers we have been testing up to the cutoff point. We form an auxiliary table showing the powers of 2 as the values of Q in the first line of Figure F4.5, and also the values of 2^Q, reduced by the modulus p, as the second line. Each value of Q is calculated by doubling the preceding value, starting with 1. Each value in the second line is calculated by squaring the preceding value and then reducing modulo p. The first value in the second line is 2.

Q	1	2	4	8	16	32	...	1048576
2^Q	2	4	16	256	65536	301964	...	448139

Figure F4.5. Auxiliary table of residues for powers of the
powers of 2 with respect to modulus 1000621

Suppose the last previous power of 2 to be tried was 2,000. The next eligible power of 2 is 2,180, as shown in Figure F4.4. Since $2^{2180} = 2^{2000} \cdot 2^{128} \cdot 2^{32} \cdot 2^{16} \cdot 2^{4}$, we can calculate it by multiplying the previous power by the values from the second line of Figure F4.5 which correspond to 128, 32, 16, and 4, reducing after each multiplication with the modulus p, of course.* If the result is not 1, we continue by calculating the next eligible power of 2, and so on up to $(p − 1)/2$.

This scheme has been found to determine the period of powers of 2 (for a prime modulus p of about a million) in 5 minutes or less with the Model I IBM 1620. The cutoff point is a critical factor, but little is known about its best value. If you choose it too high, you must calculate too many powers of 2; if you set it too low, you waste time by increasing the number of divisions. In the example, there are only 128 divisors of p − 1, compared with the 998,620 steps that would be calculated by using brute force all the way. By making the cutoff point a

_____

*We are, in effect, converting the binary equivalent of 2180 to the decimal equivalent, reducing modulo p.

parameter which can be varied easily, the student can, with a moderate amount of research, establish a new criterion for these calculations.

EXERCISE 5. (a) Elaborate the routine of Exercise 3 as suggested so that a cutoff point can be read in as well as the modulus. After the successive powers have reached the cutoff point, test only the eligible powers of 2. Print the prime and the period. (b) By varying the cutoff point, attempt to determine the best value for it when p is near one million. (c) Modify the routine of part (a) to determine the period for powers of 2 with respect to a very large "chained prime," as described in Problem F2, setting the cutoff point at zero, and starting the testing at $(p - 1)/2$, as suggested after Exercise 4.

Problem F5

REPEATING DECIMALS

It is well known that some fractions, such as the ones in Figure F5.1, repeat indefinitely when they are expressed as a decimal. Consequently, the decimals have no definite length, but we can ask, "What is the length of the period of repetition?"

> EXERCISE 1. (a) Write a routine to read in a numerator and denominator from the typewriter and to calculate and print a 20-digit quotient on the same line. Then return for additional data. (b) Use the routine of part (a) to determine the period for various fractions. Make various observations about the results, including the length of each complete period.

We could generalize the problem by regarding terminating fractions as repeating indefinitely with the single digit zero. We shall distinguish between such fractions and those which repeat a nonzero digit by giving their period as $0/1$. Thus, for $N = 25$, we have $1/N = 0.040000...$ with period $0/1$; for $N = 30$, $1/N = 0.03333...$ with period 1. Before undertaking to calculate the periods for all fractions, we make a simple observation that enables us to reduce the complexity of the problem.

We notice that the length of the period of a fraction in lowest terms depends only upon the denominator. We therefore ask, "What is the period of the fractional units, $1/2$, $1/3$, $1/4$, $1/5$, ... ?" Since a fractional unit is the reciprocal of the denominator, we may ask the same question in the form, "What are the periods of the reciprocals of the positive integers?"

Our problem is thus simplified to extending the table of Figure F5.2, making whatever further observations we can about it.

> EXERCISE 2. (a) Modify the routine of Exercise 1 so as to convert the fractional units $1/N$ into decimals, advancing N automatically after typing each line. (b) Observe the length of each period, if it is com-

Fraction	Repeating Decimal	Length of Period, p
5/7 =	0.714285 714285 714285 ...	6
1/19 =	0.052631584947368415 05263 1584947368415 05263158494736...	18
17/31 =	0.548387096774193 548387096 774193 548387096774193	15
2/3 =	0.6 6 6	1
1/25 =	0.040 0 0	0 or 1

Figure F5.1. Some repeating decimals

plete, and write it by hand or type it with any typewriter on the same line as the decimal. Supply the
decimal point in the same way. Make other appropriate observations. Does the period of repetition
necessarily start at the beginning of the decimal?
What relation, if any, does the length of the period
of the reciprocal of a prime number seem to have
with respect to the prime itself? Does the same relation hold for other (composite) numbers? What
relationships can you perceive for the length of the
period for reciprocals of composite numbers?

When we divide the numerator by the denominator in order
to convert a fraction into a decimal, as in Figure F5.3, we note
that the decimal starts repeating as soon as the remainder becomes equal to 1 or to a positive power of 10. This fact enables
us to count the length of the period in a convenient way.

EXERCISE 3. (a) Elaborate the routine of Exercise
2 so as to count and type the length of the period.
Provide also for reading in and using the length of
the quotient, and for typing the actual figures of the
period under switch control. (b) Use the routine of
part (a) to extend the results obtained in Exercise
2, printing only the number N and the length p of
the period.

N		1/N			Length of Period
2	0.50000	00000	00000	00000	0/1
3	0.33333	33333	33333	33333	1
4	0.25000	00000	00000	00000	0/1
5	0.20000	00000	00000	00000	0/1
6	0.16666	66666	66666	66666	1
7	0.14285	71428	57142	85714	6
8	0.12500	00000	00000	00000	0/1
9	0.11111	11111	11111	11111	1
10	0.10000	00000	00000	00000	0/1
11	0.09090	90909	09090	90909	2
12	0.08333	33333	33333	33333	1
13	0.07692	30769	23076	92307	6
14	0.07142	85714	28571	42857	6
15	0.06666	66666	66666	66666	1
16	0.06250	00000	00000	00000	0/1
17	0.05882	35294	11764	70588	16

Figure F5.2. Periods of reciprocals

If the student has any serious intention of calculating periods for large values of N, he should give considerable thought to improving the method. A careful consideration of the method used in Figure F5.3 to convert a fraction into a decimal will reveal that the decimal will have to start repeating whenever any remainder recurs, and therefore the period must be less than N. However, for a large prime number such as 701, we might have to develop a quotient of 700 digits. We could speed up the execution of the routine by incorporating in it a simplified division subroutine, tailored for this particular problem. This gives us a better plan, perhaps like the one in Figure F5.4.

EXERCISE 4. Write a routine to implement the flow chart of Figure F5.4. Add provisions to suppress the typing of the actual figures of the decimal under switch control

The routines considered up to this point have calculated the period for every value of N in succession so long as the routine continued. Thoughtful comparison of the results for composite (nonprime) numbers will show that this method, notwithstanding several improvements already made, is still

```
              0.07142857. . .
        14  1.00000000
              98
              20
              14
              60
              56
              40
              28
             120
             112
              80
              70
             100
              98
              20
```

Figure F5.3. Conversion of a fraction into a repeating decimal

woefully inefficient. The student can easily verify that the length of the period for the reciprocal of any composite number is divisible by the length of the period for each of its factors; it is, in fact, the least common multiple of those lengths. For these calculations, the length of period for a factor with a terminating reciprocal must, of course, be taken as 1 instead of zero. Since we can calculate the length of period for any composite number in this way, we are able to reduce the problem greatly. The problem is now simply to calculate the period for the reciprocals of the prime numbers.

EXERCISE 5. (a) Show that the fraction $1/91$ is equal to $2/13 - 1/7$, and therefore its period is the least common multiple of the periods for $1/13$ and $1/7$. (b) Rewrite the routine of Exercise 4 so as to read in from separate cards the prime numbers up to 1,000 and to calculate the period for the reciprocal of each one, printing the number and the period on the same line. The prime numbers may be generated by a routine of Problem F1, or they may be obtained from printed tables of prime numbers.

The student who has read Problem F4 may wonder whether there is a correspondence between the primes that have a least exponent of full size (i.e., for which the least exponent is $(p - 1)$

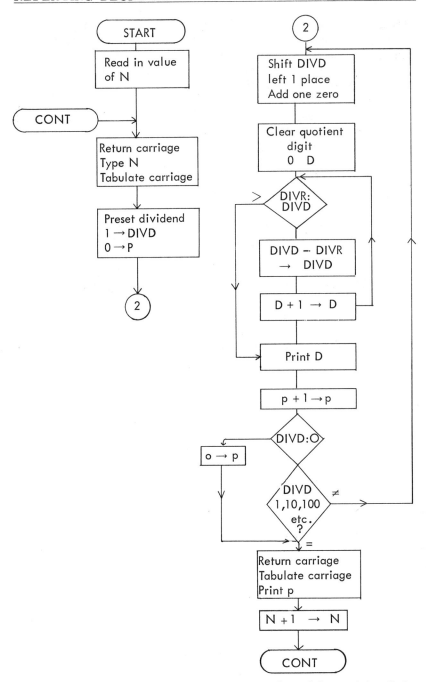

Figure F5.4. Plan for calculating reciprocals and determining their
periods

itself) and the primes that have the maximum period in the representation of their reciprocal. The results obtained in the preceding exercises may be used to throw light upon this interesting question. The student may wish to extend his results up to N = 10,000 in order to carry on this investigation. If so, he will probably wish to improve his routine still further. It might help him to notice, for instance, that if a prime has a full-length period of (p − 1) digits in its reciprocal, the two halves of the period add up to 999. . .999. Or he might observe the value of the remainder at the halfway point (where the number of digits is (p − 1)/2) and thus shorten the calculation for primes with very long periods.

> EXERCISE 6. (a) Shorten the routine for the reciprocals of prime numbers in accordance with the suggestion. Also, incorporate a prime number generator in the routine so that the investigation can be extended easily. Provide for punching the results, eight to a card under switch control. (b) Test the conjecture mentioned concerning primes with a least exponent of full size. Does the same principle seem to be operating in both cases?

Problem F6

PRIMITIVE ROOTS

Problem F4 dealt with so-called least exponents. For a prime p the least exponent is the smallest x for which $2^x = 1$ modulo p. As we have seen, x always is an integral submultiple of (p − 1).

If the least exponent of the base 2 for a given p is (p − 1), then 2 is called the least positive primitive root of p. If the least exponent (the residue index on 2) is (p − 1)/k, where k is an integer greater than one, then 2 is not a primitive root of p. We seek now the smallest value for a, such that

$$a^{p-1} \equiv 1 \bmod p$$

and for all exponents less than p − 1, $a^m \not\equiv 1 \bmod p$.

The a that satisfies will be the least positive primitive root of p.

We will not even describe a method for calculating primitive roots. For all primes up to a million, tables exist of the least positive, the least prime, the least negative, etc., primitive roots. Generally, the least positive primitive root (lppr) is a small number; it has been estimated that p would have to greatly exceed 10^8 before the lppr would exceed 100. As a very rough rule of thumb, about 1/3 of the primes have 2 for their lppr; 1/3 of those remaining have 3 as their lppr, and so on.

The term "least negative primitive root" needs some explanation, since there are no negative numbers in the theory of numbers. It is strictly a matter of convenient notation. For the modulus 23, for example, the number 22 (=p − 1) is called (−1). For p = 23, the least negative primitive root is −2; that is, 21.

Consider p = 109. Its least exponent is 36; its least positive primitive root is 6; its least negative primitive root is −6 (that is, 103); its least prime primitive root is 11. These are the basic statistics for the prime 109.

For large values of p (say, greater than 100,000), the calculation of these statistics is a complex and involved task, which calls on much more of the theory of numbers than can be given here. Efficient computer routines to develop tables of these statistics can be written only after considerable experience with inefficient routines. This is really only another expression of one of the fundamental principles outlined in the Introduction.

The student cannot be expected to produce an efficient routine for the calculation of primitive roots of prime numbers. However, all the facts are available to produce a routine.

So the problem is this: For the 14 primes in the range from 900 to 999, fill in the blanks in the table of Figure F6.1. Then write out the improvements you would consider for calculating the same table for the 879 primes between 90,000 and 99,999.

Primitive Roots

Prime	Least Positive	Least Negative	Least Prime
907		4	2
911	17		
919		5	7
929			3
937	5	5	
941	2		
947	2	3	
953			3
967			5
971	6	3	
977		3	
983			5
991	6		7
997	7	7	7

Figure F6.1. Some primitive roots

Problem F7

A DUPLICATING SERIES

Figure F7.1 shows a series of numbers. They are the first differences of part of a table of prime numbers (from 1,233 to 1,489). Let us make some observations about this list.

1. All entries are even.
2. The smallest entry is 2.
3. There cannot be two 2's in a row.
4. The most frequent entry is 6 (although this fact is not apparent from the short sample of Figure F7.1).
5. Within the sample shown, the longest repeating sequence is 2, 6, 12, 10, marked at A and B.

Suppose we had a long table like Figure F7.1, say 100,000 entries. Our problem is this: How could we determine the longest repeating sequence in the table?

6		6
2		6
6	A	8
12		18
10		10
18		14
2		4
4		2
6		4
2		6
6		8
4		4
2		2
4		6	B
12		12
2		10
2		2
6		4
34		2

Figure F7.1. Differences between consecutive primes

If the problem had to be solved, it would definitely be a computer problem. There seems no other way to attack it, however, than by sheer brute force. Assuming that sequences of 3, 4, and 5 elements are found to repeat (simply by eye examination), we would have to compare every set of 6 with every other set of 6; then every set of 7 with every other 7; and so on, perhaps right up to comparing half the table with the other half.

This problem is included (see also Problem M5) as an example of an extremely difficult problem with today's knowledge of computers. We know a way to do it, but the way is not feasible where the number of table entries is very large. There may be a way to cut the problem down to size. Until there is, the problem remains useful simply as an illustration of the limitations of our machines and our knowledge. With the basic IBM 1620, such a problem is unwieldy even for N around 2,000.

This problem should be used for class discussion. Would it help to have the table sorted? Is it really a computer problem, or would it be more suitable for punched card equipment?

Problem F8

TERMINAL DIGITS OF 2ᵀ

In the problem solution section of the May 1950 issue of The American Mathematical Monthly (p. 350) there is a proof of this theorem: For any integer r there exists a power of 2 each of whose last r digits is either 1 or 2. The proof given establishes only that such powers exist, but does not show how to find them. Our problem is to calculate a few of these powers of 2 that have terminal digits consisting of all 1's and 2's.

For r = 1, the first power of 2 satisfies the requirement. For r = 2, the lowest power to satisfy is the ninth (the ninth power of 2 is 5_1_2_). Similarly, the 89th power of 2 is

$$6189700196426901374449562112$$

and we see that it satisfies the conditions for r = 3 and also for r = 4, and, in fact, is the smallest power that will satisfy.*

We are developing entries in the table in Figure F8.1. The computer problem is to extend this table a few more lines.

We must first decide how many digits to retain (for each power) in the computer calculation. We have already noticed that only a certain number of terminal digits need be retained, first in connection with the hand calculation of 2^{89} and then in Figure F8.1. If we should decide to extend the table to r = 20, then only 20 digits need to be retained at each stage, and so on. It will turn out that going beyond r = 20 may require large amounts of machine time.

As always, we start with the working part of the problem. We raise 2 to successive powers by adding each result, x, to itself (rather than multiplying by 2). The exponent is called T. In housekeeping, x should be set up as a 20-digit number, initialized to 00000000000000000002. At the same time a counter, T, should be initialized to the value 1. We make it also 20 digits

---

*This may not be obvious, but it is easily checked by hand calculation, since we need to carry only the last 4 digits of each power in our work up to this point.

Number of Digits r	Exponent T	Terminal Digits in $x = 2^T$
1	1	2
2	9	512
3	89	562112
4	89	562112
5	589	322112
6	3089	12122112

Figure F8.1

long, lacking definite information about it. A 2-digit counter is needed for r; initialize it to 1. The flow chart of Figure F8.2 outlines the solution to the problem.

Notice the operation indicated at Reference 4. Doubling field x will result in an overflow condition every third time or so. We must arrange to ignore the overflow (46 "xxxxx" 01400) and also to turn off the overflow light. It costs us nothing extra to do this after every addition of the x field.

When we achieve success (as when r = 6, T = 3089), we increment r by 1 and retest the same value of 2^T.

The mathematical theory of the problem guarantees us that the table of results is endless. Although the routine is fast (about 500,000 values of T per hour), it will consume large amounts of machine time to break any records by this method. At this writing, the value for r = 20 is known, but not the value for r = 21 or any greater r.* Before trying the method outlined in Figure F8.2, we should consider some improvements in our method of attack.

Program switch 1 is used to allow visual monitoring of the action of the routine. Switch 2 allows for orderly restart. If the routine has been halted (and we have noted the current values of r, T, and x), it may be restarted by reading in those values at Reference 1.

This is a problem in number theory. It is easily coded, and offers a chance (given a large amount of machine time) to break a world's record. The student should be aware, however, that the problem situation is somewhat impractical.

A list of criteria for a good computer problem was given in the Introduction. Let us apply those criteria to the problem at hand. After examining some powers of 2 (the first, ninth, eighty-

---

*Extended to r = 60 by the date of publication.

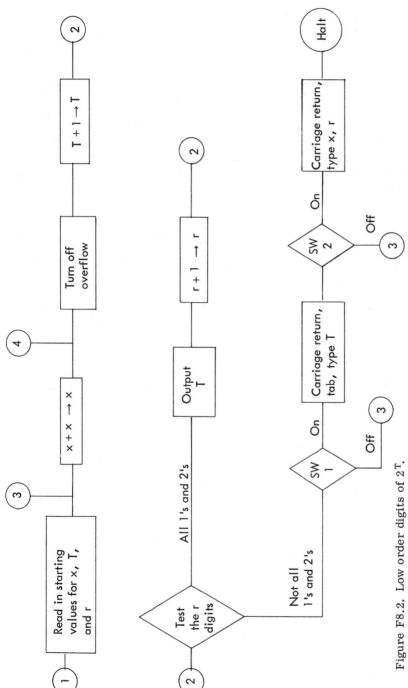

Figure F8.2. Low order digits of 2^T.

ninth, and so on), we find that the problem is immediately well defined. Moreover, we can see a method of solution; namely, to generate the powers systematically and examine their low-order digits. The problem is well within the capabilities of the IBM 1620, at least for the first several million powers. There is a large element of repetition, and the payoff is tremendous; we could not hope to fill in more than five lines of our table by hand, or even by desk calculator.

There is another point about this problem: it is purely a decimal problem. If we wished to solve it on a binary computer, we would first have to program the machine to operate decimally. Thus, the problem ideally fits the IBM 1620.

We should now consider the seventh principle given in the Introduction: Brains will always beat brute force.

The solution outlined in Figure F8.1 was strictly a brute force solution; namely, to develop sucessive powers of 2 and search each one. The most casual reference to a list of powers of 2 reveals that this procedure is wasteful. The units digit of the series repeats in a cycle of four—with the digits 2, 4, 8, 6, 2, 4, 8, 6, etc. Thus only the first, fifth, ninth, . . . , $4T + 1$ powers are even eligible. If we generate and examine all the powers, then three out of four searches are automatically fruitless. We could jump four powers at a time by multiplying by 16 (= 2^4), and thus proceed faster.

But the same kind of thinking lets us proceed much faster still. The last two digits of the powers of 2 repeat in a cycle of length 20 (as you discovered in your hand calculation of 2^{89}), and the only eligible ending is 12, found on the ninth, twenty-ninth, forty-ninth, etc., powers. So we could jump 20 powers at a time by multiplying by 1048576 (= 2^{20}).

This reasoning can be extended. (After the result for $r = 5$ is found, only every 500th value need be examined, and jumps of 500 can be made in one multiplication.)

In fact, as in all research, a little probing reveals much about the problem and at the same time uncovers fascinating new avenues to explore. For example, Figure F8.1 can be extended as in Figure F8.3. One might be led to think that the entire approach of Figure F8.2 is not the proper one.

We can now begin to see a vastly superior method. Notice, however, that this method is not apparent until some results are obtained by a straightforward approach. In solving a problem with a computer, when the best method is not clear, a good approach might well be a "quick and dirty" routine that works and produces a few results. At that point one is better equipped to consider how the programming can be improved. Questions relating to an improved algorithm, ways of increasing the speed, changes in the output format, suitable restart procedures, and the like are seen in proper context and can be attacked in sensible fashion.

r	Power, T	Difference	Multiple of
1	1		
		8	$4 \cdot 5^0$
2	9		
		80	$4 \cdot 5^1$
3, 4	89		
		500	$4 \cdot 5^3$
5	589		
		2500	$4 \cdot 5^4$
6, 7, 8	3089		
		312500	$4 \cdot 5^7$
9, 10	315589		
		7812500	$4 \cdot 5^9$
11	8128089		

Figure F8.3. Figure F8.1 extended

The student is particularly warned that elaborate output does not belong in the first phase of a program and is often a serious violation of the principle "Cut the problem down to size." After some results are obtained, it is time to consider improvements.

Our reasoning for this problem has now changed. Let's go on the machine and type the low-order digits of every fourth power until we achieve success (namely, on x = 9, when the terminal digits are 12). At this point, we want to start jumping by steps five times as big; namely, by 20's. We now look for the entry that has its last three digits all 1's or 2's. We are, at this point, examining only those powers which all have their last two digits satisfactory. The digit just to the left (called the critical digit) can be shown to maintain its parity; i.e., if it starts out odd it will stay odd, and if it starts out even it will stay even. We are thus assured of success at the next higher level for r, within the next five lines.

Each time we achieve success at the next level, we can increase the jump rate by a factor of 5 and get our next success within, at most, five stages.

In other words, our original attack was not efficient. We need a routine that will develop and type the terminal 20 (or so) digits of any arbitrary power of 2 and go on to higher powers by an increment that we can alter by a factor of 5 when success is achieved.

This is readily done by calculating first a table of powers of powers of 2, as in Figure F8.4. Fifty lines of this table (the argument is formed by doubling, the function by squaring) suffice to carry our problem to its conclusion.

We can now go on the machine with starting values of, say, T = 89 and ΔT = 100. We know from our experience with the problem that we have reached r = 4 and that we can afford to jump by 100's. A search-and-multiply loop on the table of Figure F8.4 will produce for us the last 20 digits of <u>any</u> arbitrary power of 2. For example, if we want the 89th power, we need to multiply together the functional values corresponding to the arguments 64, 16, 8, and 1 (precisely the binary representation of 89, of course).

Argument	Function
1	2
2	4
4	16
8	256
16	65536
32	4294967296
64	744073709551616
128	607431768211456
·	·
·	·
·	·

Figure F8.4. A table of powers of powers of 2

We will arrange also to alter ΔT by a factor of 5 whenever we please. We are now ready to really solve our problem. We will generate the 89th, 189th, 289th, 389th, and so on powers (all of which end in the digits 2112) and wait for the appearance of a terminal sequence of more than 4 digits that are all 1's or 2's. We know that this will occur after, at most, five lines. At that time we will alter ΔT by a factor of 5 and proceed. The process repeats from then on. In about 10 minutes (on the IBM 1620) we can develop the table shown in Figure F8.5.

r	T
1	1
2	9
3	89
4	89
5	589
6	3089
7	3089
8	3089
9	315589
10	315589
11	8128089
12	164378089
13	945628089
14	1922190589
15	11687815589
16	109344065589
17	231414378089
18	1452117503089
19	4503875315589
20	65539031565589

Figure F8.5. More results of the terminal 2^T problem

Problem F9

CONSECUTIVE ZEROS IN 2 ᵀ

Problem F8 concerned the terminal or low-order digits of the powers of 2. Consider a problem that appears, superficially, to be the same.

The 10th power of 2 contains a significant zero; it is the lowest power to have one. The 53rd power contains two consecutive zeros (these are not terminal digits). In the notation of Problem F8, we have the table of Figure F9.1.

r	T
1	10
2	53
3	242
4	377
5	1491
6	1492

Figure F9.1

We wish to extend this table to $r = 20$. The same algorithm that was used in Problem F8 comes to mind; namely, to generate successive powers of 2 and search them for r consecutive zeros. There is this significant difference: In this case we must develop the entire power (not just the low-order 20 digits), and thus the problem solution will continuously slow down.

In fact, we know of no shortcuts to this problem. At this writing, the value for $r = 8$ is known ($T = 14,007$), and it is known that the value for $r = 9$ is greater than 60,000. At $T = 11,000$, incidentally, the solution is running about 5 powers per minute on a Model I 1620 (and on an IBM 7094 it runs, at that level, at about 40 powers per minute).

This problem, as we have described it, is probably not a suitable computer problem. It lacks the regularity found in Problem F8 (or so it seems at this time); finding a few results

212

does not seem to advance us much in understanding what is going on, and does not suggest a way to cut the problem down to size.

As stated here, the problem is only a special case of a more general situation. We are seeking consecutive zeros in the powers of 2. For zeros we could substitute 1's, 2's, and so on to fill in the table shown in Figure F9.2. There are also powers of 3, and of 7, and many other primes to be investigated.

	0	1	2	3	4	5	6	7	8	9
1	10	4	1	5	2	8	4	15	3	12
2	53	40	43	25	18	16	46	24	19	33
3	242	42	43	83	44	41	157	24	39	50
4	377	313	314	219	192	41	220	181	180	421
5	1491	485	314	221	315	973	220	317	316	422
6	1492	1841	2354	2270		973	2269	972	971	2187
7	6801							972		
8	14007									

Figure F9.2. Generalized consecutive digits problem

Perhaps a better attack is this. Considering only the consecutive zeros again, Figure F9.1 showed the power for which the first appearance was noted. Now, after T = 86, every power of 2 seems to exhibit zeros (see Problem F10). However, not many powers have consecutive zeros. Thus, we might focus attention on the cases for r = 2 and search for all values and not just the first appearance. Suppose it should happen (it doesn't) that for r = 3, successive appearances were on the 242, 377, 512, and 647 powers. These figures form a progression, from which we might form a hypothesis. The true situation won't be that simple, of course.

We have deliberately included this problem to illustrate some principles. The superficial similarity to Problem F8 leads one to suspect that the problems are basically the same, whereas they are radically different. As far as we know now, this problem is far beyond the scope of an introductory course. Brute force gets us nowhere, but may provide some clues. Since the most important part of knowledge is to know its limits, some consideration of this problem is worth while.

Problem F10

POWERS OF 2 WITHOUT ZEROS

A statement appeared in Recreational Mathematics Magazine,* "The highest power of 2 that does not contain the digit zero is the 86th."

Here is another facet of this series of numbers (see Problems F8, F9, and F11) that warrants exploration.

The first nine powers of 2 contain no zeros, as well as these powers: 13, 14, 15, 16, 18, 19, 24, 25, 27, 28, 31, 32, 33, 34, 35, 36, 37, 39, 49, 51, 67, 72, 76, 77, 81, and 86. Is that the complete list?

First, let's outline an efficient method for generating the powers. Suppose we set up in storage the following numbers:

X	$\overline{8}192$	address 19000
N	$\overline{0}0013$	address 01505
F	$\overline{1}8997$	address 01500

The field X is the 13th power of 2, and is noted in the field N. F records the address of the flag on X. To generate successive powers efficiently, the flow chart of Figure F10.1 applies.

For each power of 2 that is generated, a search is made, starting at F and continuing through 19000. The presence of a zero ends the search immediately. If the entire field X contains no zeros, then the value of N should be typed.

This attack cannot prove the statement from Recreational Mathematics Magazine. However, suppose the search gets to N = 12,000, without finding any new results. At that point we would be searching a field of 3,613 digits.

Now, there is no evidence either way as to the randomness of the digits in high powers of 2. We have already some small evidence that zeros appear regularly; in fact, in clusters (from Problem F9). We might conjecture that 5's appear about one-tenth of the time, so we might guess that we have, at this stage, around 361 zeros and 361 5's. At least a third of these probably

---

*No longer published.

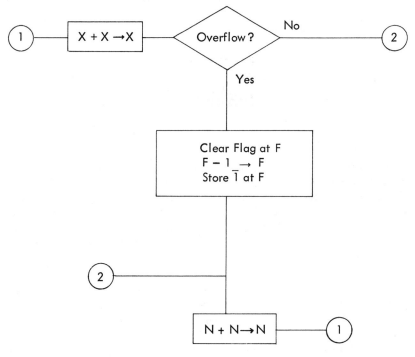

Figure F10.1. Generating powers of 2

have a digit to their right that will produce no carry when multiplied by 2. Thus, the chance of having zeros in the next power is quite high. Perhaps the conjecture from Recreational Mathematics Magazine is a certainty, but the proof will have to be done analytically.

We also have here a problem that can be generalized. What is the highest power of 2 that lacks any given decimal digit? The answer would seem to be 86 for the digit zero. Similarly, it would seem to be 91 for the digit one, 168 for the digit two, and so on.

Problem F11

BINARY 2 ^{X}

Several problems (F8, F9, and F10) have dealt with characteristics of the series 2^x; i.e., the series 2, 4, 8, 16, 32, ... These problems all relate to the <u>decimal</u> representation of the elements in the series. If these properties are to be explored on a binary machine, then the routine should be written to express the series in decimal form, or, to be precise, in a BCD (binary coded decimal) mode.

One way to do this is to allocate a computer word to each digit of the number. Thus, to store the 20th power of 2, we might store the 7 digits as shown in Figure F11.1.

In other storage words we could keep track of the power (20) and the address of the high-order digit (1002).

To double our stored number, we must operate on it digit by digit, working from right to left, using the table of Figure F11.2 and the logic of Figure F11.3.

Word	Contents
1002	0001
1003	0000
1004	0004
1005	0010
1006	0005
1007	0007
1010	0006

Figure F11.1. BCD representation for the decimal number 1048576

If, in the process of doubling, the last C (for carry) is 1, then the address of the high-order digit should be reduced by 1.

EXERCISE 1. Write a routine to calculate powers of 2, using the scheme outlined above (or a better one).

216

(Old digit)	0	0	(New digit)
	1	2	
	2	4	
	3	6	
	4	8	
	5	0	
	6	2	
	7	4	
	8	6	
	9	8	

Figure F11.2. Conversion table for doubling

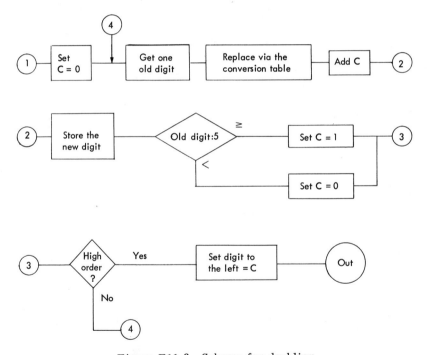

Figure F11.3. Scheme for doubling

EXERCISE 2. Apply the routine of Exercise 1 to one of the Problems F8, F9, or F10.

EXERCISE 3. Outline a method to perform BCD subtraction and multiplication in a manner analogous to the one outlined for addition.

Problem F12

3K IN BINARY

Visitors to a computing center are often fascinated by the lights blinking on the console panel as electrical circuits are turned on and off inside the computer. Many casual observers are baffled, however, in any attempt to read the numbers represented by the lights because they are not familiar with the binary representation of numbers, in which a lighted lamp is indicated by 1 and an unlighted lamp by 0, as in Figure F12.1.

Number	Binary Representation
1	0000 0001
2	0000 0010
3	0000 0011
4	0000 0100
5	0000 0101
6	0000 0110
7	0000 0111
8	0000 1000
9	0000 1001
10	0000 1010
11	0000 1011
12	0000 1100

Figure F12.1. Binary representation of integers

Dr. Mark Wells (of the Los Alamos Scientific Laboratories) once remarked that every third number seems to have an even number of 1's. That is, multiples of 3 usually cause an even number of lights to shine. This is true in Figure F12.1. Figure F12.2 shows that 9 of the first 10 multiples of 3 do have this characteristic. There is only one exception in numbers of five bits (binary digits) or less.

EXERCISE 1. (a) Show by hand calculation that 9 out of 10 of the six-bit multiples of 3 also have an even

219

number of 1's. (b) Investigate the situation for seven-bit multiples of 3.

On decimal computers, only single digits are shown in binary notation by lights on the console panel. Nevertheless it is

Decimal	Binary
3	00011
6	00110
9	01001
12	01100
15	01111
18	10010
21	10101 (Odd-one)
24	11000
27	11011
30	11110

Figure F12.2. Numbers of the form 3k in binary notation

sometimes very convenient on such a decimal machine as the IBM 1620 (Model I) to add numbers in binary notation. This is not difficult. All arithmetic is performed on this computer by means of table lookup. The arithmetic tables (which are stored between 00100 and 00399) are normally the decimal arithmetic tables. They need not be: That area can contain similar tables to perform arithmetic in any base less than ten. In particular, binary tables can be stored, and the 1620 can then operate (partially) as a binary machine. We say "partially," since instruction arithmetic (i.e., address modification) is still to be done decimally.

The procedure, then, is this. To perform binary addition, we should replace part of the decimal tables with the binary add table. This is particularly easy because the binary add table contains only 4 digits, and three of them are the same as the corresponding digits in the decimal table:

	0	1
0	0	1
1	1	$\bar{0}$

Actually, the combinations of digits that involve 2 must also be replaced because of the way carries in addition are handled by the 1620. Still more digits must be altered if the addition can be negative, which calls for complementation and, if the result can be negative, recomplementation. The point is, that for the effort of changing a few digits, the machine stands ready to perform binary addition (and other arithmetic operations as well). Suppose we store at 10000 a record consisting of the binary arithmetic tables. We also must store, say, at 11000, the normal decimal tables. Then to perform a binary operation BB, the following three instructions are needed:

$$
\begin{array}{lll}
31 & 00402 & 10000 \\
BB & \text{———} & \text{———} \\
31 & 00402 & 11000
\end{array}
$$

That is, the tables are converted to binary, the operation is performed, and the tables are then restored to decimal.

> EXERCISE 2. Write a routine to count by 3's in binary notation. Read in from the typewriter a 3-digit binary number with a leading zero. Extend the field to the left automatically whenever the sum displaces the leading zero. Type the result after each addition.

It may not be evident how to calculate the number of multiples of 3 that have an odd one, without actually generating the multiples in binary notation and counting the 1's.

> EXERCISE 3. Write a routine to count the number of multiples of 3 that have an odd number of 1's in their binary representation. Print the cumulative total for each number of binary digits from 5 onward (i.e., from the point at which you left off in your analysis by hand.)

The student may ask whether it is possible to improve the method of testing the Wells conjecture, in accordance with a principle laid down in the Introduction. To do this we note that the number of multiples with an odd-one in any set, with the same number n of binary digits, depends on the number of multiples with even-ones in the previous set. This latter number, in turn, depends on the number of multiples with an odd-one in its preceding set. Let us represent by t_n the total number of multiples with n bits (binary digits) or less. Let us use p_n (for peculiar multiples) to represent the number of multiples with an odd-one, counting all cases of n bits or less. Then by the reasoning already given, or by a careful and complete reasoning along the same lines, we guess that p_{n+2} depends in some way on p_n. We tabulate, in Figure F12.3, part of the results obtained with a routine similar to that suggested in Exercise 3.

Number of bits	Number of multiples of 3 —		
	With odd-one	With even-ones	Total
(n)	(p_n)	(r_n)	(t_n)
5	1	9	10
6	2	19	21
7	8	34	42
8	16	69	85
9	45	125	170
10	90	251	341

Figure F12.3. Occurrence of 3k with odd-ones

The student can verify that the following simple relationship actually does exist between p_{n+2} and p_n:

$$p_n = 3p_{n-2} + t_{n-3}$$

EXERCISE 4. Write a short routine to extend the table of Figure F12.3 by using the recurrence relationship given. Note that the total number of multiples of 3 is given by $\lfloor 2^n/3 \rfloor$; i.e., only the integral part of the quotient is used.

The student will find it entertaining and informative to use the IBM 1620 (Model I) for binary arithmetic. The binary multiply table is

	0	1
0	0	0
1	0	1

EXERCISE 5. Write a short routine to read in two
binary numbers from the typewriter and compute
their product.

EXERCISE 6. (a) Write a routine to complement a
negative binary number by using binary arithmetic.
(b) Write a routine to add two signed binary numbers,
taking care to recomplement the result when necessary.

Problem F13

THE FLAGSTONE PROBLEM

A man has red, gray, and black flagstones for making a walk. How shall he lay them so that no pattern of colors is immediately repeated and how many can be so laid? That is, no consecutive stones may have the same color; no consecutive pairs of stones may have the same colors in the same order; no three stones may show the same sequence of colors as the preceding three; and so on.*

This problem can be described in many different ways. A mathematical statement of it† goes like this: Is there a non-terminating decimal containing only the digits 0, 1, and 2 such that no two adjacent n-tuples are identical in digits and arrangement, for any value of n?

> EXERCISE 1. (a) State the same problem as applied to three bells, a string of beads‡ and a code of dots, dashes and spaces. (b) Write a routine to type a sequence composed of the digits 0, 1, and 2. Use a random number generator from Problem E7 to choose at random from the other 2 digits after typing each digit. (c) Examine sequences from part (b) to find portions that satisfy the conditions of the problem.

The following sequence of 77 digits satisfies the conditions of the problem, but no digit can be added to it at the end without repeating a pattern immediately:

---

*Problem 33 of the fifth book of <u>Problematical Recreations</u>, Litton Industries, Beverly Hills, California.

†See Hugh Noland, problem statement in <u>The American Mathematical</u> <u>Monthly</u>, June–July 1963, p. 675.

‡See John Leech, "A Problem on Strings of Beads," <u>The Mathematical Gazette</u> (London), Vol. 41, 1957, pp. 277-278. See also Marston Morse and Gustav Hedlund, "Unending Chess, Symbolic Dynamics and Problems in Semigroups," <u>Duke Mathematical Journal</u>, Vol. 11, March, 1944, pp. 1-7.

3 2 3 1 2 3 2 1 2 3 1 2 1 3 2 3 1 2 3 2 1 2 3 1 3 2 3
1 2 3 2 1 3 2 3 1 2 1 3 2 1 2 3 1 2 1 3 1 2 3 2 1 3 1
2 1 3 2 1 2 3 1 3 2 3 1 2 3 2 1 2 3 1 3 2 3 1

Adding a 3 would repeat a pattern, 2 3 1 3, of 4 digits at the
end. However, adding a 2 would produce a repetition of the 11-
digit pattern, 3 2 1 2 3 1 3 2 3 1 2. Similarly, the series

2 3 1 2 3 2 1 2 3 1 2 1 3 1 2 3 1 3 2 1 2 3 2 1 3
2 3 1 2 3 2 1 2 3 1 3 2 3 1 2 1 3 1 2 3 2 1 3 2 3
1 2 3 2 1 2 3 1 3 2 3 1 2 1

cannot be extended without repeating either a pattern of 2 digits
or a pattern of 23 digits. To extend a terminating sequence in
accordance with the conditions, it is necessary to back up 1 or
more digits and choose the alternate digit.

> EXERCISE 2. (a) Rewrite and elaborate the routine of
> Exercise 1 to test each new digit for a repeating
> pattern of every length from 2 up to half the length of
> the sequence. If any pattern is repeated, change the
> last digit to its alternate. In case this digit also fails,
> return to the previous digit, or, if necessary, to still
> earlier digits. (b) Use the routine of part (a) to pro-
> duce a sequence of at least 200 digits.

Before attempting to break any records in the Flagstone
Problem, the student should consider whether it is possible to
improve the method, as suggested by a principle given in the
introduction. It might be difficult to create a series in any arbitrary length by the method of Exercise 2, but there is an ingenious method for generating a sequence from the beginning
to any length whatever.* This method is based on the set of
positive integers, which furnishes a simple example of an infinite sequence. The integers are expressed in binary notation
and classified according to whether they have an even or odd
number of 1's in their binary representation (see Problem F11).
First we define the sequence $S = a_0 \, a_1 \, a_2 \, \ldots$, where $a_n =$
0 if there is an even number of 1's in the expression of n as a
binary number, and $a_n = 1$ if there is an odd number of 1's. If

---

*See C. H. Braunholtz, problem solution in The American Mathe-
matical Monthly, June–July 1963, p. 675.

we start with 20, say, then

$$S = 0\ 1\ 1\ 0\ 0\ 1\ 1\ 0\ 1\ 0\ 0\ 1\ 1\ 0\ 0\ 1\ 0\ \ldots,$$

as shown in Figure F13.1. Now we count the number of 1's between successive zeros, obtaining a new sequence T. That is, we let $T = b_1\ b_2\ b_3\ b_4\ b_5\ \ldots$, where b_i is the number of 1's between the ith zero in S and the next zero. Using the sequence in Figure F13.1, we obtain $T = 2\ 0\ 2\ 1\ 0\ 2\ 0\ 1$. It can be shown that when T is obtained in this way, starting with any integer, it satisfies the conditions of the problem.

n	a_n	b_i
20 = 010100	0	
21 = 010101	1	
		2
22 = 010110	1	
23 = 010111	0	
		0
24 = 011000	0	
25 = 011001	1	
		2
26 = 011010	1	
27 = 011011	0	
		1
28 = 011100	1	
29 = 011101	0	
		0
30 = 011110	0	
31 = 011111	1	2
32 = 100000	1	
33 = 100001	0	
		0
34 = 100010	0	
		1
35 = 100011	1	
36 = 100100	0	

Figure F13.1. Classification of binary numbers

EXERCISE 4. (a) Using a subroutine to count in

binary, as described in Problem F11, write a routine to generate a sequence for the Flagstone Problem. (b) Use the routine to type out a sequence of at
least 500 digits.

EXERCISE 5. (a) Define a_n as the sum of the binary
digits in the binary representation of n. Define b_i as
the number of a's between successive zeros as be-
fore. Then $T = b_1 \ b_2 \ b_3 \ b_4 \ldots$ gives an infinite sequence of <u>seven</u> symbols with no repeats. (b) Write
a routine to generate a sequence for seven colors of
beads on a string with no repeats.

Problem F14

THE CALCULATION OF π

There is an unlimited number of ways to form an infinite series whose sum is equal to π . The simplest is

$$\frac{\pi}{4} = 1 - 1/3 + 1/5 - 1/7 + 1/9 - 1/11 + \ldots$$

This is Leibnitz's formula (1674). It is obtained from the formula (which comes to us from the calculus) for the arctangent of an angle expressed in radians, by setting x = 1 in the series

$$\arctan x = x - \frac{x^3}{3} + \frac{x^5}{5} - \frac{x^7}{7} + \ldots \tag{1}$$

EXERCISE 1. (a) Write a routine to calculate π by using Leibnitz's formula. Place the printout under switch control. Print the number of terms and the value of $\pi/4$. (b) Experiment with the routine of part (a) to find out how many terms are required for 2-figure accuracy, 3-figure accuracy, and so forth ($\pi/4 = 0.7853981633 \ldots$).

Although Leibnitz's formula is simple, it converges very slowly to its limiting value of exactly $\pi/4$. Exercise 1 indicates that many thousands of terms would be needed to yield even 6-place accuracy. One way to speed up the convergence is to smooth out the "bouncing" (which is so noticeable in an alternating series of this kind) by grouping terms:

$$\frac{\pi}{4} = \left(1 - \frac{1}{3}\right) + \left(\frac{1}{5} - \frac{1}{7}\right) + \left(\frac{1}{9} - \frac{1}{11}\right) + \ldots$$

$$= 2\left[\frac{1}{1 \cdot 3} + \frac{1}{5 \cdot 7} + \frac{1}{9 \cdot 11} + \frac{1}{13 \cdot 15} + \ldots\right] \tag{2}$$

EXERCISE 2. (a) Write a routine to calculate $\pi/4$

by grouping terms in Leibnitz's formula as suggested. Place the output under switch control as before, and show both the number of terms and the
value for $\pi/4$. (b) Show by experimentation how
fast convergence is speeded up by the grouping
method for 100 terms, 200 terms, and 1,000 terms.

By the exercise of some ingenuity, the grouping can be
carried still further. For example, by grouping differently, we
obtain

$$\frac{\pi}{4} = 1 - \frac{1}{3 \cdot 5} - \frac{2}{7 \cdot 9} - \frac{2}{11 \cdot 13} - \frac{2}{15 \cdot 17} - \cdots$$

Averaging this with the previous series

$$\frac{\pi}{4} = \frac{2}{1 \cdot 3} + \frac{2}{5 \cdot 7} + \frac{2}{9 \cdot 11} + \frac{2}{13 \cdot 15} + \cdots$$

we arrive at

$$\frac{\pi}{4} = \frac{1}{2} + 4 \left[\frac{1}{1 \cdot 3 \cdot 5} + \frac{1}{11 \cdot 13 \cdot 15} + \frac{1}{15 \cdot 17 \cdot 19} + \cdots \right] \quad (3)$$

EXERCISE 3. (a) Write a routine to calculate $\pi/4$ by
using the series with three-factor denominators. (b)
Study the rate of convergence as before.

The student has learned from the exercises that the summation of series is an art in which mathematical imagination
can be applied to shorten the work of computation by factors of
hundreds, thousands, or even millions. He is now probably curious to know what schemes have been used to determine π to
thousands of decimal places. Exactly the same formula (for
arctangent) is used as before, but this time it is applied to

$$\frac{\pi}{4} = \tan^{-1} \frac{1}{2} + \tan^{-1} \frac{1}{3} \quad (4)$$

First we prove the correctness of the formula by using the
sum formula,

$$\tan(\alpha + \beta) = \frac{\tan \alpha + \tan \beta}{1 - \tan \alpha \tan \beta}$$

We let $\alpha = \tan^1 1/2$, $\beta = \tan^{-1} 1/3$. Then taking tangents of both sides of Equation (1), we have

$$1 = \frac{1/2 + 1/3}{1 - 1/6}$$

which is identically true. Now applying the arctangent formula (1) twice to Equation (4), we obtain

$$\frac{\pi}{4} = \left[\frac{1}{2} - \frac{1}{3} \left(\frac{1}{2} \right)^3 + \frac{1}{5} \left(\frac{1}{2} \right)^5 - \cdots \right.$$

$$\left. + \frac{1}{3} - \frac{1}{3} \left(\frac{1}{3} \right)^3 + \frac{1}{5} \left(\frac{1}{3} \right)^5 - \cdots \right] \tag{5}$$

EXERCISE 4. (a) Write a routine to calculate $\pi/4$ by Formula (5). (b) Study the rate of convergence, as before.

The student who wishes to consider breaking a record of some kind should be warned that π was determed to 3089 decimal places in 1955 and to 100,000 decimal places in 1961. There is plenty of room, however, for exercising ingenuity in developing formulas suitable for the computer that will converge rapidly. We shall therefore take the student a little farther along this road.

Machin, in 1706, elaborated the method used for developing Formulas (4) and (5), obtaining:

$$\frac{\pi}{4} = 4 \tan^{-1} \left(\frac{1}{5} \right) - \tan^{-1} \left(\frac{1}{239} \right) \tag{6}$$

This formula can be verified by applying the sum formula repeatedly. Then applying Formula (1), we come to Machin's formula:

$$\frac{\pi}{4} = 4 \left[\frac{1}{5} - \frac{1}{3} \left(\frac{1}{5} \right)^3 + \left(\frac{1}{5} \right)^5 - \cdots \right]$$

$$- \left[\frac{1}{239} - \frac{1}{3} \left(\frac{1}{239} \right)^3 + \frac{1}{5} \left(\frac{1}{239} \right)^5 - \cdots \right] \tag{7}$$

EXERCISE 4. (a) Verify Formula (6). (b) Write a routine to calculate $\pi/4$ by using Machin's formula. Take care to add terms to the sum in decreasing order of absolute magnitude, so that the sum will proceed steadily toward its limiting value of $\pi/4$. Plan your routine so it can be used for 10 or 100 decimal places.

Machin's formula was used by Edward Shanks, in 1873, to calculate π by hand to 707 decimal places.* That record was engraved on his tombstone as a tribute to his tremendous perseverance. Daniel Shanks and John W. Wrench, Jr., used an IBM computer in 1961, applying two similar series:

$$\frac{\pi}{4} = 6 \tan^{-1} \frac{1}{8} + 2 \tan^{-1} \frac{1}{57} + \tan^{-1} \frac{1}{239} \qquad (8)$$

$$\frac{\pi}{4} = 12 \tan^{-1} \frac{1}{18} + 8 \tan^{-1} \frac{1}{57} - 5 \tan^{-1} \frac{1}{139} \qquad (9)$$

Formula (8) is due to Störmer; Formula (9) is due to Gauss.

EXERCISE 5. (a) Verify Formulas (8) and (9). (b) Write a routine to calculate π using Gauss' formula. As before, arrange to check out the routine to 10-digit accuracy, but to run production to 100 digits.

---

*With, alas, an error in the 528th place.

PICK A NUMBER

Here is an old trick. Ask someone to select an integer and perform the following operations:

1. Multiply by one million.
2. Subtract from the product the original number.
3. Divide by 7.
4. If the result contains more than 6 digits, cross off all digits to the left of the low-order 6 digits, and add the number crossed off to the remaining 6 digits.
5. Repeat step 4 if necessary, until the final result is just 6 digits.

If he now tells you any specific digit of the final result, you can tell him all the rest. Let us analyze this trick.

Steps 1 and 2 form 999999x. Step 3 forms 142857x.

The number 142857 (the repetitive part of the reciprocal of 7) has the curious property that it can be multiplied by any integer and, when the product is reduced to 6 digits as in steps 4 and 5, one of the numbers in Figure G1.1 will appear.

$$142857$$
$$285714$$
$$428571$$
$$571428$$
$$714285$$
$$857142$$
$$999999$$

Figure G1.1

You can test this theory for various values of x; the programming of step 4 is tricky.

The particular number 142857 is not unique (though it is the smallest number with the required property). The reciprocal of any prime number that is full size (i.e., for which the length of the period is one less than the number) will behave in the same way. Thus the number

526315789473684210

(the reciprocal of 19) will act in an analogous manner. Problem
F5 suggests ways of finding more such numbers.

The proof that a number such as 142857 behaves in the way
it does is complex.

Write a routine to test this behavior empirically. Use
RNG (from Problem E7) to produce a random number. Multiply
it by 142857. Reduce the result to 6 digits, and test to verify
that it is one of the 7 numbers in Figure G1.1.

For example, suppose RNG furnishes as output the number
3870522174. Multiplying by 142857 yields 552931186211118. The
steps in the reduction are as follows:

$$
\begin{array}{r}
211118 \\
552931186 \\
\hline
553142304 \\
\end{array}
$$

$$
\begin{array}{r}
142304 \\
553 \\
\hline
142857 \\
\end{array}
$$

and the result satisfies the theory.

Problem G2

THE INSTALLATION MANAGEMENT GAME

Figure G2.1 shows the layout for a game called "Installation Management." A pair of dice is required, and a colored marker for each player.

Installation Management resembles other games (particularly the game of Chutes and Ladders, published by the Milton Bradley Company for the 4-to-6-year-old set), with three small differences. Landing on square 36 causes the loss of two turns; landing on square 24 takes the player out of the game; and squares 18 and 21 are interlocked in a loop.

The number of dice throws it takes to reach (or surpass) cell 50 is variable. It cannot be less than four throws of the dice. In theory, it could take an indefinitely large number of throws, but there is a very high probability that the game will be over by the time one player has had 12 turns.

We wish to investigate the distribution of the number of plays it takes to complete a game. To put it another way, we ask: What is the probability of reaching "Success" in each number of plays from 4 to 20, and what is the probability of failure caused by squares 24, 18, and 21?

In the latter form, the game resembles questions in many problems of business management, where the elements of the game involve decisions in investments, manufacture, distribution, and sale of products.

There are two ways to determine the required distribution:

1. Knowing the distribution of the tosses of two dice (see Problem E7), we could calculate the probabilities, cell by cell, and determine analytically the probability distribution. The complexity of the problem is staggering.

The problem could be set up in the form of 50 equations in 50 unknowns. Even assuming that that were done, there would still remain the problem of solving a 50 × 50 set of equations.

2. We could simulate (and then play) the game a few hundred thousand times, record the results of each game, and form the distribution. Given a computer, this latter method is attractive.

234

INSTALLATION MANAGEMENT
(Computing One-upmanship)

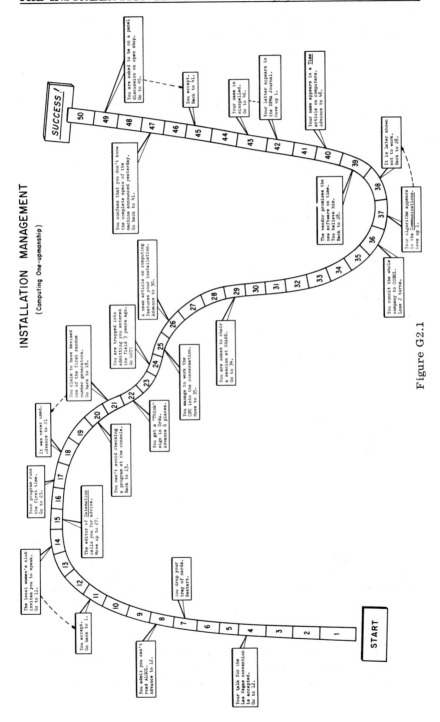

Figure G2.1

The process of simulating a real situation, sampling its ramifications extensively, is called the "Monte Carlo technique." We can simulate the game of Installation Management perfectly in the computer and play it (in the sense of executing the game) extensively. Although this may not appear too useful for this particular game, the principle is quite general and is widely used. Practical applications are widespread (in fields ranging from nuclear physics to pure mathematics), and the principle may be easier to explore in this somewhat trivial situation.

We may already have coded a subroutine for tossing dice (as in Problem E7).

The flow chart of Figure G2.2 shows the broad pattern of attack on Installation Management. We will need several counters in storage (they can all be 5-digit counters):

1. Counter T, to record the number of games played.
2. Counter S, to record the score, i.e., the number of turns taken within one game.
3. Counter C, to record the number of times a game ends on cell 24. No entry is made to the D-counters for this case.
4. A set of counters D, to record the desired distribution.

We will need a separate counter for each expected value of S. Since S cannot be less than 4 in any game, the first D counter records 4's; the next D counter, 5's; and so on, to the maximum. We have chosen arbitrarily to set the maximum at 30 (thus, there are 27 D counters) and record any game for which S exceeds 30 in a special counter.

5. Counter E, to record the number of games for which S exceeds 30.
6. Counter B, to record the board position. The B counter has a range from zero to 61 (throwing a 12 after landing on cell 49). (If we test first, the value of B need never exceed 50.)

The flow chart of Figure G2.2 has a feature that may be new to you: namely, an insert. At the point indicated by the asterisk, another test had to be inserted. The natural procedure would be to redraw the flow chart and incorporate the missing piece of logic. Published flow charts normally do this, but, in real life, patching flow charts is as common as patching codes. The return from the patch (the lower asterisk) is to the box "Apply dice toss to B."

The application of the dice toss to B is simple. If the output of the dice tossing subroutine is X, then $B + X \rightarrow B$.

Reference 3 requires some explanation. Figure G2.3 shows

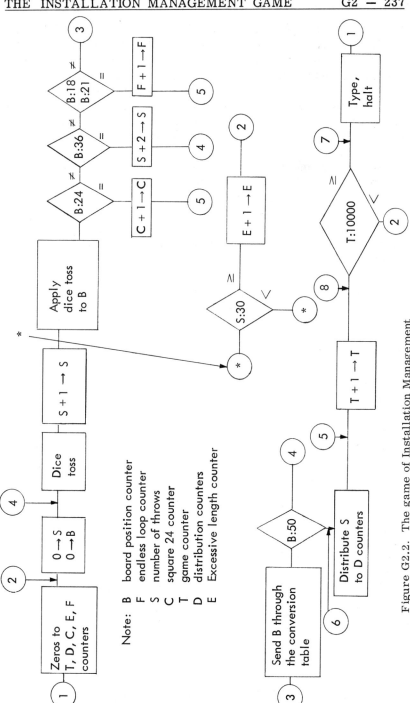

Figure G2.2. The game of Installation Management

a portion of the conversion table. The value of counter B (board position) is to be converted by means of this table. Actually, the left-hand side of the table need not appear in storage. The position on the right-hand side can be calculated as a function of the old value of B. The conversion table thus implements the actual jumps of the board. To enable the conversion subroutine (you would write it as a subroutine, wouldn't you?) to operate under all conditions, the conversion table should contain entries up to 61.

When B reaches or exceeds 50, a game has ended in success, and the number of plays, S, should be entered into the D table of counters. Suppose the D counters are all 5-digit counters, and the 4 counter is addressed at D itself (with the 5 counter at D + 5, the 6 counter at D + 10, and so on.) Then the address of the counter into which we wish to tally one for this game is given by Y:

$$Y = 5(S - 3) + (D - 5)$$
$$Y = 5S + D - 20$$

			1	1
			2	2
			3	3
			4	12
			5	9
			6	6
When	B has	the	7	0	Replace B with the
value	shown	here	8	12	value shown here
			·	·
			·	·
			·	·
			45	41
			46	46
			47	41
			48	48
			49	41
			50	50
			51	51
			·	·
			·	·
			·	·

Figure G2.3. The conversion table

At reference 8, it is assumed that in production we would want to play 10,000 games at a clip. During debugging and testing, a more realistic limit might be 10 or so.

At reference 7, we would arrange to type whatever it is we want to see. Again, for production we would want to see only the D, C, and E counters. For debugging, it might be sensible to set the limit (reference 8) to one and arrange to type out the contents of all the counters.

The following procedure is suggested for testing the routine. Initialize RNG to known values. Write a routine to use the dice tossing routine and type out a list of results from it. Then use those dice tosses to play a few games by hand. Now, with RNG reinitialized to the same starting values, play single games and compare the results.

Problem G5

GUESS-WORD PUZZLES

The competitors in many types of guessing games must combine a broad knowledge in some particular area with skill in deduction and inference based on incomplete information. Typical in this respect is the word-guessing game.* It will require alphabetic sorting of large amounts of stored data as described in Problem L3, and also elaborate logical decisions. The game is played as follows:

A player selects a 7-letter word, which he writes down but keeps concealed from his opponent. Each player tries to guess his opponent's word, using only 7-letter words for trials. His opponent must tell him how many letters of the guess agree with letters in the same position of his word but is not required to tell which positions. The player who requires the least number of guesses to discover his opponent's word wins the game, and his score is the difference between the number of guesses required by his opponent and the number he himself makes.

The student will recognize that the words used in Problem L3 are taken from this game. Suppose player A selects BA-ZOOKA, and player B guesses ODOROUS. Player A must respond with the count of one, since only one letter of the guess agrees with the letter in the same position in his word.

We consider whether it is possible to program the computer to play this guessing game. We see quickly that it is not too difficult to write a routine that allows the computer to select a word and count the matching letters in guesses made by the human player.

> EXERCISE 1. (a) Write a routine to read a card containing a 7-letter word into an area that already contains suitable flags, so that the letters can be compared with the letters of a word typed in by the player. Provide for correcting the guess under

---

*The name "Guess-word Puzzles" (by analogy to crossword puzzles) is attached to this game, even though the word "puzzle" is a misnomer.

switch control if an error is made in typing. Count
the number of matching letters and type it. When
the player succeeds in guessing the hidden word
stored in the computer, type RIGHT and the number
of guesses. (b) Elaborate the routine of part (a) so
that 100 cards selected at random from a large deck
are read into storage. Each card is to contain 10 7-
digit words. Select the word at random from this
collection, using the random number generator of
Problem E7.

Any attempt at writing a routine for the computer to guess
a word chosen by the human player is likely to show the awesome
superiority of the human memory over the storage of the computer. Even if 10,000 positions are made available in the computer for a collection of possible guesses, only 700 words can
be stored. A more striking contrast, however, is the uncanny
ability of the human player to make inspired guesses. Experienced players often succeed in discovering the hidden word in
very few guesses, and some can maintain an average count of
less than 12 when playing against a person with whom they are
well acquainted. Such skill seems to involve a vast amount of
generalization and deduction based on numerous observations of
the opponent and even of the environment where the choice of
hidden word is made. The student may question whether the computer could compete successfully with a human player even if
it were equipped with a magnetic tape drive or disc drive to
provide very large auxiliary storage. Nevertheless, much can
be learned about programming (and a little about logic) by
writing as good a routine as possible.

Before we try to program the computer to make the guesses
in the word-guessing game, we should cut the problem down to
size, according to the basic principle of abstraction laid down
in the Introduction. We therefore start with a much easier
problem: to have the machine discover a hidden 4-digit number.
Figure G3.1 shows a set of possible steps in such a game, where
the number to be guessed was 5208.

At A, the zero in the hidden number has been located; at B,
the 2; at C, the 5; and at D, the 8. It is left to the student to for-
mulate the logic completely. He will find that it is the zero
guesses that finally fix a digit. Fifteen guesses were required in
the sample game to discover the hidden number. The student is
challenged to reduce the number of guesses.

Guess	Count	
0000	1	
1111	0	
1000	1	
1100	1	
1110	0	A
2222	1	
1222	1	
1122	0	B
3333	0	
4444	0	
5555	1	
1555	0	C
5206	3	
5207	3	
5208	4	D

Figure G3.1. A sample game of guessing numbers

EXERCISE 2. (a) Write down a logical series of guesses for a hidden number such as 8373. (b) Write a routine to guess a hidden 4-digit number. (c) Improve the routine by using the random number generator of Problem E7 to select the starting number.

By experimenting with the 4-digit version of the guessing game, ths student will discover the basic principle of establishing the location of a digit. He will also find that it is never necessary to try all possible 4-digit numbers. He may now wish to advance to a 4-letter word-guessing game. This modification makes the game far more attractive, but introduces a good many complications. For example, the routine must have available a list of legitimate 4-letter English words that contain every letter in every position in which it can occur in any English word. The student can expect to compile such a list with about 50 carefully chosen words.

The competitive aspect of the game can be modified slightly so that two (or more) teams of programmers play against each other. Each team selects a set of test words for the routine written by the other team. The routines may also be tested against the same set of test words. The winning team is the one that requires the lowest number of guesses. Methods for reducing the number of guesses are left to the programming teams. It is clear, however, that the winning team will use logical deductions based on an understanding of letter frequencies in English words. Further lists beyond the basic list of 50 words will certainly be needed, by analogy with the 4-digit game, but any attempt to list all possible 4-letter words is obviously not only impractical but wholly unnecessary. Crossword puzzle lists, spelling lists, and Walker's Rhyming Dictionary* are better arranged for selecting suitable lists than an ordinary dictionary.

EXERCISE 3. (a) Prepare lists of suitable 4-letter words for guessing a hidden word. (b) Write a routine to guess any legitimate 4-letter word.

A few remarks may be added concerning a routine to guess 7-letter words. If auxiliary storage is available as magnetic tape or discs, so that all 7-letter words can be stored, we could attempt to simulate a human player in making partly random guesses. Unless all 7-letter words can be stored, the letters must be determined individually. A more advanced method than changing a single letter at a time will be required. To prepare suitable lists becomes a major part of the problem, and this task might itself be accomplished with the aid of the computer.

EXERCISE 4. (a) Show that a 7-digit <u>number</u> can be guessed even if 3 digits are required to be changed at a time. (b) Write a routine to guess 7-digit numbers by always changing at least 3 digits at a time.

EXERCISE 5. (a) Prepare lists of words that will detect letters of high frequency, such as vowels. For example, the pair of words

adamant
bananas

will detect an "a" anywhere in a hidden word. (b) Write a routine to guess any one of 700 7-letter words. You may store the words in any desired order, such as alphabetically by vowels. (c) Modify the routine of part (b) to read in any list of 700 7-letter words and sort them into the required order.

---

*Published by E. P. Dutton & Co., Inc., New York, 1924.

The student may wish to allow the computer to play independent games even if the human player chooses the same word twice. This makes the play more interesting and also makes it more difficult for the human player to bamboozle the computer.

EXERCISE 6. Elaborate the routine of Exercise 5 so that the first pair of guesses is chosen at random from the lists. Further, whenever there are several choices available that satisfy the criterion being used, make the choice at random.

Problem G4

BUZZ

There is a children's game, called "Buzz," in which the players count rapidly out loud, starting with one. For any number containing the figure 7, or any number that is exactly divisible by 7, the player says "Buzz" instead of the number. Then the next player continues the counting. For numbers that contain the figure 7 and are also divisible by 7, the player says "Buzz-Buzz." After 100 is reached, the game starts over.

The student is invited to consider the flow chart in Figure G4.1 for a routine to type according to this pattern. The output should thus begin

1 2 3 4 5 6 BB 8 9 10 11 12 13 B

and so on.

Before writing a routine in accordance with the proposed flow chart, the student should judge the suitability of the problem for a computer in accordance with the principles given in the Introduction. Besides furnishing an amusing demonstration, the problem has value only as an exercise in programming. As an exercise, the problem involves numerical and alphabetical typing and loop writing and testing. We list the requirements as follows:

Initialize the number
Return typewriter carriage
Advance the number
Test for divisibility and branch
Test units' digit and branch
Test for tens' digit and branch
Test for N = 100 and branch
Type B
Type BB
Type N and space
Test for leading zero and suppress
Return

The student is challenged to see how close he can come, as an exercise in routine writing, to meeting these requirements in

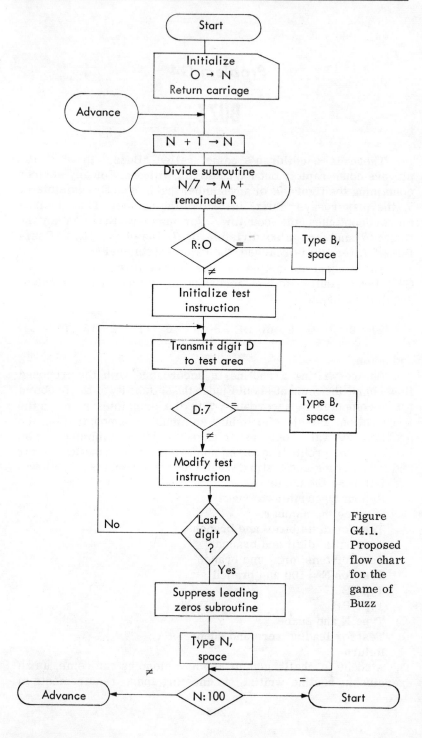

Figure G4.1. Proposed flow chart for the game of Buzz

20 or less machine language instructions for the IBM 1620, without the use of any subroutine.

> EXERCISE 1. Write a machine language routine in
> not more than 20 instructions, plus constants and
> data fields, to count and type as in the game of Buzz.

The application of logical planning, as in this exercise, will help the student to write accurate and concise routines. He should be warned, however, not to sacrifice simplicity in an effort to save a few steps. Completing Exercise 1 in 20 instructions or less depends on skillful use of the test operations provided by the 1620, without loss of simplicity.

Given a problem that is well defined, what is the best routine for its solution? Is it the one with the fewest instructions (which may minimize storage space or, as is suggested above, merely be the most elegant)? Or is it the one that minimizes execution time? Or is it the one that gets into operation soonest (i.e., that minimizes the elapsed time to solution)? The answer, of course, depends on the situation. If our primary concern is saving elapsed time, then often a "crowbar" solution is the best, with no consideration given to storage space or execution time. The important thing is to be aware of the differences in these various approaches. The Buzz Problem is designed to focus on just one mode of optimization.

Problem G5

OLD PUZZLE PROBLEMS

Here are two old problems.

1. Arrange the digits from 1 to 9 in order, using only addition and subtraction, to total 100. Some examples are:

$$1 + 2 + 3 - 4 + 5 + 6 + 78 + 9 = 100$$
$$1 + 23 - 4 + 56 + 7 + 8 + 9 = 100$$
$$12 + 3 + 4 + 5 - 6 - 7 + 89 = 100$$
$$123 - 45 - 67 + 89 = 100$$

There are many other possible ways.

2. Using four 4's and any mathematical operations you please, express each of the integers from 1 to 112. A few examples of these known results are given in Figure G5.1.

$$3 = \frac{4 + 4 + 4}{4}$$

$$4 = 4 + \frac{4 - 4}{4}$$

$$10 = \frac{4}{4} \cdot \frac{4}{.4}$$

$$13 = \frac{44}{4} + \sqrt{4}$$

$$19 = 4! - 4 - \frac{4}{4}$$

$$25 = 4! + 4^{4-4}$$

$$31 = \frac{(4!/.4) + \sqrt{4}}{\sqrt{4}}$$

248

$$39 = 4! \sqrt{4} - \frac{4}{.4} \left(\text{Note: } .\dot{4} = .44444 \ldots = \frac{4}{9}\right)$$

$$54 = \frac{(4 + \sqrt{4})!}{4!} + 4!$$

$$71 = \frac{4! + 4.4}{.4}$$

Figure G5.1. The four 4's problem

EXERCISE 1. Recall or invent as many criteria as you can for distinguishing problems suitable for a computer. Apply them to these puzzle problems, and write a report stating your conclusions. It is important to know when not to use a computer.

Problem H1

THE CALENDAR ODOMETER

You are familiar with many counting devices, such as the registers on a desk calculator, or the mileage counter on an automobile (i.e., the odometer). For all such devices, there must be a simple mechanism to deal with carrying from wheel to wheel. If an odometer stands at 12345 (in whole miles) and one more mile is to register, the unit wheel rolls to 6. When the device stands at 12349, however, the addition of one more unit must not only roll the unit wheel to zero but must sense the special case that dictates also rolling the ten wheel to 5. Again, at 19999, this mechanism must arrange to carry over four wheels, and so on. In the odometer, the carry-over is achieved mechanically. In the computer, special circuits are usually provided. In some cases, however, the mechanism for carrying must be programmed. For example:

EXERCISE 1. Write a routine to add 1 to an alpha-numeric field that represents a 5-digit positive number.

EXERCISE 2. (a) Write a subroutine to add 1 to any alphanumeric field that represents a positive number up to 10 digits in length. (b) Compare the logic of your routine with this method: Convert the alpha field to pure numeric, perform the addition, and convert back to the alpha format.

Suppose, now, that we postulate a counting mechanism for British currency, in pounds, shillings, and pence, as in Figure H1.1.

Between the first and second wheels (counting from the right) there must be the usual decimal carry, so that after 09d comes 10d. But after 11d comes 00, with a carry of one to the shilling wheels since 12d = 1 shilling. Similarly, the two shilling wheels must count decimally to 19 (since 20s = 1£) and then roll to zero and carry one to the pound wheels (all of the pound wheels add decimally).

250

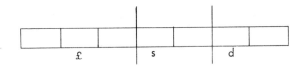

Figure H1.1

EXERCISE 3. (a) Construct a flow chart for counting (by single pennies) in the British currency system. (b) Write a routine for such a counter, following your flow chart. Arrange to type results under switch control.

EXERCISE 4. Write a routine to count in inches, feet, yards, and miles.

We wish to program a counter for a Gregorian calendar, capable of counting days, months, years, and days of the week, from January 1, 1800, through December 31, 2199. By Zeller's congruence (see Problem H2) or by consulting a calendar, we find that January 1, 1800, was a Wednesday, and January 1, 2200, will be a Wednesday. Thus, the Gregorian calendar repeats every 400 years. (Zeller's congruence shows that a change of 4 in the number of centuries does not alter the value of the day of the week.)

We want a counter that looks like Figure H1.2.

Figure H1.2

The unit wheel will roll from zero to 6 as the days advance. Zero stands for Sunday, 1 for Monday, . . . , 6 for Saturday. The wheel will be initially set to 3 for January 1, 1800. There is no carry out of this wheel.

The day wheels will advance decimally, but with a variable upper limit of 28, 29, 30, or 31, depending on the month and, if February, on the year.

The month wheels advance decimally to 12, and then carry one to the year wheels.

The year wheels advance decimally to 2199. The total advance of the entire device should halt when the counter shows

219912312

The flow chart for our counter will be quite large. It will contain many decision boxes, including those listed below (not necessarily in order, and not exhaustive):

1. Is the day now 28?
2. Is the month 02?
3. Is the year divisible by 4?
4. Is the year divisible by 100?
5. Is the year divisible by 400?
6. Is the month 09, 04, 06, or 11?
7. Is the counter now at 219912312?
8. Is the month 12?

And so on. You should complete this list and then arrange it in logical order. Question 7, for example, may come first; many computer routines begin with the logical question, "Are we finished?" Is the terminal 2 in the test constant of Question 7 necessary? Should it be included, as a nice check?

There could be other useful checks. December 7, 1941, was a Sunday. January 14, 1964, was a Tuesday. November 11, 1991, will be a Monday.

Your "calendar" may run fast or slow on the machine, depending on how clever you are. For example, the first test for leap years (to be made only on the 28th of February) is, Is the year divisible by 4? How would you make this test? Would you actually divide the year number by 4 and compare the remainder to zero? Or would you multiply the year by 25? Or multiply just the last 2 digits of the year? These are small points, but there will be many of them.

How long will it take to cycle through the entire 400 years? If this amount of machine time exceeds, say, 15 minutes, you should provide a restart procedure, so that you can finish the problem later if it is necessary to interrupt your use of the computer.

> EXERCISE 5. (a) Construct a flow chart for the calendar odometer. (b) Write a routine for the calendar odometer, following your flow chart. (You might consider using a table of 12 entries for the number of days in a month during common years.) Change your routine into a subroutine for use in further investigations.

Given our calendar odometer as a checked-out subroutine, we can now apply it to the following problem: Does the 13th of the month fall on Friday as often as on any of the other six days of the week? While we are at it, we might as well check all the days of the month in the same way.

	S	M	T	W	T	F	S
1							
2							
3							
4							
.							
.							
.							
.							
.							
31							

Figure H1.3

EXERCISE 6. Fill in the entire table of Figure H1.3.

What size counters should be assigned to the cells in this table? What numbers would you expect to have typed? What checks can you devise to ensure that the final table is correct? For example, if the calendar counter is initialized to the first of _this_ month, and terminates with the last day of this month, the table would present a condensed version of this month's calendar. Does that constitute a good check?

Could your calendar be operated backward? How far back could it go correctly?

* * *

A note about leap years. The rule is this: If the year is a multiple of four, it is a leap year, except that a multiple of 100 is a leap year only if it is also a multiple of 400. Thus, 1900 was not a leap year, but 2000 will be. The calendar will repeat exactly every 400 years due to the construction of this rule.

By the Gregorian calendar, there are 97 leap years in 400 consecutive years. These 400 years will thus have exactly 146,097 days in them. But an astronomical year (i.e., one revolution of the earth around the sun) takes place in 365 days, 5 hours, 48 minutes, 45.974 seconds.* Thus 400 years will be 146, 096 days, 21 hours, 6 minutes, and 29.6 seconds (check our arithmetic). The error will be, in 400 years, just 2 hours, 53 minutes, and 30.4 seconds. This error will accumulate to a full day in 3320 years. Since the Gregorian calendar was started in 1582, it will be off by one full day in 4902. The Gregorian formula is thus amazingly accurate.

The Gregorian calendar was calculated from the date of the first Nicene council in 385 A.D. and was established October 15, 1582. It was adopted by Great Britain and the English colonies in America in 1752.

---

*As defined for January 1, 1900, by the U.S. Bureau of Standards.

Problem H2

ZELLER'S CONGRUENCE (DAY of the WEEK)

To calculate the day of the week for a given date, Zeller's congruence can be applied.*

A date is expressed as follows:

m = month number, with January and February taken as months 11 and 12 of the preceding year. March is then 01, April is 02, . . . , December is 10; k = day of the month; C = century; D = year in the century.

Thus, for August 23, 1963, m = 06, k = 23, C = 19, D = 63. For January 1, 1800, m = 11, k = 01, C = 17, D = 99, and so on. The congruence is

$$f = \left\{ \left[2.6m - 0.2 \right] + k + D + \left[\frac{D}{4} \right] + \left[\frac{C}{4} \right] - 2C \right\} \bmod 7$$

The square brackets denote "greatest integer in." Let us illustrate with August 23, 1963, a Friday.

For m = 06, the quantity (2.6m − 0.2) is 15.6; dropping the decimal (as indicated by the square brackets) gives 15.

We add 23 for k and 63 for D; [D/4] is 15, and [C/4] is 4. We subtract from this sum 38 for 2C, for a net of 82. The remainder on division by 7 is 5, for Friday. (Sunday is zero, Monday is 1, and so on.) The formula works for this case.

The formula is readily programmed. The divisions by 4 are best done by multiplying by 25 (and dropping two decimal places) The division by 7 (if your machine lacks the division circuitry, or even if it doesn't) can be programmed simply by subtracting 7 repeatedly. The sum field should be initialized to some high multiple of 7 (such as 77, for example) to avoid negative totals (are they possible?). Is 77 too much? The routine can be packaged as a neat demonstration.(But be sure that it is not represented as a good computer problem! If a worthy goal is to find

---

*See J. V. Uspensky and M. A. Heaslet, <u>Elementary Number Theory</u>, McGraw-Hill Book Company, Inc., New York, 1939, p. 206.

the day of the week, then the proper tool is called a calendar.)

The input to the demonstration is a date, perhaps in the form 08231963 for August 23, 1963. (To be elegant, the input should be in the latter familiar English form.) The output is a message of the form THE DAY IS FRIDAY.

The demonstration can be dressed up for effectiveness. It runs much too fast, for one thing. Casual observers tend to be more impressed if a Time Waster* routine is used to delay the typeout for about 2 seconds, to give the appearance of mulling over the problem. The wasted time should come between THE DAY IS and the answer.

The input can be arranged to contain a hidden trigger, such as an extra space after the inserted date (or anything else that is not readily detected by the audience). For such dates, the routine can be instructed to yield an incorrect result (not as easy as it sounds—first the correct result must be calculated) and then correct itself.

This trick must be used with caution. A good technique is for the demonstrator to use two or three known dates (such as Monday for November 11, 1991) and then call for a date from the audience. It is vital, of course, that the person furnishing the test date know the correct answer—today's date is ideal. The typeout then reads (say, for August 23, 1963):

THE DAY IS MONDAY

followed by 4 seconds' delay (just enough time for the audience to notice the error), followed by:

. . . OOPS, FRIDAY

If you rig your demonstration this way, be prepared to explain in detail what happened, and be honest about it. You will not want to add to the stock of misconceptions about computers. Such a demonstration, if handled properly, can create genuine interest in programming.

The trick data entry (to force an incorrect result) can be handled on the IBM 1620 in the following way. The routine has two READ instructions in sequence. The first of these calls for reading the 8 digits of the date. The second calls for reading alphabetically into an area of storage that has been preset to

---

*See Fred J. Gruenberger and Daniel D. McCracken, Introduction to Electronic Computers, John Wiley & Sons, Inc., New York, 1963, p. 127.

nonzero characters. Then the normal course of action is to type the 8 digits, followed by the action RELEASE, START, RELEASE, START. The routine then tests for nonzero and proceeds to furnish the correct result. For the trick, however, the action is RELEASE, START, type a space on the typewriter, RELEASE, START (the extra action being unnoticed by the audience). Now there are zeros in the preset area of storage, and these zeros can be detected by the routine.

Another test can be this: Read in the digits 66666666. This is meaningless as a date, but the routine will faithfully calculate the day of the week as Tuesday. The point can be made that (when input data is not properly edited) a computer exercises no judgment but proceeds on its way blindly. You could, of course, arrange to edit the input data, and type a suitable error message for improper data. In either case, you are prepared for the situation in which the input is inadvertently garbled.

The trick data entry can be similarly rigged on other computers.

9 TO THE 9th TO THE 9th

Simply by virtue of being the largest number that can be expressed with 3 decimal digits, the number 9^{9^9} has attracted interest for many years.* It is a number whose decimal expansion would contain 369,693,100 digits. Until recently (i.e., up to 1962) the high-order 131 digits were known, and the low-order 26 digits, and no more. Since the ability to handle large numbers directly is one of the outstanding characteristics of the IBM 1620, it is a simple matter to break both records. Dealing with very large numbers on a word-oriented computer involves multiple-precision routines. The problem described here would be somewhat difficult on such machines.

We will describe first the calculation of digits at the low-order end, since that task is somewhat easier. Suppose we wish to calculate the low-order 100 digits of $N = 9^{9^9}$. We create a 100-digit field with the value 9. For this field $k = 0$ in the expression 9^{2^k}. When the field is squared, we get a 200-digit field with the value 81. This new field is $k = 1$ in the above expression. We reduce it back to 100-digit size (the low-order 100 digits), by setting a flag, and square again (now $k = 2$). The process of truncating to the low-order 100 digits each time is valid because of the way multiplication works, i.e., the low-order 100 digits of a 200-digit product are correct.

This squaring process continues to $k = 28$, so that we have $9^{2^{28}}$, or $9^{268435456}$. Along the way, the values corresponding to $k = 0, 3, 6, 8, 12, 15, 16, 17, 18, 20, 24, 25, 26$, and 28 are themselves multiplied together (and each of these products is also cut back to 100 digits). A total of forty-one 100×100 multiplications are made (each one taking 1.68 seconds on a Model I 1620), and the final product is the desired result.†

What we were doing was developing the 387,420,489th power

---

*It is clear that we mean $9^{\left(9^9\right)}$ rather than $(9^9)^9$—the latter figure being merely 9^{81}.

† The same result could be obtained by cubing the number 9 eighteen times. There would then be thirty-six multiplications. Would the details of coding be easier or harder?

of 9 by expressing the exponent as a sum of powers of 2; in other words, precisely its binary expansion.

We have described what was done to calculate the low-order 100 digits of N. The reasoning is the same for any number of digits, for example, 2 digits. Before proceeding further, calculate the 2 low-order digits of N by hand (using a desk calculator). You will need to perform twenty-eight squarings of 2-digit numbers (recording all the results). Then the proper ones are selected and multiplied together (retaining only 2 digits in all multiplications), and the end result should be 89.

This step is vital, not only in this problem but in most problems. You will not only have a better "feel" for the problem, but you will know what fields to set up, how many digits to allow for, and so on.

Now you are ready to consider using the computer. Write a routine to calculate the low-order 100 digits of N, keeping in mind at all stages that 100 is a parameter that will be changed later. Each multiplication is 100 × 100 (making a 200-digit product).

The programming is exactly the same for longer field lengths; all that changes is the running time. This time goes up by the square of the field length, so the calculation for, say, 2,000 digits (the current record) takes 400 times as long, or about 8 hours. The details of such a routine are left to the student. The work should be arranged as a collection of subroutines, of course. The trickiest part of the problem is picking off the proper products along the way (i.e., the third, sixth, eighth, and so on). Be sure to provide for a restart procedure.

For the calculation of the high-order digits, one further refinement is needed. What is to be saved after each multiplication (speaking in terms of 100-digit numbers again) is the high-order <u>nonzero</u> digits. Suppose that there is a 100-digit field at some stage. This number is squared, to produce a 200-digit field. Now, even if the original number had a leading nonzero digit, the product may begin with a zero. In that case, we want the digits in positions 2 through 101 (counting from the left). But it gets even trickier. The first seven squarings (and their associated multiplications) have lots of leading zeros. This whole idea will become clearer if you calculate, on paper, the first <u>2</u> digits of N.

Again, before proceding to a computer routine, make a hand calculation of the high-order digits. If you have tried the low-order end already, this hand calculation should be tried with the 10 high-order digits (10-digit accuracy being the limit of working with ease with a desk calculator).

As of the time of writing, the low-order 2,000 digits and the high-order 1,200 digits of N are known. There are thus some 369,689,900 digits still unknown.

Problem H4

BASEBALL STANDINGS

Every day, during the baseball season, there appears in the newspaper a table similar to Figure H4.1. The ten teams in the league are listed in rank order, the rank being determined by their percentage of wins out of the number of games played. These percentages are carried to three decimal places, rounded from the fourth place.

Team	W	L	Pct.	GBL
3	95	59	.617	. . .
8	91	65	.583	5
4	84	70	.545	11
1	81	73	.526	14
10	82	74	.526	14
2	81	74	.523	14 1/2
6	78	77	.503	17 1/2
7	72	82	.468	23
9	60	94	.390	35
5	49	105	.318	46

Figure H4.1. Baseball standings

The GBL (games behind leader) is calculated by this formula:

$$GBL = \frac{(W_1 - L_1) - (W_2 - L_2)}{2}$$

using the Win and Lose figures for the leader and the other team. Thus, in Figure H4.1, team No. 8 is 5 games behind:

$$GBL = \frac{(95 - 59) - (91 - 65)}{2} = 5$$

and team No. 5 is 46 games behind:

261

$$GBL = \frac{(95 - 59) - (49 - 105)}{2} = 46$$

The information of the table of Figure H4.1 is on a deck of cards. Additional input consists of one new game on each card, as follows:

Card	1	1007
	2	0508
	3	0102
	4	0102
	5	0604
	6	0406

These six cards indicate the total activity for a day. Team 10 beat team 7, and team 5 beat team 8. Team 1 beat team 2 twice. Teams 4 and 6 split a doubleheader.

EXERCISE 1. Write a routine to update and type out Figure H4.1 from such information, as well as to punch out a new deck of input cards for the next day's updating.

ABSTRACT ART

It often seems to the casual observer that modern abstract paintings are made with random selections of geometric shapes that are colored at random and placed on the canvas in a random position. If this were so, we could program a computer to compose such a painting, using a random number generator to make the necessary choices. (Of course the actual execution of the painting remains to be done.) The student will see that here, as in the playing of games with the computer, he is attempting to make an opening in the study of thought processes. By endowing the computer with the apparent "intelligence" to make choices, we simulate in a very crude way one function of the creative artist.

As in many new investigations we must first simplify the problem by limiting the choice of shapes and colors to some small set available to the painter. Suppose that there are six possible shapes, including, say, squares, rectangles, triangles, ellipses, and two less regular figures such as trapezoids or parallelograms; for these choices we need a random number in the range from 1 to 6. For most shapes we need a number to specify the aspect ratio, i.e., the ratio of height to width, and another number to indicate its orientation. Further random numbers can be chosen to specify the size of each shape (perhaps one of five possible sizes) and its color from eight available colors.

We need 2 numbers to give the location of each shape. If we produce our abstraction on a 22- × 30-inch sheet, we might choose the origin of coordinates in the lower left-hand corner. Then the abscissa should be a number in the range from 00 to 30, while the ordinate should be in the range from 00 to 22. Smaller ranges may be used if it is desired to allow a margin.

A further decision remains: when to stop. The number of shapes may be chosen at random, or the decision may be made to depend on the total area of the shapes already chosen. In the latter case, the total area may be chosen at random.

EXERCISE 1. (a) Write a routine to compose an abstract painting, as suggested, and to type out the specifications in numerical codes. (b) Make the specifications much easier to follow by printing them in words. Thus:

No. 3 triangle, 1:3, 90 deg., lt. blue,
x = 22, y = 14

would give the size, shape, aspect ratio, orientation, color, and position.

The random numbers specifying the abstract painting can be typed out in a few minutes of computer time; the time required to execute the painting directly from the specifications may be exorbitant. Some sort of quick layout may appear desirable. For example, the shapes may be cut out of stiff colored paper and assembled on a flannel board or pasted on a background sheet. A temporary frame may be used to show ordinates and abscissas, so that the shapes can be located quickly.

EXERCISE 2. Vary the sizes, the colors, and the total area until abstract compositions of satisfactory "quality" are obtained.

The first crude compositions designed by the computer are likely to be displeasing to most people. Even people who profess to see nothing of value in modern art will usually find these compositions somewhat worse. The student will find it instructive to refine his routine by placing in it restrictions on free choice and placement of shapes and colors. For example, he might force the selection of neutral colors for other large shapes after the color for one large shape has been determined. Or he might force very bright colors or very prominent shapes into centers of interest away from the borders. In these ways he may explore various theories of artistic composition.

EXERCISE 3. (a) Modify your routine to increase the number of colors but with the restriction that brilliant colors are not permitted near the border. (b) Increase the number of shapes but restrict the choice of bright colors to small shapes after a dominant color has been determined by a random number.

(c) Add other restrictions to your routine and compare results. Write a report describing the theories that have been tested by your routine.

THE GAME of BOWLING

Read from a punched card the number of pins knocked down per delivery of a bowling ball and print the adjusted score for each half-frame, the cumulative total for each frame, and the score for the game. Some test cases are shown in Figure H6.1.

Pins knocked down	Score	Case
8 1 7 3 9 1 9 0 9 1 10 10 7 1 7 3 9 1 9	167	(1)
9 1 9 0 8 2 8 2 7 2 10 6 0 10 9 0 9 0	131	(2)
0 0 0 0 0 0 0 0 0 0 0 0 0 0 0 0 0 0 0 0	000	(3)
10 10 10 10 10 10 10 10 10 10 10 10	300	(4)
10 10 10 10 10 10 10 10 10 9 0	267	(5)
10 10 7 2 9 1 10 10 8 2 7 0 8 2 7 3 9	183	(6)

Figure H6.1. Sample lines of bowling

The automatic scoring of a line (a complete game of bowling is called a line) at a bowling alley could be done with a very simple calculator designed for that particular application. Such special-purpose calculators are widely used. (Another familiar example is the calculating device on a gasoline pump.)

A routine for a general-purpose computer to score a line of bowling is an interesting and educational application of a computer to make logical decisions. The student should simplify the problem considerably, however, for a first approach. Accordingly, we start by asking only for the separate score at the end of each half-frame. Assuming that the number of pins for each delivery of the ball is punched in a separate column of an input card, we are to print the two scores for each frame on the same line.

Since the number of pins knocked down by the ball can vary from 0 to 10, some scheme must be adopted to punch one of 11 different numbers in one card column. This scheme must then be decoded into a field of at least 2 digits after the card is read in. The number of times a ball is delivered can vary in a game from 11 to 21. The routine must separate these into frames, according to the rules of the game. To guard against error, the routine should also check to see that the remainder of the card is blank up to some specified column, say column 30.

> EXERCISE 1. (a) Devise a coding scheme for punching the number of pins knocked down in each delivery, so that a complete game is contained in 11 to 21 columns.* (b) Write a routine to read in a card representing one game. Decode the input and determine the separate score for each half-frame, printing the two scores for one frame on the same line. Test for a maximum of eleven frames, checking up to column 30.

The routine for Exercise 1 required the use of a tally for counting the number of frames to determine when the game was complete. It was also necessary for the routine to distinguish between the halves of a single frame. A convenient way to accomplish this is to use one position in storage as a trigger.† A zero can be stored in the trigger when the current score corresponds to the first half-frame, for example, and a one can be stored to indicate the second half-frame. Triggers are frequently used in computer routines that must make logical decisions.

The rules for scoring a complete line suggest the use of two more triggers. We can set up a trigger A to show whether the previous frame was a spare or a strike or neither and a trigger C to show whether or not the second previous frame was a strike. After the trigger A has been used in connection with the current score, according to the scoring rules, the current

---

*If the choice for zero pins is a punched zero, then a blank card is case (3) in Figure H6.1, since a blank card column reads in as a zero on the 1620. If a flagged zero is used for 10, then case (1) would be punched as 8173919091$\overline{0}$07173919.

† This nomenclature is unfortunate, since trigger also refers to hardware devices in computers. A better word here might be signal, but trigger is the accepted term.

score is used to determine the correct status of the trigger for the next delivery. The trigger is then set to this status.

The A trigger may not only require that the current score be added to the total as if it were part of the score for the previous frame, but it may also demand that the C trigger be set to show additional scoring for the next delivery. The C trigger should therefore be used for a decision concerning the scoring of the present delivery before the A trigger is considered. The proper timing is of special importance in simplifying the logic and shortening the routine for problems involving logical decisions.

> EXERCISE 2. (a) Assign two triggers as suggested, taking care to provide three alternatives where necessary. (b) Construct a careful flow chart for calculating the cumulative score at the end of each frame, and print it on the same line with the separate scores for that frame. Assume for now that no game runs into the eleventh frame. (c) Write a routine to implement the flow chart of part (b).

A careful consideration of the scoring rules reveals that scores in the extra frame are not handled in exactly the same way as earlier scores. The slight change should be analyzed closely to see how it can be accomplished without introducing unnecessary complications in the program. Again, as before, it is important in problems involving decisionmaking to place the tests for exceptional cases in the most appropriate place.

> EXERCISE 3. Modify the routine of Exercise 2 in the simplest manner to allow for the correct scoring of pins in the extra frame.

The scoring rules suggest that the score for each frame in which all the pins are knocked down should be adjusted after the next one or two deliveries. This procedure would require placing the scores in storage instead of typing them out immediately. The routine is consequently longer and more complicated.

The situation in bowling is complicated by the necessity (according to the rules of the game) of adjusting the cumulative score at the end of a frame according to what happens in the next one or two frames. Before proceeding to Exercise 4, outline or flow chart very carefully a scheme whereby the necessary decisions can be made efficiently.

EXERCISE 4. Rewrite the routine for scoring a line of bowling so that the separate scores for spares and strikes are augmented, as provided for in the rules, by the succeeding scores.

The preceding exercises have shown the need for careful planning when a computer routine is to make logical decisions. Scoring a line of bowling represents a difficult programming exercise for a beginner.

LATIN ARITHMETIC

Can you program the computer to accept any two Roman numerals less than MMD (2,500) and type their sum in Roman numerals? Or multiply and divide Roman numerals? And convert the number of a year to or from Roman numerals?

A routine to accomplish some of these things would make a very attractive demonstration. It could serve also to illustrate the very important topic of list processing.

The letters commonly used as Roman numerals are shown with their 2-digit equivalents for the IBM 1620 in Figure H7.1. There are two rules:

1. If a letter precedes one of smaller value, its value is added.
2. If a letter precedes one of larger value, its value is subtracted; then the difference is added to the rest of the number.

It is customary to write a number in as simple a way as possible using only C, X, and I as subtrahends. Examples are MCMLXIV, 1964; DXLIX, 549.

The Romans themselves performed their calculations with small stones (calculi) on a counting board. In this way they did their arithmetic in the decimal system. We shall arrange to have the computer, also, perform the arithmetic in the decimal system, using one subroutine, RODEC (for "Roman to decimal"), to convert from Roman to Arabic numerals, and using another subroutine, DECRO (for "decimal to Roman"), to convert from Arabic to Roman numerals.

Rule 2, above, adds considerable complication to the conversions, both from and to Roman numerals. As a first simplification, we disregard it, writing 4 as IIII, 9 as VIIII, 40 as XXXX, and so on, which actually was the old style and is sometimes seen on clocks.

The Roman numeral is read into a work area, ROMAN, which is divided by flags into 2-digit fields to facilitate the interpretation of the numeral. These flags are not disturbed by reading into the area in alphameric mode. The numeral thus has

270

Symbol	Alphameric code	Value
M	54	01000
D	44	00500
C	43	00100
L	53	00050
X	67	00010
V	65	00005
I	49	00001

Figure H7.1. Table of Roman numerals and their equivalents

the form of a list of 2-digit characters. To reduce the number of "red tape" instructions in our program, we shall always deal with the letter in the first two positions of the work area. We call this field the "bottom" of the list,* or BOX. We interpret each character in turn as it reaches the BOX and then shift the rest of the list two positions to the left. This is a push-up list. We shall use a push-down list later. List processing is of very great importance in many applications of computers; special circuits are being designed continually to accomplish it more effectively.

We use another push-up list, INDEX, as a dictionary for interpreting the character in the BOX. This list is "stacked" by using a TABLE of equivalents, containing every letter used as a Roman numeral and its value, as shown in Figure H7.1. We shift this list, INDEX, to the left, one character at a time until we find a letter matching in the numeral. We add the corresponding value to the sum, SUM, which will eventually become the number that is equivalent to the Roman numeral. The INDEX is most easily reset to its original position by providing a TABLE of equivalents. The TABLE of equivalents, and therefore the INDEX also, ends with a record mark, so that we can easily test for the end. Arriving at the record mark signals an error. The first flow chart in Figure H7.2 shows the plan.

EXERCISE 1. (a) Write an independent routine to convert a Roman numeral into an Arabic numeral, following the plan in Figure H7.2. (b) After careful

---

*We think of the first element placed in a list as being at the top of the list, even though it may have a lower address than succeeding elements.

checking, convert the routine of part (a) into a sub-routine, RODEC.

When the second rule is disregarded, the process of converting the answer from an Arabic numeral to a Roman numeral is just the reverse of the previous process. We test the number, NUM, against each value in the INDEX, until we find one that is less. We subtract this value and place the corresponding letter at the lower (or right-hand) end of the work area, ROMAN. We shift the whole list to the left before continuing, to make room for the next letter. We shall call the field where each new letter is to be inserted the "bottom" of the list and give it the label BIN. We place a record mark at the end of the list, so that the result can be typed out or transmitted to a punchout area.

The calling sequence should place the Arabic number (itself, not its address) in the reference location, NUM, immediately preceding the subroutine. The Roman equivalent is left in the work area, ROMAN, justified to the right.

EXERCISE 2. (a) Write an independent routine to convert an Arabic numeral to a Roman numeral, following the second flow chart in Figure H7.2. (b) After careful checking, convert the routine of part (a) into a subroutine, DECRO.

EXERCISE 3. (a) Write a routine to read in two Roman numerals, one at a time, calling on the subroutine RODEC to convert them. Then add the results and call on the subroutine DECRO to reconvert the sum to a Roman numeral. Finally, type the answer and return for additional data. (b) Extend the routine of part (a) slightly to permit simple conversion and typing of the Roman numerals under switch control.

The student who has completed Exercises 1 through 3 may now wish to accept the complications introduced by Rule 2 and produce a much more sophisticated demonstration routine.

In the RODEC subroutine, to change a Roman numeral under Rule 2 to an Arabic numeral, we must save and compare the value of the previous character. If the value is less than the value of the current character, we must subtract it twice: once to cancel the previous addition and once in accordance with Rule 2. Then we replace the previous value with the current value

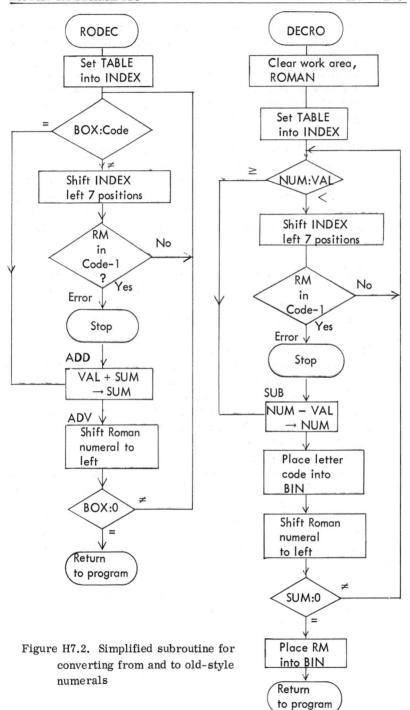

Figure H7.2. Simplified subroutine for
converting from and to old-style
numerals

and restore the INDEX before we advance to the next letter. This complication thus adds some five instructions to the subroutine.

EXERCISE 4. (a) Rewrite the subroutine RODEC so as to follow Rule 2 as well as Rule 1. (b) Extend a routine of Exercise 3 to permit multiplication, under switch control, instead of addition.

The DECRO subroutine is no longer the simple reverse of its companion subroutine when Rule 2 is to be followed. We must now compare the number, NUM, with the values of the 2-letter combinations as well as with the values of the single letters. This alone makes the table of equivalents twice as long. If NUM is equal to 900, for example, we must place CM into the BOX as the next two letters.

EXERCISE 5. Rewrite the table of equivalents and make the small modifications required in both subroutines in order to follow Rule 2 as well as Rule 1 for converting to and from Roman numerals.

The demonstration routine can be embellished in various ways. Messages can be typed asking for input. Editing may be supplied to detect illegal Roman numerals, or Arabic numerals over 4999 or less than 1. Appropriate messages may be typed, reporting the errors. Subtraction and division of Roman numerals can be provided for, with minus signs for negative numbers and printout of both quotient and remainder (if any) in the case of division. Simple conversion from Arabic to Roman numerals may be provided for. The routine may allow the operation to be indicated by a sign, $+$, $-$, $*$, or $/$, typed between the two numbers of the input. The student may allow his imagination to run rampant in polishing up the demonstration. The proper time to add these ornaments is, of course, after the basic problem has been solved and the routine is thoroughly checked out and documented.

EXERCISE 6. Write as elaborate a demonstration routine as time permits to call on the RODEC and DECRO subroutines.

Problem J1

COMPOUND INTEREST

Savings institutions attract deposits by offering to pay interest periodically, usually every quarter year. If the interest is not withdrawn, it is compounded; i.e., it becomes part of the principal and in turn draws interest. As an additional inducement, to attract more depositors, some institutions advertise that they compound interest <u>daily</u>. Is there a significant difference?

One way to compare the offers is to calculate the interest in both ways for a particular principal P and some given annual rate r. If interest is compounded f times per year, the rate for each period is r/f. The amount A of principal and interest at the end of one period is

$$A = P + \frac{r}{f} \cdot P$$

or

$$A = P\left(1 + \frac{r}{f}\right) \tag{1}$$

where r is taken in decimal form. This amount becomes the principal for the next period. We indicate this fact by the "replacement" statement.

$$A \rightarrow P$$

EXERCISE 1. (a) Write a Fortran routine to read from cards the principal P, the annual rate r (as a decimal), the frequency f of compounding, and the number n of periods, and to calculate the (final) amount. Print the original principal, the amount, and the total interest. (b) Use the routine of part (a) to calculate the amount for a principal of $100 at an annual rate of 4%, but for frequencies of 1, 2, 4, 8, 12, 24, and 365 times per year. (c) Draw a conclusion about the effective rate on an annual basis if interest is "paid daily." Explain how many separate calculations are required in practice to calculate the total daily interest on $100 for a full year.*

Another way to compare daily interest with quarterly interest is to calculate how long it would take $100 to be doubled for each method.

EXERCISE 2. (a) Rewrite the compound interest routine to calculate how many periods are required for $100 to be doubled at an annual rate r and a frequency f of compounding. Calculate also the years required, by dividing the number n of periods by f. Print the rate, the frequency, and the number of years. (b) Use the routine of part (a) to prepare a table showing the time required to double at 4% annual interest for various frequencies of compounding from 1 to 365 times per year. (c) Draw a conclusion comparing (in days) the time required for doubling an amount at 4% when interest is compounded daily instead of quarterly.

The time required for money to be doubled at compound interest may be expected to vary inversely with the annual rate, even though a strict proportionality does not hold. If we write

$$A = P(1 + r)^n \tag{2}$$

for the compound amount for a total of n years at an annual rate of r, we can use logarithms to calculate the doubling time exactly.

EXERCISE 3. (a) Apply logarithms to Equation (2) to obtain an exact relation between r and the number of years for money to double at compound interest. (b) Write a short Fortran routine to calculate the exact doubling time according to the formula obtained in part (a). (c) Use your routine to prepare a table showing the exact doubling time for various rates of interest from 2 to 10% annually. (d) Plot the doubling

---

*In 1964, some lending agencies were advertising that their interest rate on deposits, while nominally 4.85%, was effectively 4.97% due to daily compounding. With small modification, your routine or Exercise 1(b) can check this claim.

time against the rate on logarithmic (loglog) coor-
dinate paper. Invent a rough rule for calculating the
doubling time, and state it in words.

The striking effect on the doubling time of changing the
annual rate suggests that daily interest might be significantly
different from quarterly interest for higher annual rates.

EXERCISE 4. (a) Use the routines of previous exercises to study the effect of daily compounding at
various interest rates. (b) Write a short report giving
a reasonable definition of significant difference in
connection with interest rates and discussing the effects of increasing the frequency of compounding at
various annual rates. Define effective annual rate of
interest. Suggest a meaning for continuous compounding of interest and explain how it would be calculated. This is to suggest that the frequencies used
in Exercise 1(b) be increased even more. When
f = 730, interest is being compounded twice a day;
when f = 36,500, the compounding is done 100 times
per day, and so on. The amount of interest earned
goes up continuously as f increases, of course, but
it approaches a limit.

Now lending agencies don't offer such services (continuous
compounding). But many things in nature do behave in this fashion.
The growth rate of a bacteria culture, or the rate of decay of a
radioactive substance, both exhibit this so-called continuous
compounding.
When interest is actually credited to a savings account and
entered in the passbook, it is rounded to cents. The usual
method of "forcing" is to add 1 cent if the fraction dropped is
half or more. The student will find it desirable to have a Fortran
subroutine for dropping the 2 least significant digits and rounding
the last one retained.

EXERCISE 5. (a) Write a function subroutine for your
Fortran system to round off floating-point results
to 6 significant figures. (b) After testing the subroutine of part (a), insert it in your deck of Fortran
subroutines, taking care to change the index card in
the deck and to include title heading and trailer cards.
You might call the subroutine RND. (c) Place a

carefully written description of your RND subroutine
on file, so that others may make use of it when writing
Fortran routines.

Most people buy on time at least once in their life and are
keenly interested in the "amortization" of their loan. The loan
is usually repaid in equal monthly installments, which include
accrued interest on the loan and a partial repayment. As the
outstanding balance is reduced month by month, a greater proportion of the payment is applied toward repayment because the
interest is less. Although the other payments are equal, the
last payment will usually be somewhat less, since the payments
are necessarily rounded to cents. The routine in Exercise 6
will make an excellent demonstration.

EXERCISE 6. (a) Write a Fortran routine to read in
from the typewriter the amount of the loan, the annual
rate of interest, and the monthly payment. Type or
punch under switch control for each month the
amount applied on the principal, the interest paid, and
the balance. Stop when the balance becomes negative.
(b) Elaborate the routine of part (a) to print headings
for each column. Round off the interest payments to
the nearest cent, using the RND subroutine of Exercise 5. Adjust the last payment so that the balance
will be exactly zero, and type the payment.

Problem J2

THE MANHATTAN PROBLEM

We are told that the purchase price of Manhattan Island in 1627 was $24. If the $24 had been invested at 8%, compounded annually, what would its value be today?

We might calculate the amount in four different ways, and get four different answers.

1. With a computer, using a word length of 10 or 12 digits, we apply the formula $A_m = A_{m-1} \cdot (1 + i)$ to calculate the amount year by year, dropping fractions of a cent.
2. We use Method 1, but round the result each year to the nearest cent.
3. We use Method 1, but retain all digits at every step, to obtain an "exact" answer.
4. With logarithms, using either tables or a computer routine, we apply the formula $A = P(1 + i)^n$.

The problem will become even more interesting and instructive if an estimate is first made of the total amount and of the variations to be expected in the results obtained by different methods.

EXERCISE 1. (a) Obtain from your friends several estimates of the total amount and the differences. (b) Write a routine to calculate the compound amount according to Method 1.

The result obtained in Exercise 1 may be compared with the present assessed value of the land.* It should immediately be checked by some other method, to guard against error. Since the fourth method seems quite different from the first, we should use that one.

EXERCISE 2. (a) Make the calculation using 5-place logarithms, estimating the uncertainty in your answer on the basis that the logarithms are accurate only to

---

*Some $4 billion in 1964.

0.000005. If 7-place logarithms are available for the lower part of the logarithm table, be sure to use them. (b) Write a short Fortran routine to solve the problem by Method 4.

Although the result obtained by Method 4 can be used to verify the order of magnitude of the first result, it is clear that the two methods are not equivalent. More comparable results should be obtained if Method 1 is modified as suggested for Method 2.

EXERCISE 3. Modify the routine of Exercise 1 to round the result each year to the nearest cent. Place this modification under switch control, so that the new routine can be used for either Method 1 or Method 2.

The IBM 1620 computer is especially well adapted for solving the problem by Method 3 because the word length is not fixed and because there is no limit to the size of the product that can be obtained (other than the storage capacity of the machine).

EXERCISE 4. (a) Write a routine to calculate the amount by Method 3. (b) Compare the results obtained by the four different methods. How are the differences to be explained for Methods 2, 3, and 4?

The reader may ask which of the four results is the correct one, or whether each can be called correct in some sense. In order to discuss the variations more definitely, we give in Figure J2.1 the results calculated for 336 years, using the modest interest rate of 3%.*

Although each result can be called "correct" in some sense, the result for Method 1 is about $3,400 less than for Method 3 or 4. We ask whether this is a reasonable difference, assuming that half a cent on the average is lost each year.

EXERCISE 5. (a) Write a short routine to accumulate half a cent per year at 3% for 336 years.

---

*For many years, 3% has been a standard rate for calculating the legal reserves on life insurance policies. Results 1 and 2 were calculated on an IBM 7094; result 3 on an IBM 1620; result 4 by hand, using 5-place logarithms.

Method	Amount
1	$490,341
2	493,919
3	493,763
4	493,752

Figure J2.1. Comparison of compound amount calculated by different methods

In Method 3, the result is rounded once at the end. In Method 2, the result is rounded each year. The errors in Method 2 tend to cancel each other out, but if by chance an additional half-cent were added in the early years, the accumulated amount would be $100 more, since the original $24 increased 20,000 times. This consideration seems to offer an adequate explanation for a difference of $150 between the results for the two methods.

EXERCISE 6. (a) Modify the routine of Exercise 5 so as to obtain an explanation for the result by Method 1 at 8%. (b) Test the results at 8% by Methods 2, 3, and 4 as done above for the results at 3%.

Other ways can also be used to obtain estimates of the fluctuation in round-off error due to chance.

EXERCISE 7. (a) Modify the routine of Exercise 1 so that the initial amount can be varied from $23.00 to $25.00, but arrange to have the routine reduce the final result by proportion so that it is comparable to the result for $24.00. (b) Use the routine of part (a) to verify that the discrepancies between the results by Methods 2, 3, and 4 can be explained as round-off error.

The student should often use similar reasoning or experimentation to establish the extent of round-off error, so that he can judge the reliability of his results. He is warned, however, against a trap into which even experienced programmers sometimes fall. No allowance for round-off error is permissible while testing a routine. The results must be checked exactly against hand calculated results, using double-precision methods with a desk calculator if necessary. No inaccuracy in the routine can be tolerated. The Manhattan Problem shows how rapidly an error can grow during repeated operations with a computer if even the smallest inaccuracy is left in the routine itself.

EXERCISE 8. (a) Modify the routine of Exercise 2(b) so that the rate of interest is a parameter to be read in by the routine. Prepare a table of results for various rates of interest, say, from 1 to 10%. (b) Estimate the reliability of the results shown in the table of part (a). (c) Modify the routines of Exercises 3 and 4 so that the rate of interest can be varied. Verify the estimates made in part (b) by actually making the calculation for selected rates different from 8%.

Problem J3

THE CORPORATION DIVIDEND PROBLEM

Consider an idealized business situation. A company is worth A dollars and earns 6% of A in a year, available for distribution as profit. A man holding shares that represent $100 of the company's worth is thus eligible to receive $6 in dividends, if all the profit is so distributed. In 25 years, at this rate, he would receive $150. We are ignoring what he might do with his earnings.

The directors of the company can choose to distribute the earnings in any way they please. They could, for example, plow them all back into the company. In 12 years, then, the company would be worth 2A dollars (since the money now compounds at 6%), and the $100 investment could be earning $12 per year in subsequent years. If that plan were followed (i.e., plow back for 12 years, then pay out everything), the man would receive a total of $156 at the end of 25 years.

Two things are fixed: the initial value of A (or $100, to keep it simple) and the 6% rate of annual earnings on A. But there are now several parameters that can be juggled:

1. The portion of each year's earnings to be paid out, ranging from zero to the full 6%. It need not be the same, or even the same fraction, each year.

2. The length of the run. Do we want to maximize the return to the investor each year, or over a 20-year period, or what?

Although we have grossly oversimplified the problem, it is a real one, faced by every corporation. Some companies are famous for never having paid a dividend; the net worth of the company keeps increasing (as does the "value" of its shares in terms of the stock market quotations). Others pride themselves on paying out most of their annual earnings, resulting usually in great stability of both stock prices and annual dividends.

Put yourself in the position of the man having an initial $100 of true value in a company. Decide on the time span over which you want to maximize (say, 30 years). Now probe for the optimum strategy of (constant) dividend payment to achieve that maximum.

Problem J4

AMORTIZATION TABLES

The table shown in Figure J4.1 is a section of an amortization table for a loan. The loan is for $7,493 at 5.9% per year, payable in equal monthly payments of $218 over a period of 38 months. As of the early 1960's, few money lending agencies would write such a loan, for the simple reason that they had no means of calculating the table. A bank would gladly make a loan for $7,500 at, say, 6%, for 36 months. The latter figures are a good approximation to the desired loan, and the monthly figures corresponding to those shown in Figure J4.1 can be looked up in standard tables of compound interest.

Month	Balance ($)	Interest ($)	To principle ($)
1	7,493.00	36.84	181.16
2	7,311.84	35.95	182.05
3	7,129.79	35.05	182.95
4	6,946.84	34.16	183.84
5	6,763.00	33.25	184.75
6	6,578.25	32.34	185.66
.	.	.	.
.	.	.	.
.	.	.	.
36	592.63	2.91	215.09
37	377.54	1.86	216.14
38	161.40	.79	161.40

Figure J4.1. An amortization table

Thus, there is no great need yet to be able to calculate odd amounts. However, the following problems are real, and means to handle them are needed.

1. The value of money changes. A borrower might legitimately ask to renegotiate a loan after 24 months at a

lower rate. How does this affect the monthly payments?
2. The borrower can foresee a greater ability to repay after 13 months and is willing to add $10 per month to his payments. By how many months will this shorten the loan, and by how much will the total interest payments be decreased?

And so on. The conditions of a loan can change in many ways during its course, and the effects of the change can be calculated.

Consider first the simplest case. For a loan of $7,943 at 5.9% (the interest being calculated on the unpaid balance), with payments of $100 per month, what will the schedule of payments be? At the end of the first month, there is due $36.84 in interest (i.e., $1/12 \times 0.059 \times \$7,493$). Of the $100 paid, $36.84 goes to service the debt, and the balance ($100.00 − $36.84 = $63.18) goes to reduce the principal. We have now one complete line of a new table:

Month	Amount ($)	To interest ($)	To Principal ($)	New balance ($)
1	7,493.00	36.84	63.16	7,429.84
2	7,429.84			

The calculation is now repetitive. Each entry of the table is calculated as follows:
1. The month number is the previous month number plus one.
2. The amount is the same as the "New balance" from the previous line.
3. "To interest" is calculated by multiplying the amount on that line by 0.0049166667 (=1/12 times 0.059).
4. "To principal" is $100 minus the amount calculated in item 3.
5. "New balance" is "Amount" on that line minus the amount calculated in item 4.
6. When "New balance" becomes negative, the table is complete.
7. The "New balance" figure on line 1 must be less than the original amount; otherwise the monthly payment is insufficient, and there is no point in calculating further. This is obvious, but we wish to generalize the solution, and this simple check avoids embarrassment.

The figures used in the example are all really parameters. A routine can be written (usually in floating point) for which the input consists of the variable information—namely, the initial amount, the rate of interest (usually expressed per year), and the monthly payment. The routine can now grind out any number of tables. None of them are like Figure J4.1, since we are specifying the monthly payment and letting the number of months go where it will. We could, to be sure, work the problem backward by calculating enough tables until the number of months "came out right." There must be a more direct way. Find it.

Problem K1

ECONOMIC LOT SIZE

Pretend that you are running a factory and you use widgets as a part of a larger product. The usage varies from month to month, and you have the figures for usage for the last several years. Future usage can be expected to follow past history.

When the stock of widgets runs low, the proper machinery must be put in motion to fabricate a new batch. The problem is this: How many widgets per batch should be made? Setup costs are high, so you should make a large lot, to spread out the setup costs. On the other hand, you can make too many very easily, for many reasons. Widgets are perishable. They consume costly warehouse space. They tie up capital, and money is worth money. As valuable property, they are subject to property taxes.

We are weighing two opposing forces. Figure K1.1 shows the effect of setup costs. The more units made in a batch, the cheaper they get, since the setup cost is spread over more units.

The other factors in the cost of production are generally linear; i.e., the costs go up directly per unit. For example, warehouse space costs twice as much for twice as many units.

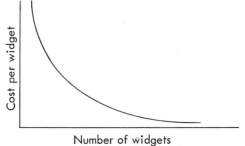

Figure K1.1. The Setup Cost Curve

If the factors were strictly proportional to the number of units produced, they could be expressed as in Figure K1.2. The intersection of the two curves, as in Figure K1.3, dictates the quantity, x, of widgets to be made.

The problem of Economic Lot Size (ELS) isn't that simple.

287

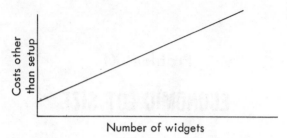

Figure K1.2. Cost curve for other factors

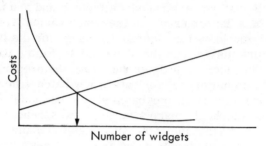

Figure K1.3. The combined cost curve

For one thing, the other factors aren't strictly linear. Perhaps they can be expressed as a gently sloping parabola (i.e., a second-degree curve), in which case we merely seek the intersection of a hyperbola and a parabola.

But there are other considerations. The fabrication of widgets involves fidgets, and for fidgets (which are bought) there is an Economic Order Quantity (EOQ). The EOQ is a calculated figure like ELS, and it may be that a value for EOQ for fidgets that differs for the ELS for widgets could materially increase the costs. The combined cost curve of Figure K1.3 (i.e., the sum of the two curves shown) is usually very flat, so the point x is not critical. Frequently (2x) or (x/2) would yield a cost figure well within reason. But values of (2y) or (y/2) for EOQ might easily double the costs.

Then, too, ELS is intimately tied to the reorder point; this is the number of widgets on hand below which we shall not go before restocking. The reorder point is a function of usage, coupled with the lead time (i.e., how long does it take to get the new batch into the inventory?). Your computing laboratory has an example of reorder points and lead time. Blank cards must be ordered periodically. Let's assume the following conditions:

1. The lead time is 14 weeks. That is, 14 weeks will elapse

between the day the lab initiates a purchase order and the day the cards arrive. The 14 weeks is a steady figure; i.e., the lead time has never gone as long as 16 weeks, and the lowest figure was 13 weeks. Most of this time is red-tape time in the purchasing routine, plus some red-tape time in the vendor's procedures.

2. The minimum order is 30,000 cards, to avoid penalties and nuisance charges. A significant price break will occur if the order exceeds 300,000 cards, and another if the order exceeds 1,000,000 cards.

3. Assume also that usage figures for the last year show an average monthly use of 178,333 and a standard deviation of 28,666. In crude terms, then, a given month has a probability of about 0.6 of using between 149,667 and 207,000 cards. What is a sensible reorder point, and what quantity of cards should be ordered when the quantity on hand falls to or below the reorder point? Would the inventory problem be simpler or more complex if a standing order were in effect to deliver 300,000 cards every seventh week?

How can you tell whether or not your formula for the reorder point is correct? If, month after month, you run out of cards in the lab, then the reorder point is too low, or the quantity ordered is too low, or both, or usage is increasing. Which is it? You might be able to devise a simulation of the card usage situation and run it (varying the parameters from run to run). On the other hand, if you never run out of cards, the chances are that the formulas are too conservative. This should show up in a continuously increasing inventory.

It has been suggested that the following formula be used to determine the reorder point for card inventory:

$$ROP = S \cdot L(A + V)$$

where L is the lead time in months, A is the average monthly usage, V is the standard deviation of the monthly usage, and S is a safety factor.

This is probably the most poorly defined problem in this book and, at the same time, one of the most important to industry. Inventory costs money, and industrialists continually seek ways to control their inventory better. By this they mean to decrease the inventory with minimum risk of running out. The problem is complex. You can afford to run out of No. 2 pencils; you probably can't afford to run out of 10,000-hp motors. Identical formulas for reorder point, ELS, and EOQ may not apply to the pencils and the motors.

We suggest that you take an inventory problem (perhaps the problem of stocking the computer lab with cards), explore it, study it, and simulate it.

There is much in the literature on this subject. Consider, for example, Camp's formula for ELS. It is this:

$$ELS = \sqrt{\frac{2SU}{RC}}$$

where S is the setup cost, U is usage, R is the cost of using money (expressed as an interest rate), and C is the total cost per unit other than setup cost. The formula implies that you already know more about the article in question than most businesses do. It also implies that all costs other than setup cost are linear, which may not even be true for the cost of using money.

But even if Camp's formula were ever valid, it could not be valid for all cases. Consider the concept of lot sizes for (a) vitamin pills, (b) steam turbines, and (c) diamond rings. For vitamin pills, the most important unusual factor is obsolescence, both in the sense of spoilage and that of being outmoded by new discoveries or competition. For steam turbines, warehouse space for the lot is a dominant factor. And for diamond rings, property taxes and safeguarding the lot might be the overriding considerations.

It might be possible to devise one formula (say, a polynomial) to cover all such cases, with appropriate coefficients having the value zero as needed (for example, the term for the cost of warehouse space could have a zero coefficient when seeking the ELS for diamond rings). But consider another factor: what is a continuous function for one item might be a stepwise function for another. The obsolescence term for vitamin pills is a case in point: for a certain period of time the term might be constant and after that time the term is zero (i.e., the pills are worthless). In some industries, the cost of obsolescence is considered as increasing continuously up to a limit, after which the cost jumps sharply due to engineering changes that take place periodically.

We are suggesting that for those students of computing who have connections with industry (particularly manufacturing industry), the ELS problem is fascinating and is wide open for endless research. The computer is one tool for this research.

You will probably not develop an ELS formula that is satisfactory in all respects, even for a given industry. It is one of those situations where the more you discover, the less you seem to know for sure about the subject. Let us list some additional points to consider:

1. A formula will yield a value for the ELS for a given item. How critical is this value? That is, by how much will the cost per unit vary for deviation up or down from the calculated ELS figure? The curves are not symmetric, so the deviations in both directions must be taken into account.

2. Formulas tend to regard variables as continuous; more frequently, in real life, variables are discontinuous, or undefined over some ranges, or are step functions. You can't order 2/3 of an electric motor, or borrow money at any arbitrary interest rate or for fractional months.

3. Values for the input parameters may not be known; it is a rare company that can furnish historical statistics in the form you may want them. Fortunately, the critical variables are usually the best known; if this were not so, industry would not have advanced as far as it has.

4. A given formula, applied to a given lot, does not take into account the interference effect of other lots. If the lot sizes for a number of items are all small, and they are all ordered to be fabricated at once, they will interfere with each other and introduce additional cost factors due to logjamming. These cost factors are difficult to predict, but are certainly real.

5. No formula, however scientifically produced, should be expected to fly in the face of common sense. A lot size that turns out to be a 1-day supply (or a 5-year supply) may call for some human review.

The possibilities for better management control through better decisionmaking are very large. The points listed above are simply intended to caution you against claiming success (in a competitive field) too soon. Above all, avoid the trap of claiming that "the computer says we should do thus and so."

Problem K2

FREE CHOICE

The mathematical analysis of games of chance led to the development of the science of statistics. The importance of statistics as a basis for modern business decisions is widely recognized. We may ask whether the study of other simple games can lead to principles of fundamental importance in business management. Accordingly, we undertake the study of a simple game that involves <u>deliberate choice</u> rather than the chance fall of a coin or die.

Two players, A and B, each place a coin on a table without letting their opponent see it. Then the coins are uncovered. If the coins are both tails, A wins a stipulated amount from B; if they are both heads, he wins triple the amount. If the coins are unlike, A pays B double the amount.

It is clear that our problem here is to study the strategy of the players. Therefore we are not concerned with the outcome of a single game, but with the results of many thousands of games. We shall use the computer to simulate these games.

We assume at first that both players choose at random; i.e., this is their strategy. We simulate a random choice of heads or tails by generating a random number with one of the subroutines of Problem E7 and prefixing an imaginary decimal point. If the number is under 0.5, we choose heads; if over 0.5, we choose tails.

EXERCISE 1. (a) Write a routine to simulate the Free Choice Game for random choices by both players and with a fixed amount of $1. Print the cumulative result after each additional 100 games as a positive or negative number. (b) Calculate A's expectation for 1,000 games by using the laws of probability, noting that there are four equally likely possibilities. Compare with the results of part (a).

292

By changing the division point p between heads and tails for the human player, we can modify his strategy. We thus specify by p the probability that the player will select heads. In a similar way, we control the probability that the machine will choose heads by changing the point q dividing heads from tails for its decisions.

EXERCISE 2. (a) Rewrite the routine for the Free Choice Game as a subroutine with both p and q as parameters. (b) Write a routine to estimate A's expectation with different strategies by simulating 1,000 games each with p varying from 0 to 1 by steps of 1/8. Keep q constant at 1/2. (c) Show by using the laws of probability that A's expectation for 1,000 games when $q = 1/2$ is $E = 1000 (p - 1/2)$, and hence that he should choose heads every time if he observes that B's coin is breaking evenly.

The student can easily see from the exercises that A's choice of strategy will depend on B's. Therefore, there are two variables to study. He accomplishes this task by simulating 9,000 games for each choice of strategy by B. In this way he uses the computer to compress, within a short time, the experience that could be obtained in 81,000 games with A and B both varying their strategy.

EXERCISE 3. (a) Use the routine of Exercise 2 (b) to calculate A's expectation for 1,000 games when A's strategy is varied from $p = 0$ to $p = 1$ by steps of 1/8, while B's strategy varies from $q = 0$ to $q = 1$ by steps of 1/8. (b) Tabulate the results of part (a) by hand and draw a conclusion concerning the choice of B's strategy.

The Free Choice Game has been made extremely simple so that the student can check by hand calculation the results obtained in simulating the game with a computer. In this particular game, the expectations can be calculated by applying the principles of probability. This circumstance develops the student's confidence in his own ability to apply the computer method in situations where hand calculations would not be feasible.

EXERCISE 4. (a) Show by applying the laws of probability that the expectation for a single play of the Free Choice Game is

$$E = 8pq - 3p - 3q + 1$$

Hence show that setting $q = 3/8$ guarantees B a "house percentage" of 12.5 per cent in the long run. (b) Show that the house percentage can be reduced to 5.26 per cent as in roulette by making the payoff 11 for both heads, 1 for both tails, and the loss 4 or 3, depending on whether A chooses heads or tails. (c) Rewrite the routine of Exercise 2(b) according to the rules of 4(b).

The student is aware that when the Game of Free Choice is played by human opponents,* a player may attempt to "read the mind" of his opponent by noting tenseness in his facial muscles, twitching in hands or feet, certain mannerisms of play, or casual remarks. This factor is usually undesirable because it does not correspond to specific elements in the problems of industrial management for which the Game of Free Choice serves as a simplified trial exercise. It can be eliminated by having the human players choose their strategy ahead of time. Of course the strategy may cause the actual choice to depend on the results preceding it. In particular, any desired betting system, perhaps one discussed in Problem E1, may be combined with an arbitrary method of placing the coin, such as changing from heads to tails only after winning. Alternatively, a player may wish to modify the placing of his coin according to the pattern set by his opponent if he observes that the opponent tends to equalize his choices. In this way he turns to his own advantage the widely accepted fallacy that random numbers are equally spaced. (See also Problem E4.)

---

*The name "Psych-out" has been given to this game by its author, Robert N. Reinstedt.

Problem K3

QUEUEING

In many businesses, successful operation depends on giving prompt service. If customers must wait too long in a queue, the business loses customers. There are many factors affecting the tolerance that customers will display toward a queue. Similarly, there are important cost factors involved in providing quicker service. The problem of queueing is therefore an important one. Since it is often difficult or impracticable to solve such a problem by direct calculation, the problem offers an excellent illustration of the application of a computer to simulate a practical situation.

The length of queue that can be permitted varies greatly. In some situations, customers will show great patience. For example, they will wait a long time for long distance service at reduced rates on Christmas Day, or for tickets to a World Series baseball game. In some other situations, the tolerance is low. The appearance of even a short queue of cars at a service station will discourage customers from stopping. Let us consider the relatively simple case of the cashiers at a supermarket.

Suppose that a supermarket in your community is open 8 1/3 hours per day and has an average of 1,000 customers per day who require a checkout time of 4 minutes each, on the average. How many checkout stations are required if no queue of more than 4 persons is permissible more than one-tenth of the time? If further information is required, describe a reasonable plan for obtaining it. It is understood that customers will always choose the shortest queue.

It is clear that the problem involves random factors. Calculations based on averages alone without considering probabilities can only determine the <u>minimum</u> number of checkout stations.

EXERCISE 1. (a) If <u>exactly</u> 2 customers come to the checking point every minute and require <u>exactly</u> 4 minutes each, show that 8 checking stations are required and that there will be no queues. (b) If there

295

are only 7 checking stations under the same conditions, show that queues will form and grow steadily
longer up to a maximum of 15 persons, with an average waiting time of 30 minutes. Explain why 8 checkout stations are properly described as the <u>minimum</u>
for the 8 1/3-hour day of the original problem.

The exercise has shown that a minimum of 8 checkout stations is required to accomplish the work. We shall now consider
the effect of random fluctuations on the formation of queues.
As in many other problems, we find it expedient to make some
important, simplifying assumptions for a preliminary study of
the problem. We still assume, as at first, that the checkout time
is always exactly 4 minutes, but now we assume that the probability of a customer's coming to the checkout stations in any
particular 10-second interval is 1/3. Then we ask, "For how
many minutes during the day will queues of more than 4 persons
exist?" (There are still 8 stations.)

We can write a computer routine to simulate this simple
situation. We use a random number generator to generate a
number between zero and 1. If the number turns out to be less
than 1/3, we count a new customer at the checkout point by adding 1 to a tally. After every 24 random numbers, we simulate
the leaving of one customer by subtracting 1 from the tally.
Whenever the tally exceeds 32, we count that 10-second interval
as a time when at least one queue exceeds 4 in length.

EXERCISE 2. (a) Show that the plan just outlined will
produce the same average number of persons as the
conditions used for Exercise 1; show also that it will
count an interval only when at least one queue exceeds 4 persons in length and that the checkout time
is exactly 4 minutes, as specified. (b) Write a routine
to count the number of 10-second intervals during a
day when a queue of more than 4 persons exists at
one of the 8 checkout stations.

The results obtained in Exercise 2 allow for random fluctuations in the number of persons appearing at the checkout stands.
We should like to allow also for random fluctuations in the time
required for checkout. These fluctuations will depend on many
circumstances, such as the size of the area served by the store,
the average size of family living there, the affluence of the customers, special sales, holidays, and the like. The student has an

opportunity to develop his skill in analyzing practical situations by undertaking a real survey of some particular supermarket. After enlisting the manager's interest and assistance, he should determine the actual times required for checking, and calculate the mean and the variance of that distribution by using a routine from Problem M6. As an illustration, we suppose the mean to be 4 minutes and the variance to be 4. Since many chance factors influence the number of items bought, and consequently the checkout time, the distribution of checkout times may be expected to resemble a normal distribution, as described in Problem M6. Accordingly, we can simulate the actual situation more closely if we no longer make the checkout time exactly 4 minutes for every customer, but choose the checkout time at random from a normal distribution with 4 minutes as the mean value and a variance of 4. In terms of 10-second intervals, the numerical value of the mean for this assumed distribution would be 24, and the numerical value of the variance would be 144. The values obtained for some particular supermarket may be expected to come out somewhat different from these assumed values.

EXERCISE 3. (a) Determine the checkout times for a carefully chosen sample of the customers at an actual supermarket in your community. Use a routine from Problem M6 to calculate the mean checkout time and the variance. Convert these values so that they correspond to 10-second intervals. (b) Incorporate (in the routine of Exercise 2) a routine from Problem M6 to select the checkout time at random from a normal distribution with the appropriate mean and variance. Print the total number of intervals for which some queue is longer than 4 persons.

The student may develop this investigation along various lines, according to his own analysis of some particular supermarket or perhaps as suggested by the store manager. For example, he may wish to calculate the average waiting time in a queue.

EXERCISE 4. (a) Modify the program of Exercise 3(b) so as to count the number of customers exceeding 8 for each 10-second interval and to accumulate a total of these numbers. (b) Calculate the average waiting time for each customer from the result of part (a).

Another line of inquiry is to investigate the effectiveness of adding a ninth checkout station.

EXERCISE 5. (a) Alter the routine of Exercise 4 so that the number of checking stations is a parameter to be read in from the typewriter. (b) Use the routine as altered in part (a) to study the effect of adding a ninth checkout station. (c) By counting the number of customers for each interval when the number is less than 9, you can determine the amount of time during which checking stations are idle. Modify your routine to obtain this information. Check the result by making a simple calculation involving averages. (d) Discuss human factors that would operate to reduce the time during which checking stations are idle.

EXERCISE 6. (a) Plan a computer routine that will simulate the natural action of an alert store manager by adding a tenth checking station whenever the queues exceed 4 in length for a period of 15 minutes, and that will eliminate the extra station when the queues remain at 4 or under for 15 minutes. (b) Write a routine to implement the plan of part (a), printing the number of minutes the extra station is in operation for each opening.

EXERCISE 7. (a) Discuss various methods of reducing the checkout time in order to control the length of the queues. (b) Use the routine of Exercise 6 to study the length of queues if the average checkout time can be reduced to 3 minutes (with the same variance as before) when the queues exceed 4 persons in length for 15 minutes.

The various investigations of the queueing problem up to this point have assumed that a person is as likely to come to the checkout counter at one time as another. This assumption is not in accord with the experience of actual stores, which have some relatively quiet periods during a day and some rush periods. The mathematical model that we are using to simulate the actual situation in a supermarket can be improved by incorporating in it the fluctuations according to the time of day. These fluctuations must be determined for the particular supermarket being studied. The number of customers during each hour can sometimes be determined by inspecting the cash register tapes. Another way is for two or more students to work as a team, using simple hand counters to count the number of customers. A further investigation might be made to study the variation in the number of customers on different days of the week, and before and after holidays.

EXERCISE 8. (a) Use or modify a previous routine to study the length of queues when the number of customers varies in different hours according to the results obtained by an actual count, or else according to the illustrative results given in Figure K3.1.

Hours	Customers
9:00-10:00	86
10:00-11:00	147
11:00-12:00	103
12:00-1:00	48
1:00-2:00	79
2:00-3:00	114
3:00-4:00	195
4:00-5:00	156
5:00-5:15	72

Total 1,000

Figure K3.1. Distribution of customers by time of day

(b) Write a report summarizing the results obtained and recommending a procedure for controlling the length of queues.

MERGING ACCOUNTING FILES

Suppose we have 325 5-digit account numbers arranged in ascending order in a single block of storage. As one small part of an accounting procedure, we need to add 68 account numbers throughout the block, placing them in the correct order. Since the new account numbers would ordinarily be punched in separate cards, we may assume that they have been placed in ascending order by using a card sorter. Our problem is to "merge" the two files.

This apparently simple problem deserves very careful planning, since merging two files is a basic procedure in business data processing. We shall disregard the additional information that we expect to find in the cards and in storage, postponing a general discussion of sorting to Problem L3. Suppose that the old file starts in 10000 and ends with the dummy account number 99999 followed by a record mark, and that the new (merged) file is to start in 15000. Suppose further that the new account numbers are punched in the first five columns of the cards, with at least one blank card at the end of the pack.

It is convenient to place each old account number, in turn, into a field, BOX, for comparison. We start with the working part of the routine after the next old account number is in BOX. Also, we start after a card (bearing the next new account number) has been read into a working area, AREA. We need to choose between the next new account number and the next old account number (to select which number goes into the updated file) according to which is lower. A common technique is to place the new account number in the updated file at once as an arbitrary choice, and then replace it if comparison shows that the next account number in the old file is lower. This technique is shown in Figure L1.1.

A little experimentation will show that this trial-and-error procedure leads to a very simple straightline flow chart and often (as in this case) shortens the routine besides. The student should recognize how important it is for him to acquire the habit of constructing simple, straightforward flow charts even for short problems. The consequent shortening of his routines and reduction of errors will contribute greatly to his success in programming very long problems later. The student should now plan his merging routine by completing the flow chart of Figure L1.1. His constant aim while doing this should be to keep the logic simple while providing for all necessary special cases.

EXERCISE 1. (a) Complete the flow chart for merging two files. Consider the following cases:

(1) Will the routine work properly if no flag is punched as a field mark? If not, modify your flow chart to provide this protection.

(2) Will the routine place a record mark at the end of the new (merged) file and then stop? Why is this provision desirable?

(3) After the 1st card has been read in, will the routine continue up to the end of the old file?

(4) After the last account number in the old file has been reached, will the routine read in the remainder (if any) of the new account numbers?

(5) Are the modified addresses preset, so that the routine can be used repeatedly?

(6) Is the logic simple and straightforward, leading to a short routine (about 16 or 17 instruc- (b) Write a routine to implement the plan of part (a).

The merging procedure in the preceding discussion presumes that both the old file and the card deck of new accounts are in exact, ascending order. If they are not, the merged file will not be in order either. Provision should therefore be made to test the order of both the old and new files at the same time by checking the sequence of the resulting merged file. It was also assumed that no account number in the card deck is in the old file. If a new account number duplicates a number in the old file, one of them should be omitted.

EXERCISE 2. (a) Modify the routine of Exercise 1 to save the previous account number for comparison. Print a special message if an error is found. (b) Modify the routine of part (a) so as to disregard any new account number that is equal to a number in the old file. Also provide for replacing the old file by the current file after the merging is complete.

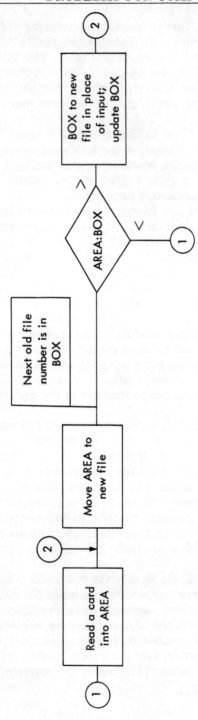

Figure L1.1. Trial-and-error method for the merge.

Two files already in storage may be merged by using a method similar to the one already described. If neither file is known to end with 99999, special care must be taken to include all of both files.

> EXERCISE 3. (a) Construct a flow chart to merge a file, A, of 5-digit numbers (starting at address 05004) with a file, B, of 5-digit numbers (starting at address 10004) to form a file, C (starting at address 15004). (b) Write a routine in accordance with the plan in part (a). Assume that both files end with a record mark, and that a record mark is required at the end of the merged file. Suppress duplicate account numbers. Check the merged file as it is formed, and print an appropriate message if an error in sequence is detected.

When it is not convenient to sort a set of new account numbers before they are read into storage, the sorting can be done by a computer routine. The computer is not well-adapted for this task, but many different methods have been devised to reduce the inefficiency as much as possible. The literature of data processing abounds with articles on various methods of sorting.* The best method for a particular situation depends on the previous arrangement of the file. A method that is satisfactory when the file is almost in order may be very slow for a file in random order. If the file consists of a relatively small number of random items at the end of a long list that is already in sequence, it will usually be desirable to sort the random items separately and then merge them with the rest of the file. The following method is suitable for sorting a small number of items. It is not very efficient when the number of items exceeds 100, but it is simple and easy to code. It is therefore widely used.

The file is to be arranged in ascending sequence. A counter, T (for tally), is set to zero. Each item is compared with the following one. If the first of each pair is not greater than the second, these two are in relative order, and no action is taken. Otherwise they are interchanged, using a third field, HOLD, as a work area, and a tally is made in the counter. After the end of the file is reached, the counter is examined. If it is zero, that pass completed the sorting, and the file is now in order. If not,

---

*For example, the May 1963 issue of <u>Communications of the Association for Computing Machinery</u> is devoted entirely to methods of sorting.

further passes are needed. The counter is reset to zero, the modified instructions are initialized once more, and the process is repeated. The scheme is pictured in Figure L1.2. The student should notice the careful distinction made between the address y used in the test for the end of the file and the contents, c(y), or number at that address which is tested in the previous comparison.

> EXERCISE 4. (a) Write a routine to sort a file by the successive interchange method.* Provide for printing, under switch control, the number of interchanges on each pass. (b) Write a short routine to load about 100 5-digit numbers from separate cards into a block of storage. Take care to provide field marks either in the cards or by programming. Use the routine of part (a) to sort the file.

The preceding plan for sorting a file has obvious weaknesses. We can see at once that it is unnecessarily slow. The first pass will place the largest number in the last place. The second pass guarantees the number in the place next to the last. Hence, the process could be shortened by reducing the address of the last item after each pass.

> EXERCISE 5. (a) Modify the routine of Exercise 4 so as to shorten each succeeding pass. (b) Read the card deck into storage ten times, shuffling it in between, thus producing a file of about 1,000 items. Compare the time required for sorting the file by the two different routines of Exercises 4 and 5(a).

A small improvement in the sorting routine was made by shortening each pass, but the number of passes remained unchanged. A very large improvement would be realized by reducing the number of passes required. If only the last card is out of sequence, the successive interchange method will place the file in order in one pass. However, if only the first card is out of order, and fifty cards precede it, fifty passes will be required. This dissymetry suggests that the file should be sorted in opposite directions during alternate passes.

---

*Sometimes called a "bubble sort," since each item being sorted bubbles up to the top of the list.

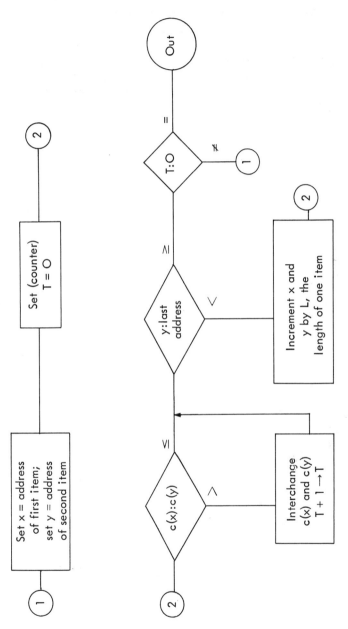

Figure L1.2. A sorting scheme (successive interchange method)

EXERCISE 6. (a) Elaborate the routine of Exercise 4 or 5 so as to sort forward in ascending sequence and then to sort backward in descending sequence on alternate passes. (b) Determine the number of passes required, by typing the value of T under switch control for each pass. Verify in this way the superiority of the alternating interchange method for files that are nearly in order.

Problem L2

PRINTING PAYCHECKS

Customarily, in writing checks, one writes the amount in figures at the end of the line that begins "Pay to the order of _____." Then, to prevent the check's being altered, the amount is repeated in words on the next line. Some examples are shown in Figure L2.1.

$123.45   ONE HUNDRED TWENTY-THREE AND 45/100

$306.10   THREE HUNDRED SIX AND TEN/100
      or,
      THREE HUNDRED AND SIX AND 10/100

$250.00   TWO HUNDRED FIFTY AND NO/100
      or,
      TWO HUNDRED FIFTY EXACTLY

$6.50   SIX AND 50/100

Figure L2.1. Check amounts

When checks are produced for payroll purposes, this latter protection is frequently omitted. The figure amount is sometimes "check protected" by filling out the field with asterisks, for example, $**98.17. It is felt that since the figures are printed, rather than written, alterations would show up visibly. However, many firms protect themselves even more by also printing the amount in words.

> EXERCISE 1. Assuming that no check is written for less than $1 or for more than $500, write a routine to translate the amount into words (in conventional terminology), and print the result.

Part of this problem is mechanical. For an amount such as $423, the hundreds' digit, 4, must be converted, through lookup

307

in a stored table, into the alphabetic word FOUR. This part of the task is straightforward, except for the minor adjustments to take care for the fact that the number of letters in such a word varies from 3 (for example, "TWO") to 5 (for example, "SEVEN").

The bulk of the problem is logical. For the fourth example in Figure L2.1 ($6.50), no information should be typed for the hundreds' figure, for instance. Also, a zero in the tens' digit is handled still differently, as in the second example. Note too that the English for the tens' digit of a number is not consistent, since numbers such as 17 and 47 are handled differently.

Your routine should perform some editing on the input data. The amount of the check should be in the form $\overline{xxxxx}$ (for example, $123.45). This amount may not exceed 50000, according to the conditions of the problem, nor may it be less than 00100. If either condition is violated, your routine should type an error message.

Problem L2 is a real and practical problem in the business world.

Problem L3

SORTING BY COMPUTER

What is the best way to sort a list of names in storage? Suppose the list contains 350 names in random order, with 20 letters or blanks in each name.

The computer is not well adapted for sorting, and yet sorting is an important task in business data processing. Names or employee numbers may be sorted for a payroll, item numbers may be sorted for an inventory, or a sort may be made according to salesman number for commission accounting. It is easy to think of many other applications of sorting in business. At college, names or student numbers may be sorted for recording attendance or grades. (The sorting of names is also useful in Problem G3.)

If the list is on separate cards, the cards would ordinarily be arranged in order with a card sorter before entering them in storage. The list could then be combined with a list that is already in storage by merging, as described in Problem L1. This procedure avoids the necessity of sorting by computer. If the list is on magnetic tape or on magnetic discs, we might want to use the computer for sorting. A great many schemes have been devised for sorting by computer. These methods attempt to reduce the inefficiency of the process to a minimum for different situations by making some allowable compromise.

Because of the necessary compromises, a sorting scheme should be judged with reference to a particular application. In general, any sorting scheme can be measured according to the following criteria:

1. How does the execution time vary with the number of items to be sorted? Is the method relatively good for short lists but very slow for long ones?

2. To what extent does the scheme capitalize on whatever order that may already exist in the list? Is the method especially quick when the list is already almost in order? Is it greatly hampered when the items are in the worst possible order, rather than merely in random order?

3. How is the speed affected by the length of the field to be

sorted? Is the time of execution sharply reduced if the "key" (i.e., the part of the field to be sorted) is much shorter than the field itself?

Additional considerations might include the storage requirements of the method and the ease with which it can be adapted to different situations.

One method of sorting by computer, the successive interchange method, has already been described in Problem L1. In the worst possible case (i.e., when the file is originally in exact reverse order), that method can require as many as $N(N-1)/2$ interchanges (where N is the number of items to be sorted). The execution time therefore tends to increase as the square of the number of items. This tendency makes the method unsuitable for long lists. On the other hand, if only the last item is out of order, the sorting would be complete after two passes, involving less than N interchanges. The method checks out well on the second criterion, but not on the first.

The sorting of cards with a card sorter depends strongly on the number of columns in the key and the number of possible holes in each column. When the key consists of alphabetic data in 20 columns, as in the present problem, the entire deck of cards must ordinarily be run through the machine 40 times. Since each pass may take several minutes, depending on the speed of the machine, the total task might require considerable time by this method. If such a deck is to be sorted repeatedly, a short numerical key is usually assigned to each name to make the sorting several times faster. Card sorting is weak on criterion number 3. The successive interchange method of sorting with a computer meets this criterion satisfactorily.

The problem of sorting names is equivalent to that of sorting numbers because the alphabetic characters are read into storage as 2-digit numbers according to a code in which the alphabet runs from a low number for A up to a high number for Z. A blank is represented by double zero; it will therefore precede any letter in the sorted list.*

---

*The internal representation of alphabetic characters in the IBM 1620 is such that this will work. Since A is 41 and B is 42, a numerical comparison will establish that A is "low" with respect to B. The entire alphabet will compare in normal order, and, what is more, a sequence is established for all the characters that can be stored. This is the collating sequence of the machine. (It is, unfortunately, different for almost any two computers made.) The collating sequence for the 1620 is (from low to high) as follows: blank, period, right parenthesis, plus, dollar, as-

EXERCISE 1. (a) Write a short (two-card) routine
to place a list in storage by reading in a deck of name
cards.* (b) If a routine using an interchange method
(as described in Problem L1) is available in your
computer laboratory, use it to sort a list produced
by reading in a well-shuffled deck of name cards
with the routine of part (a).

We shall now investigate a simple and natural method that
depends on simple replacement rather than interchange. We
first simplify our problem by limiting the list to 20 names.

On the first pass through the list we pick out the smallest
number, but we also determine its address. This enables us to
blank out the name in the list by replacing it with zeros. We store
the name from our comparison location, SML, as the first name
of a new list. We repeat this procedure 20 times, producing a
new list in alphabetical order.

EXERCISE 2. (a) Make a detailed flow chart for the
sequence method, just described, to sort a list of 20
names. (b) Write a routine to implement the flow
chart of part (a).

The method of Exercise 2 could have been used to select
the largest number in the list instead of the samllest. In this
case, the name would have been placed at the end of the new
list. The second pass would then select the next largest number,
and so on, until the new list was complete. This possibility
suggests that the new list could be built up from both ends toward
the middle, so that two words are added to it at the end of each
pass. We may call this the double sequence method.

EXERCISE 3. (a) Make a careful flow chart for the
double sequence method of sorting, and write a rou-

---

terisk, minus, virgule, comma, left parenthesis, equal, "at" sign, A-Z,
0-9. For example, the "word" 1620 is higher than HIGH, and the word
)*$ is lower than LOW. It sounds tricky, doesn't it? In this system, a
string of 9's is the highest thing you can have; a string of blanks is the
lowest (notice that blank is 00 but zero itself is 70).

*A sample deck may sometimes be obtained from the admissions of-
fice of a college or from a nearby firm that uses a computer for preparing its payroll.

tine, in accordance with that flow chart, to sort 20 names in ten passes. (b) Elaborate the routine of part (a) so that the number N of items is a parameter of the routine, to be read in from the typewriter.

Given a collection of 14-digit fields, each representing a 7-letter English word, we have the means to put them into alphabetic sequence. For example, the left-hand column of Figure L3.1 shows 20 words in alphabetic order, i.e., in what most people call alphabetic order. The middle column is in order, too: the sort has been made considering the second and third letters as the high-order part of the word. In other words, the second and third letters have been used as the sorting key, as it is called. The third column of words is also in sort. Can you deduce the key?

ADAMANT	BANANAS	PLEASED
AVERAGE	SCHOOLS	BANANAS
BANANAS	ICICLES	PYRAMID
BOLOGNA	ECSTASY	SUCCUMB
BOWLING	ADAMANT	ICICLES
ECSTASY	ODOROUS	ROADMAP
ELEMENT	GENERAL	GENERAL
FUTURES	SHERIFF	LITHIUM
GENERAL	PLEASED	MINIMUM
ICICLES	ELEMENT	BOWLING
LITHIUM	MINIMUM	ADAMANT
MINIMUM	LITHIUM	ELEMENT
ODOROUS	UNUSUAL	SCHOOLS
PLEASED	ROADMAP	BOLOGNA
PYRAMID	BOLOGNA	SHERIFF
ROADMAP	BOWLING	AVERAGE
SCHOOLS	SUCCUMB	ODOROUS
SHERIFF	FUTURES	UNUSUAL
SUCCUMB	AVERAGE	ECSTASY
UNUSUAL	PYRAMID	FUTURES

Figure L3.1. Twenty words, three orderings

All the fields involved in these sorts have been the same length. Indeed, it is frequently a standard practice in data processing to force fields that must interact to the same length.

Returning now to the original problem, we consider the complications and the possibilities involved when the list is very long, requiring 14,000 positions of storage. First we ask whether it is necessary to run through the full 14,000 positions on each pass, or if it is not possible to shorten the list as each name is removed. Since we know where each name is blanked out, can we not shift the rest of the list 40 positions to take up that space? The second question is, Is this shifting procedure necessary in order to solve the problem if storage is limited to 20,000 positions?

The answer to both questions is Yes. In the (single) sequence method, we choose the largest number and build up the new list from the end. We need a record mark at the end of the list, so that we can use the TRANSMIT RECORD operation, code 31, for shifting the remainder of the list to the left. The new, sorted list will thus replace the original list. It is possible, but not very convenient, to apply this replacement scheme to the double sequence method.

> EXERCISE 4. (a) Write a routine that will sort 350 names by the sequence method and replace the original list by the sorted list. (b) Discuss the difficulties that would be encountered in applying this scheme to the double sequence method, and suggest a procedure for overcoming them.

The student should now evaluate the sequence method of sorting, using the criteria given at the beginning of this problem.

> EXERCISE 5. (a) Write a short report answering, for the sequence method, the same questions that were considered for the interchange method. Compare the two methods with respect to these criteria and also with respect to storage requirements and ease of altering the routine to fit various lists. (b) If a routine for sorting by the interchange method is available, compare the time required to sort a list by that method with the time required by the sequence method. Vary the original order of the list by rearranging the deck of practice cards in a controlled way, so as to study the effect on the speed of sorting by each method.

The basic importance of sorting in business data processing makes it desirable to write a flexible routine that will fit many situations. For example, the number of items in the list should be a parameter of the routine, to be read in from the typewriter or from a card, or determined by the computer run itself. Other parameters might include the length of each item and the location of the first one. Since the key is frequently only a reference number at the beginning of the item, the location of the key could also be made a parameter.

> EXERCISE 6. Modify the routine of Exercise 4 (a) so as to read in the four parameters mentioned.

We could adopt a different policy with respect to sorting routines. Instead of writing a long routine to take care of every conceivable variation, we might decide to produce a separate short routine for each new application. Then each routine would be tailored to fit the exact situation. Of course all these separate routines would have much in common. We therefore reject at once the notion of writing them out by hand and then punching and assembling them. We use instead a routine like that of Exercise 6, adding to it a section that will punch out the working part of the routine when the parameters have been used to adapt it to the new application. The original routine, with this addition, thus becomes a "generator." It is no longer actually used for sorting but for producing various new sorting routines. It is convenient to have the generator punch a loading routine, so that the new deck produced will be complete, ready to run. The loading routine will, of course, be tailored to fit the new routine, so that we continue to apply the idea of a generator.

> EXERCISE 7. (a) Modify and enlarge the routine of Exercise 6 so that it becomes a generator for sorting routines. (b) Use the generator of part (a) to produce a routine equivalent to the one in Exercise 4 (a). Compare the two routines and discuss any differences that appear.

It is clear that the idea of generators can be applied to many other programming tasks. The preparation of monthly reports, for example, is an essential part of business data processing. Contrary to common expectation, these reports do not remain the same month after month; frequent changes are necessary, sometimes because exceptional cases were overlooked, but more often because of changing business or management conditions. Patching the old routine and checking it out is a costly process, subject to many errors. It may be far more efficient simply to generate a new routine. Generator routines have become a vital part of programming for business applications. They have been called the key to future developments in business data processing.*

*See W. C. McGee, "Generalization: Key to Successful Electronic Data Processing, Journal of the Association for Computing Machinery, Vol. 6, No. 1, January 1959, p. 1.

BUSINESS DATA PROCESSING

It has been pointed out that most uses of a computer involve simulation of some real-life situation. Now, the business uses of computers center around <u>files</u> of information; typically, a file consists of many thousands of records.

To illustrate business data processing, we propose to simulate on two levels. Our problem concerns an inventory situation (which would simulate an actual physical inventory), and we will simulate <u>that</u> by operating in miniature.

Figure L4.1 shows our tiny inventory file for the warehouse stock of a company. Keep in mind throughout this problem that in the real-world situation, the file might easily be 10,000 times as large; it would be stored on magnetic tape or on discs, and each record would contain much more information than that shown in Figure L4.1.

The file is a deck of cards. In columns 1-3 is the item number (of the active items). Columns 4-6 show the <u>quantity on hand</u> (QOH) as of the last time this file was updated. The next four columns show the average price per unit of the item (in cents). For example, the 773 units of item 701 have an average value of 93 cents. Some were bought at 80 cents, some at a dollar, and so on. Columns 11-13 show the reorder point (ROP); when the QOH falls at or below ROP, a new supply should be obtained (see also Problem K1 on Economic Lot Size). Item 098, for example, has already passed its ROP; a new supply has presumably been ordered.

An inventory file would probably contain much more information, such as

1. The date of last acquisition.
2. The last reorder date.
3. Monthly usage figures.
4. Part description (in English).

A file is of use only if it can be maintained and if its information can be furnished on time to those who need it. Figure L4.2 shows six activity items that represent information to be used to update our file. The code number is as follows:

1 = IN (i.e., increases to the inventory)
2 = OUT (i.e., decreases or withdrawals)
3 = DELETE the item

Notice that the file itself, as well as the activity cards, is in order by item number. This is typical of file maintenance; for a large batch of activity cards (which are created in chronological order) there would have to be a preliminary ordering to arrange the cards in order of item number.

Item no.	QOH	Price	ROP
067	012	6342	005
098	256	1222	300
123	800	0237	100
167	654	1257	100
285	277	3218	100
304	163	0515	050
400	001	1600	002
519	017	0850	012
604	221	0845	200
650	846	0063	500
701	773	0093	500
709	018	0775	005
805	074	1277	070
812	900	0123	600
888	165	1004	100
916	008	1983	005
967	061	2761	050

Figure L4.1. The inventory file

The object is this: to write a routine that will update this file and furnish all information calling for action. The output will be this information, plus a new updated file of cards.

Listed below are some of the things that the business programmer would have to consider in preparing a routine for this job.

1. Both the file and the activity cards should be sequence checked as they are read into the computer. If a step-down in item number should occur, some action must be taken; this action might be to type an error message and HALT. If a card of the activity file were out of sort, would it ever be possible to recover?

Item no.	Code	Quantity	Price
078	1	100	0367
304	2	030	0000
400	1	005	1650
805	2	010	0000
916	3	000	0000
976	2	012	0000

Figure L4.2. Current activity

2. For each activity item, the corresponding file record should be adjusted. If it is an OUT activity, the quantity on hand is reduced, and the new QOH is checked against the ROP. What should be done if the QOH is less than the ROP? And what if the new value for QOH is negative?

If it is an IN activity, a new average price must be calculated. If, for the IN activity, there was no item number in the file, then a new record is to be created (as for 078 in the example).

3. The value of the entire inventory should be calculated and typed out at the end of the run.

4. Some action must be taken when an OUT activity calls on a nonexistent item, as 976 in the example.

5. At the end of the run, the sum of all the item numbers in the new file should be typed. This is a hash total, meaningless as a number by itself, but vital as a control figure. At the start of the run, the sum of the item numbers for the old file is typed. The hash total at the start of this run must agree with the output hash total from the last run. Such a control figure is much more powerful as an audit control than a simple card count, since the hash totals tell you when to stop looking for a discrepancy. (An even more powerful check would be furnished by hash totaling the entire record.)

You might consider one more aspect of such an inventory system. It would be nice, now and then, to go to the warehouse and count the actual quantity on hand for some items, to bring the file into agreement with reality. Seldom would any item agree precisely with the file. How often should this be done, and for what fraction of the inventory? Could we use the computer to help us (say, by producing sampling lists)?

Problem M1

A SIMPLE DISTRIBUTION

We have in storage 100 5-digit numbers, addressed at A, A + 5, A + 10, . . ., A + 495. Each number is to be examined and a tally made in the proper cells for the following distribution:
1. The number of positive numbers.
2. The number of negative numbers.
3. The number of zero numbers.
4. The number of nonzero numbers.
5. The number of numbers greater than 50000.
6. The number of numbers less than −50000.
7. The number of odd numbers.
8. The number of even numbers.
9. The number of numbers whose absolute value is less than 50000.
10. The number of numbers whose absolute value is greater than 50000.

* * *

The above assignment is simple, easily flowcharted, and readily coded. Problem M1 is the following:

EXERCISE 1. Devise sets of test data to check the resulting routine thoroughly to ensure that all ten counts are made correctly.

Problem M2

CURVE FITTING

It is frequently necessary, in all sorts of scientific work, to find the equation of a curve that best fits (in some sense) a given set of points. If the resulting curve is a straight line, we speak of the process as linear curve fitting; for a second-degree curve it is called quadratic (or parabolic) curve fitting, and so on. A good discussion of the elementary theory of curve fitting can be found in Ross R. Middlemiss, Analytic Geometry, Chapter 14 (McGraw-Hill Book Company, Inc., New York, 1955).

We need to define a residual as shown in Figure M2.1.

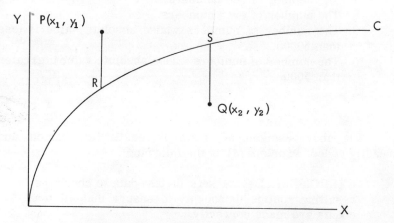

Figure M2.1. Residuals

Points P and Q are two (of many) points for which the curve C represents a fit; R and S are points on the curve having the same abscissas as P and Q. The residual of a point is the difference between the ordinate of the point and the ordinate of the corresponding point of the curve. The residual is a signed quantity; the definition fixes the sign by the rule "observed minus expected." In Figure M2.1, the residual for P is the segment RP which is positive); the residual for Q is the segment SQ (which is negative).

320

The best fitting curve of a given type is defined to be the one for which the sum of the squares of the residuals is a minimum. We use the sum of the squares of the residuals, rather than the algebraic sum of the residuals themselves, for two reasons.

1. By squaring, the direction of the residual is suppressed. In a sense, each residual represents an error, or an amount by which the curve does not fit its points perfectly. The direction of an error is not as important as its size.

2. By squaring, the effect of small errors is minimized and the effect of large errors is exaggerated.

There are many ways in which a curve could be fitted to a set of points (by eye, for example). The method of least squares, however, provides an objective way, universally agreed upon.

We can proceed directly from the definition to derive curve fitting equations for any given type (for the linear case, Middlemiss shows a derivation that does not use calculus). In any event, we arrive at a set of equations for the best fitting straight line, of the form

$$y = ax + b$$

to a given set of points, as follows:

$$\left.\begin{array}{l} a\Sigma X^2 + b\Sigma X = \Sigma XY \\ a\Sigma X + bN = \Sigma Y \end{array}\right\} \tag{1}$$

The use of these equations can be illustrated by a simple example. Suppose we have four points, as in Figure M2.2.

Figure M2.3 shows the necessary arithmetic to apply the linear curve fitting equations to the given data. The solution of the system of two simultaneous equations is

$$a = 0.34675$$
$$b = 2.13932$$

and the line $y = ax + b$ with those coefficients has been drawn in Figure M2.2. By the method of least squares, it is the best possible straightline fit to the four points.

The corresponding sets of equations for fitting a second-degree curve ($y = ax^2 + bx^2 + c$) and a third-degree curve ($y = ax^3 + bx^2 + cx + d$) are shown in Figure M2.4.

The pattern should be clear from these examples. The matrix of coefficients of the unknowns is symmetric. The first

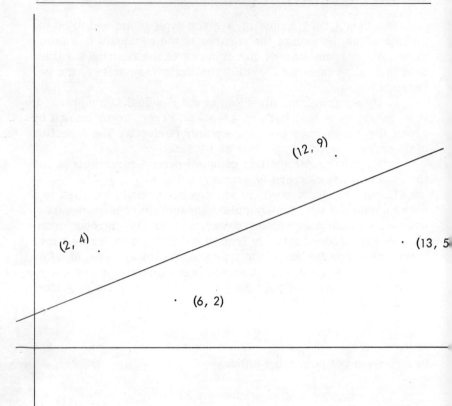

Figure M2.2. A simple case of linear curve fitting

X	Y	XY	X²	
2	4	8	4	$353a + 33b = 193$
6	2	12	36	$33a + 4b = 20$
13	5	65	169	
12	9	108	144	
33	20	193	353	

Figure M2.3. The arithmetic for Figure M2.2

coefficient is ΣX^k, where k is twice the degree. The coefficient in the lower right has k = 0, for which the sum is N, the number of points. The constant term in each equation is of the form

$\Sigma X^m Y$, where m is the same as the lowest power of X in that equation. And so on.

$$a\Sigma X^4 + b\Sigma X^3 + c\Sigma X^2 = \Sigma X^2 Y$$
$$a\Sigma X^3 + b\Sigma X^2 + c\Sigma X = \Sigma XY \qquad (2)$$
$$a\Sigma X^2 + b\Sigma X + cN = \Sigma Y$$

$$a\Sigma X^6 + b\Sigma X^5 + c\Sigma X^4 + d\Sigma X^3 = \Sigma X^3 Y$$
$$a\Sigma X^5 + b\Sigma X^4 + c\Sigma X^3 + d\Sigma X^2 = \Sigma X^2 Y$$
$$a\Sigma X^4 + b\Sigma X^3 + c\Sigma X^2 + d\Sigma X = \Sigma XY \qquad (3)$$
$$a\Sigma X^3 + b\Sigma X^2 + c\Sigma X + dN = \Sigma Y$$

Figure M2.4. Curve fitting equations for second- and
third-degree curves

The basic problem, then, is this: Fit a second-degree curve to a set of points entered on cards. Each card bears one pair of coordinates as floating-point numbers. The number of cards is not known in advance, but will be more than 2 and less than 100, with some sort of signal for the end of the data deck. As the deck is read, the summations of the Equations (2) of Figure M2.4 will have to be calculated. After the deck is read, the three simultaneous Equations (2) will have to be solved. The output is the three values for a, b, and c.

All this assumes that what we want to do is fit a parabola to the data points; i.e., we know in advance that the data is essentially parabolic. Such knowledge is frequently avaliable because of the nature or source of the data. The student should obtain (or invent) data that are, indeed, parabolic, to use as test data for this problem.

Sometimes this knowledge is not available. It might then be feasible to calculate the coefficients for degrees 1, 2, 3, . . . in turn and end the process with the last set that is meaningful. An objective measure of what is meaningful is beyond the scope of this problem.

CORRELATION

The input to the computer is a deck of cards. Each card bears 2 numbers, X and Y, each a 3-digit integer. The number of cards is unknown and variable (but is at least 3), but the last card of the deck has both variables X and Y recorded as 999. The 999 is a flag or sentinel; no real pair of variables (in our problem) can have these values, and so they signal the end of the deck for us.

We wish to compute the coefficient of correlation between X and Y. The formula is this:

$$r = \frac{N\Sigma XY - \Sigma X\,\Sigma Y}{\sqrt{N\Sigma X^2 - (\Sigma X)^2}\ \sqrt{N\Sigma Y^2 - (\Sigma Y)^2}} \qquad (1)$$

and it may have any value between −1 and +1. It will be a bit easier to calculate

$$r^2 = \frac{(N\Sigma XY - \Sigma X\,\Sigma Y)^2}{(N\Sigma X^2 - (\Sigma X)^2)\ (N\Sigma Y^2 - (\Sigma Y)^2)} \qquad (2)$$

and calculate $(r^2)^{1/2}$, assigning to the result the sign of the quantity inside the parentheses in the numerator of Formula (2). (We thus have to extract only one root.)

For each card except the last card of the deck, we must thus accumulate the following information:

1. The card count, N. Assume for now that every card is active; i.e., that it bears true values for X and Y. Thus for each card, we add <u>one</u> to a field called N that is initialized to zero at the start of reading.

2. The fields ΣX and ΣY: the simple sums of both variables.

3. The fields ΣX^2 and ΣY^2: the sums of the squares of the incoming variables.

4. The field ΣXY: the sum of the cross products of the two variables.

These fields are <u>not</u> augmented for the card bearing the signal 999.

After reading the signal card, the calculation of Equation (2) can proceed, and the result can be typed.

A statistician may also want the individual fields that were accumulated along the way. From the simple sums, the means of the two variables can be calculated:

$$\overline{X} = \frac{\Sigma X}{N}$$

and so forth. The factors in the denominator of Equation (2) can be used to calculate the <u>variances</u> of the two variables, and from them the standard deviations:

$$\sigma_X^2 = (1/N)(N\Sigma X^2 - (\Sigma X)^2)$$

$$\sigma_X = \sqrt{\sigma_X^2}$$

All these quantities make statisticians very happy. In fact, it is rare that it would happen that a deck of cards would bear just two variables. There could be, say, twenty 3-digit variables on each card, and the statistician wants the above information for each pair. For twenty variables, there are $(1/2)(20 \times 19) = 190$ pairs. For even a small deck, there is thus considerable arithmetic to be done.

The purpose of the signal card, of course, is to enable us to stack many decks in the hopper, so that many arrays of correlations can be calculated without intervention. The problem of arranging the output in meaningful fashion is not trivial.

We assumed that every variable is present on every card. This is not always true. The variables could be quiz grades, for example, and it is not uncommon for an individual grade to be missing, due to a student's absence. We have several choices possible:

1. For all correlations involving that variable, we could disregard all other figures (and not increment N).

2. The missing entry could be replaced by the mean of all other values for that variable (which requires a preliminary pass just for this purpose).

3. The missing value could be replaced by the mean up to that point (which would cause a drop-dead halt if it happened on the first card of the deck—why?), or by a standard figure from experience, or by the mean from the preceding deck. All such procedures are inherently dangerous, since they assume that some situation is so rare as to be negligible. It is a firm rule in computing that any such assumptions are usually rewarded by

having the rare situation occur the first time the routine is used in an important situation.

For your correlation routine, you must make a decision: Either tolerate no missing variables (but then be sure to edit your input data in order to check), or else take some meaningful action when they occur.

We stated that a deck must have at least two data cards. What would happen with a one-card deck?

It was also stated that the value of r cannot exceed (in absolute value) the number <u>one.</u> That statement is true and can be proved, provided Equation (1) is evaluated mathematically; i.e., with infinite arithmetic. But the arithmetic of a computer is finite; indeed, in floating point, may be restricted to 8 digits. In any real situation, it could happen that r could become greater than one. If r is actually close to (or equal to) one, the numerator and denominator in Equation (1) are nearly equal. They then represent different measures of the same thing, but they are calculated differently. Any of the three factors in Equation (1) can be small, and each is calculated by subtracting two similar numbers. This is precisely the booby trap in floating-point arithmetic, namely, that the difference of two numbers, both large and both known to 8-digit precision, may be small and "good" to less than 8 digits. For example:

$$
\begin{array}{rrrrrrrrr}
54 & 1 & 2 & 3 & 4 & 5 & 6 & 7 & 8 \\[4pt]
\hline
-54 & 1 & 2 & 3 & 4 & 1 & 1 & 1 & 1 \\
\hline
54 & 0 & 0 & 0 & 0 & 4 & 5 & 6 & 7 \quad = \\[8pt]
50 & 4 & 5 & 6 & 7 & 0 & 0 & 0 & 0
\end{array}
$$

The trouble here is intrinsic to the numbers involved, of course, and the loss of significance is unavoidable, whether in floating point or any other system of arithmetic. The real booby trap is that floating point gives no warning of the sudden loss of significance, and further calculation proceeds to a final answer that can be meaningless. In just a few arithmetic operations it is possible (using only figures that are each correct to 8 digits) to arrive at a figure for which even the exponent is incorrect. Think of what can happen when such troubles are compounded through several million arithmetic operations. Several solutions have been suggested and tried. Among these are the following.

1. The trouble arises largely when a subtraction produces a non-normalized number, as in our example. The subroutine

(buried somewhere in the floating-point package that we didn't write) that normalizes numbers after addition can be rigged to keep track of the amount of normalization that is done (in our example, it did 4 units of normalization). But now we have a new trouble—namely, what to do with this information? We might find that we have done, say, ten million arithmetic operations and have lost a total of 173 units of significance. What does that tell us about the meaning of our results?

2. The same problem can be run several times with the same input data but using floating-point arithmetic of 8-, 15-, and 25-digit precision (this is particularly easy on the IBM 1620). If the results differ widely, it can indicate extreme loss of significance. Usually, however, the results of such experiments are in good agreement. The experiment itself is expensive in machine time. What is happening is that there may be loss of significance, but most of the time there is not; i.e., the errors of floating-point arithmetic largely cancel out.

Most people quickly conclude that it is fairly safe to have faith and not worry about it. This is fine, but one should be warned that things such as a correlation coefficient of 1.00003, or sine $(\pi/2)$ = 1.00004, can happen and must be accounted for.

Can either factor in the denominator of Equation (2) be zero? What would a zero imply? What will your routine do about it?

The final value of r is to bear the sign of the unsquared numerator of Equation (2). How can we assign a sign from one number to another, in floating point and Fortran?

Can the numerator of Equation (2) go to zero? What would that imply?

Can either factor in the denominator of Equation (2) go negative? Does your routine check for this? Should it?

How does the time of calculation vary with N? How does it vary with the number of variables? If a given run is limited to, say, an hour, what limits should you set on N and the number of variables?

Using floating-point 8-digit arithmetic, is there any upper bound on N? That is, to what extent does r become meaningless as N increases?

Devising test data for this routine is a problem in itself. You must devise decks that will produce an r of 0, +1, −1, and some other known value, at a minimum.

We have assumed that a given deck bears a fixed and known number of variables. Can you adjust your routine so that the number of variables may vary from deck to deck? Would it suffice to precede each data deck with another nondata card that states the number of variables to be met?

Nothing was said concerning the decimalization of the input data; in fact, it was assumed to be in the form of 3-digit integers. Using floating-point arithmetic, each value would then have to be "floated" on input. For the calculation of r itself, the decimalization could be ignored; i.e., the values could be assumed to be integers with no harm done. For calculating the other statistics, however, the placing of the decimal points is important. How can this be handled?

The library of canned routines for most computers contains a stock routine similar to the one described here. Look up such a routine and deduce, from its description, the answers to some of the questions given above. Would the library routine satisfy the conditions of this problem?

You could also ask, "Aren't the answers to all the questions raised well known?" Well, no, they're not. But therein lies one of the challenging aspects of learning computing. Much is still un-known—and you may be the one who can tell us. Moreover, you have access to the tool to be used: the computer itself. In most cases, the answer to "What would happen if?" is "Why not try it and find out?" All we lack is time and ambition, and these are things you can furnish to the profession. One warning, though: For every question you resolve, two new ones will make them-selves apparent. That's the way research goes. You need not worry too much about duplicating research that has already been done. For one thing, when you have done it, it is then yours (and, once you start on the path of research, you will inevitably stumble quickly on an area about which nothing is known). The field is wide open to receive your contribution.

Problem M4

CONTINGENCY TABLES

The numbers in Figure M4.1 show some observed frequencies of 1,000 generated random digits in the column headed f_0. The theoretical frequencies are shown in the next column; in this case, since we reason that random digits should show a flat distribution, they are all 100. The column headed D shows the differences $(f_0 - f_t)$, and the final column shows the squares of those differences.

We wish to apply the statistical test known as chi-squared to these figures, to test whether or not the observed frequencies fit the theoretical. In using chi-squared for this purpose,* the following formula is applied:

$$\chi^2 = \Sigma \; \frac{(f_0 - f_t)^2}{f_t} \tag{1}$$

The squares that were formed (in Figure M4.1) are each to be divided by the corresponding theoretical frequency, and the resulting quotients are summed over all cases. In our example, chi-squared is then 2.56, and there are 9 degrees of freedom. Reference to a table of chi-squared (Figure M4.2) shows a value of p (probability) of 0.98. The data of our example is not significant.

Consider now the situation shown in Figure M4.3. Suppose four groups of people (called A, B, C, and D) have responded as shown to a question on a questionnaire; i.e., 307 persons of the 1,000 in group C responded with a 3. A casual inspection shows the data to be remarkably consistent (or associated). The row totals have been labeled with R's, the column totals with C's, and the grand total of all entries with G.

If we had the data of Figure M4.4, on the other hand (wherein rows B and D of Figure M4.3 have been reversed), we wouldn't need a statistical technique to convince ourselves that the figures

---

*The reader is referred to texts on statistics for details of chi-squared.

are independent or inconsistent. Again, we wish to use chi-squared as a test to discriminate between these two obvious cases. We seek an objective measure of the borderline between a table that is obviously associated and one that is obviously independent. The previous application of chi-squared for goodness of fit doesn't seem to apply, since we lack theoretical frequencies.

Digit	f_0	f_t	D	D^2
0	96	100	−4	16
1	103	100	3	9
2	105	100	5	25
3	94	100	−6	36
4	93	100	−7	49
5	104	100	4	16
6	102	100	2	4
7	96	100	−4	16
8	98	100	−2	4
9	109	100	9	81
	1,000	1,000	0	256

Figure M4.1. Data for testing goodness of fit

Refer to Figure M4.3. We reason that the marginal totals (the R and C values) are the best information we have of the trend of the table. The row totals reflect the over-all picture of the column distribution; similarly, the column totals reflect the row distribution. Therefore, we reason that a suitable "theoretical frequency" for, say, cell B2 can be formed by the calculation:

$$f_{t_{B2}} = \frac{C_2 R_2}{G} \qquad (2)$$

In our example, this would be

$$f_t = \frac{788 \cdot 1000}{4000} = 197$$

Notice that if the table were entirely homogeneous (that is, all rows were alike), these theoretical frequencies would agree precisely with the observed frequencies, which is as it should be. Similarly, the more scattered the table is, the more these calculated frequencies will disagree with the observations. This

TABLE 9.2
VALUES OF CHI-SQUARE*

| | Probability of a Larger Value of Chi-square | | | | | | | | | | | | |
D.f.	0.01	0.02	0.05	0.10	0.20	0.30	0.50	0.70	0.80	0.90	0.95	0.98	0.99
1	6.635	5.412	3.841	2.706	1.642	1.074	.455	.148	.064	.016	.004	.001	.000
2	9.210	7.824	5.991	4.605	3.219	2.408	1.386	.713	.446	.211	.103	.040	.020
3	11.341	9.837	7.815	6.251	4.642	3.665	2.366	1.424	1.005	.584	.352	.185	.115
4	13.277	11.668	9.488	7.779	5.989	4.878	3.357	2.195	1.649	1.064	.711	.429	.297
5	15.086	13.388	11.070	9.236	7.289	6.064	4.351	3.000	2.343	1.610	1.145	.752	.554
6	16.812	15.033	12.592	10.645	8.558	7.231	5.348	3.828	3.070	2.204	1.635	1.134	.872
7	18.475	16.622	14.067	12.017	9.803	8.383	6.346	4.671	3.822	2.833	2.167	1.564	1.239
8	20.090	18.168	15.507	13.362	11.030	9.524	7.344	5.527	4.594	3.490	2.733	2.032	1.646
9	21.666	19.679	16.919	14.684	12.242	10.656	8.343	6.393	5.380	4.168	3.325	2.532	2.088
10	23.209	21.161	18.307	15.987	13.442	11.781	9.342	7.267	6.179	4.865	3.940	3.059	2.558
11	24.725	22.618	19.675	17.275	14.631	12.899	10.341	8.148	6.989	5.578	4.575	3.609	3.053
12	26.217	24.054	21.026	18.549	15.812	14.011	11.340	9.034	7.807	6.304	5.226	4.178	3.571
13	27.688	25.472	22.362	19.812	16.985	15.119	12.340	9.926	8.634	7.042	5.892	4.765	4.107
14	29.141	26.873	23.685	21.064	18.151	16.222	13.339	10.821	9.467	7.790	6.571	5.368	4.660
15	30.578	28.259	24.996	22.307	19.311	17.322	14.339	11.721	10.307	8.547	7.261	5.985	5.229
16	32.000	29.633	26.296	23.542	20.465	18.418	15.338	12.624	11.152	9.312	7.962	6.614	5.812
17	33.409	30.995	27.587	24.769	21.615	19.511	16.338	13.531	12.002	10.085	8.672	7.255	6.408
18	34.805	32.346	28.869	25.989	22.760	20.601	17.338	14.440	12.857	10.865	9.390	7.906	7.015
19	36.191	33.687	30.144	27.204	23.900	21.689	18.338	15.352	13.716	11.651	10.117	8.567	7.633
20	37.566	35.020	31.410	28.412	25.038	22.775	19.337	16.266	14.578	12.443	10.851	9.237	8.260
21	38.932	36.343	32.671	29.615	26.171	23.858	20.337	17.182	15.445	13.240	11.591	9.915	8.897
22	40.289	37.659	33.924	30.813	27.301	24.939	21.337	18.101	16.314	14.041	12.338	10.600	9.542
23	41.638	38.968	35.172	32.007	28.429	26.018	22.337	19.021	17.187	14.848	13.091	11.293	10.196
24	42.980	40.270	36.415	33.196	29.553	27.096	23.337	19.943	18.062	15.659	13.848	11.992	10.856
25	44.314	41.566	37.652	34.382	30.675	28.172	24.337	20.867	18.940	16.473	14.611	12.697	11.524
26	45.642	42.856	38.885	35.563	31.795	29.246	25.336	21.792	19.820	17.292	15.379	13.409	12.198
27	46.963	44.140	40.113	36.741	32.912	30.319	26.336	22.719	20.703	18.114	16.151	14.125	12.879
28	48.278	45.419	41.337	37.916	34.027	31.391	27.336	23.647	21.588	18.939	16.928	14.847	13.565
29	49.588	46.693	42.557	39.087	35.139	32.461	28.336	24.577	22.475	19.768	17.708	15.574	14.256
30	50.892	47.962	43.773	40.256	36.250	33.530	29.336	25.508	23.364	20.599	18.493	16.306	14.953

* From table III of reference(8) with permission of Professor Fisher and of his publishers, Oliver and Boyd, Edinburgh.

Figure M4.2.

	1	2	3	4		
A	100	200	300	400	1000	R_1
B	110	190	308	392	1000	R_2
C	93	194	307	406	1000	R_3
D	106	204	296	394	1000	R_4
	409	788	1211	1592	4000	G
	C_1	C_2	C_3	C_4		

Figure M4.3. A two-way contingency table

	1	2	3	4
A	100	200	300	400
B	392	308	190	110
C	93	194	307	406
D	394	296	204	106

Figure M4.4. Another two-way table

line of reasoning may not be the best in the world, but there are three things in its favor:
1. It's all we have.
2. Everyone has agreed to use this technique.
3. It works, on known cases.

We can thus furnish the sixteen (for our 4×4 table) theoretical frequencies we need, and apply Formula (1) as before.

A straightforward approach now would be to apply Formula (2) sixteen times, and then apply Formula (1). This is not only a great deal of calculation, but it will involve fractions at every stage. Some algebraic manipulation will cut down the work considerably.

Formula (1) can be expanded as follows:

$$\chi^2 = \Sigma \left[\frac{f_0^2 - 2f_0 f_t + f_t^2}{f_t} \right]$$

$$= \Sigma \frac{f_0^2}{f_t} - 2\Sigma \frac{f_0 f_t}{f_t} + \Sigma \frac{f_t^2}{f_t}$$

$$= \Sigma \frac{f_0^2}{f_t} - 2\Sigma f_0 + \Sigma f_t$$

and it is not difficult to show that Σf_0 and Σf_t (using the definition of f_t (given by formula (2)) are equal to each other and, of course, equal to G. We thus have

$$\chi^2 = \Sigma \frac{f_0^2}{f.} - G \qquad (3)$$

Now we can substitute Formula (2) into Formula (3) and obtain

$$\chi^2 = \Sigma \frac{G f_0^2}{RC} - G$$

where the R and C in each term are the ones corresponding to the given f_0. We thus arrive at

$$\chi^2 = G \left(\Sigma \frac{f_0^2}{RC} - 1 \right)$$

In this form, the calculation is much simpler.

In practical work, we might expect many tables such as Figure M4.3 (i.e., the body of the tables, not the marginal totals). Let us simplify the computing problem by specifying the input format. Each table will appear on four cards with this layout:

Card columns   1-2:   Table number
                  3:   Row number
               4-6, ⎫
               7-9, ⎪
              10-12, ⎬ cell value for that row
              13-15, ⎭

For example, if the table of Figure M4.3 were the seventeenth table in a set to be calculated, its third card would be punched

1 7 3 0 9 3 1 9 4 3 0 7 4 0 6

in the first 15 columns. We are agreeing that all cell values can be contained in 3 digits and that the value of G cannot exceed 4 digits. We further specify that no row or column total for any table can be zero.

The task of reading in a table and calculating and printing its value of chi-squared can now be broken into logical parts. We suggest that this be made a class project, with teams set up responsible for producing a subroutine for each part. We will merely outline the job for each part.

1. The input. The code should arrange to read four cards, check that they all have the same table number, check for proper line numbers, and transmit their cell information to an area labeled TABLE (consisting of sixteen 3-digit fields). The card data is not flagged. Suitable error messages should be devised for those conditions that demand it.

2. Row totals. Four-digit fields are set up to receive the values of R1, R2, R3, and R4. Test for overflow (is it possible?). Sum the R values and produce the 4-digit value of G. Test for overflow (is it possible?). Arrange for error messages. Devise a test case of input data for the error conditions.

3. Column totals. Four-digit fields are set up to receive the column totals, C1, C2, C3, C4. The sums are formed with loops, of course. Notice that C3 is formed by summing TABLE + 6, TABLE + 18, TABLE + 30, TABLE + 42, and so forth. Sum the C values and compare this sum with the value of G produced by the previous subroutine. Devise an error message if these sums don't compare. This subroutine must be tested, then, together with the previous one. Devise test data for this subroutine.

4. The chi-squared subroutine. This is the difficult one. For each cell value (at TABLE, TABLE + 3, TABLE + 6, . . . , TABLE + 45), the square of the number must be divided by the product of the corresponding R and C values. It might be convenient, in the housekeeping phase of the entire problem, to calculate just once a new table such as the following:

TABLE + 0,	A(R1),	A(C1)
TABLE + 3,	A(R1),	A(C2)
TABLE + 6,	A(R1),	A(C3)
TABLE + 9,	(AR1),	A(C4)
TABLE + 12,	(AR2),	A(C1)

| TABLE + 45, | A(R4), | A(C4) |

where A means "address of." This new table will occupy 240 cells of storage (i.e., 16 groups of three 5-digit addresses). It is, of course, possible to devise formulas for calculating your way to the address of the proper R and C values corresponding to a given TABLE entry.

For each of the 16 cells of the data table, the cell value is to be squared, and the square is to be divided by a product of two 4-digit fields. The quotient is to have at least three decimal places. The dividend, therefore, should have at least three zeros appended to its low-order end, and the division can be effected by any scheme available (i.e., using built-in division, SPS divide, or a division subroutine).

5. Output. The fourth subroutine (above) should have calculated a value called CS (for chi-squared). That value should allow for four positions before the decimal point and three after it. Arrange to type, for each table, the table number and the value of chi-squared. Devise an error message for the extreme case where chi-squared exceeds 10,000.

6. Degrees of freedom. In general, the number of degrees of freedom for a two-way contingency table is given by

d.f. = (No. of rows minus 1) · (No. of columns minus 1)

Since we have restricted our attention to the 4×4 case, the number of degrees of freedom is always 9. To be neat, we should store in the computer that part of Figure M4.2 for 9 degrees of freedom, and type after each result one asterisk for "significant" (i.e., for which p is less than or equal to 0.05) and two asterisks for "highly significant" (i.e., for which p is less than or equal to 0.01).

7. Master routine. Finally, we need a master routine to trigger all the subroutines in proper order. This is the easiest job.

8. Generalization. A suitable term project in an advanced course would be to generalize the entire problem. Thus, the input might be two-way tables of any size between, say, 2×2 and 5×5 (and not necessarily square). Moreover, attention must be paid to the exceptional conditions that we blithely defined out of the simple case. For example, there is the problem of continuity. The texts all agree that the chi-squared test cannot be applied validly when the cell values are too small; they disagree somewhat as to what is "too small." Some research is in order, as well as statements of restrictions to apply to the final routine. It should also be noted that in the 2×2 case (calling the cell

values a, b, c, and d), the entire calculation can be done algebraically to produce one formula for the final answer. The 2 × 2 case, considered as a separate problem, could thus be used as a term problem in an elementary course

The entire battery of subroutines, for the main problem described in this problem, should be filed in the computing laboratory as a service routine. The biological science people in particular can make good use of it.

Problem M5

THE STATISTICAL CONTROL GROUP

A group of sociologists wish to perform an experiment involving members of the freshman class of a school. They wish to take a group of the freshmen and give them a new form of special help with a teaching machine. It is hoped that the special help will improve their grades.

But improve their grades over what? To provide any sort of measurement of the efficiency of the experiment, the test group of students must have a matching control group (who receive no special help). A comparison of the subsequent grades of the two groups would then provide the desired measure. It is hoped that there will be a significant difference between the grades of the two groups some time after the end of the experiment.

The key word is "matching." The two groups should be as nearly alike as possible. The whole experiment might be vitiated if it should turn out that a high percentage of just one group were from the same high school, or were girls, or were orphans, or were Protestants, or what have you.

Now, some factors can be expected to cancel out simply by picking both groups at random from the freshman class. All the factors listed in the paragraph above are of this sort; it would be remarkable if one group differed significantly from the other in such characteristics. They could differ very easily in other characteristics, however. The problem is to match the groups as well as possible on those characteristics that can be controlled.

A punched card exists for each student in the freshman class, bearing his student number, his age, his sex, his IQ, his last year's grade point average (GPA), and the city where he got his high school diploma.

Picking the test group is easy. By any of a dozen methods, a random selection can be made from these cards. Assume that the total population of the freshman class is 2,000 and that 100 students are picked for the test group. As one possible method, the cards can be punched with 4-digit random numbers, sorted on those numbers, and the first 100 of the resulting scrambled deck can be the test group.

337

Picking the 100 members of the control group is another thing again. We want the best possible match on the five available characteristics. We might arrange them in priority number: GPA, age, sex, IQ, and city. The 100 cards of the test group can, for convenience, be sorted in that order, i.e., in GPA order, and in age order within each GPA grouping, and so on.

Suppose that the first member of the test group has three statistics:

$$2.56, \ 18, \ M, \ 128, \ 5$$

i.e., his previous GPA was 2.56 (out of a possible 3.00), he is 18 years old and male, has an IQ of 128, and came from city number 5. Of the 1,900 other persons in the freshman class, there are 56 having a 2.56 GPA; of these, 45 are 18 years old; of these, 22 are male; of these, just two have an IQ of 128, and neither of these two comes from city number 5. One of them is from city number 7; the other from city 99 (i.e., out of state). We pick the one from city number 7, and one match is completed.

What we have just described is about the only process known today to perform the matching. We compare two lists, both in the same order, of 100 and 1,900 students, and we pick from the 1,900 as best we can to match each of the 100. Frequently, after 50 or so matches have been made, we find that a student who was already selected is a better match for the next member of the test group.

So this problem is an odd one. There is no standard technique for doing it mechanically (i.e., without human judgment). The most important part of knowledge is to know where it ends. Here is a problem situation that is vital to scientific research, and there is no algorithm on file. Offhand, it sounds like an excellent computer problem, but the computer solution (for the best possible match) has yet to be written.

Problem M6

QUALITY CONTROL

The screws produced in a long run on an automatic machine were sampled from time to time and carefully measured, with the results shown in Figure M6.1. If a deviation of 0.005 inch can be tolerated from the nominal value of 1/4 inch, how many screws will have to be rejected in an average lot of 100 screws? What tolerance would permit 90 per cent of the screws to be accepted?

Diameter (inch)	Frequency (number)	Deviation (from 0.250 inch)
0.238	3	−0.012
0.240	8	−0.010
0.242	9	−0.008
0.244	15	−0.006
0.246	45	−0.004
0.248	132	−0.002
0.250	373	0.000
0.252	208	0.002
0.254	119	0.004
0.256	48	0.006
0.258	26	0.008
0.260	11	0.010
0.262	2	0.012
0.264	1	0.014
Total	1,000	

Figure M6.1. Frequency distribution showing the variation in the diameters of screws

Questions of this kind involve the dispersion or scattering of values on either side of a given value. Although the screws are all intended to be of 1/4-inch diameter, the combination of many small effects produces fluctuations in the actual diameter. This is the kind of situation that gives rise to a "normal" distribution, as pictured in Figure M6.2.

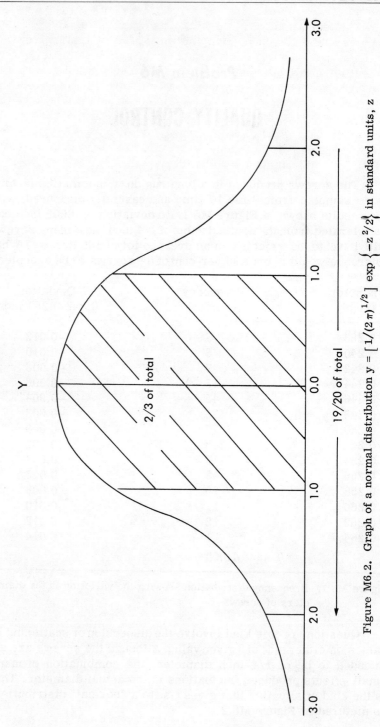

Figure M6.2. Graph of a normal distribution $y = [\,1/(2\pi)^{1/2}\,]\,\exp\left\{-z^2/2\right\}$ in standard units, z

The deviations are calculated by subtracting the nominal diameter of 0.250 inch from the measured diameter. We wish to form an idea of the average deviation. It is clear that we would not merely form the arithmetic mean of the deviations, because the negative deviations would tend to cancel out the positive deviations, so that we would not have a fair idea of the variability of the diameter. One way to form the average would be to take the absolute value of each deviation, and calculate the mean of these. This simple way is not the best. The absolute value $|b|$ of a number b is the value without regard to sign; in mathematical notation,

$$|b| = \sqrt{b^2}$$

The usual way to judge the variability of a set of values x is to square the deviation of each value from the mean value, and then to calculate the average of the squares. The squaring procedure not only makes all the results positive, but also gives greater emphasis to the larger fluctuations. Since these large fluctuations are usually the more important ones, in one way or another, the variability of the set is more clearly indicated. The mean of the squares is called the variance. The variance is of fundamental importance in studying the distribution of a set of values. For some purposes, the square root of the variance is also used; it is a kind of average deviation, and is called the standard deviation. Using the summation sign Σ , we write for the variance, v,

$$v = \frac{\Sigma (x - \bar{x})^2}{n}$$

and for the standard deviation SD,

$$SD = \sqrt{v} = \sqrt{\frac{\Sigma (x - \bar{x})^2}{n}}$$

where $\bar{x}$ is the mean and $(x - \bar{x})$ is the deviation of each value, x, from the mean.

EXERCISE 1. (a) We can use a plotting routine from Problem B1 to plot the frequency distribution given in Figure M6.1, or plot the curve by hand. Compare the result with the graph of a normal distribution shown in Figure M6.2. (b) Write a short Fortran routine to read in from cards the values of the diameter and the frequency of occurrence. Calculate the deviation of each value from 0.250 inch, and calculate and print the average square of the deviations.

The variance may be described as the average square of the deviations, but the deviations refer to the difference between each value x and the mean $\bar{x}$. On first consideration, the student might suppose that the calculation must be performed in two steps, i.e., first calculate the mean, and then calculate each deviation and its square. This would require reading the values in twice, or else storing them. Indeed, many beginners do make the calculation in just this way. A better method is given by the formula

$$v = \frac{\Sigma x^2}{n} - \bar{X}^2$$

which simplifies the calculation. The situation here is common to many computational problems. We take the definitions

$$\bar{x} = \frac{1}{n} \sum_{1}^{n} x \quad \text{and} \quad v = \sum_{1}^{n} \frac{(x - \bar{x})^2}{n}$$

and expand the latter:

$$v = \sum_{1}^{n} \frac{x^2 - 2x\bar{x} + \bar{x}^2}{n}$$

$$= \frac{\Sigma x^2}{n} - \frac{2\bar{x}\Sigma x}{n} + \frac{\Sigma \bar{x}^2}{n}$$

$$= \frac{\Sigma x^2}{n} - \frac{2\Sigma x \Sigma x}{n^2} + n\frac{(\Sigma x/n)^2}{n}$$

$$= \frac{\Sigma x^2}{n} - \frac{2(\Sigma x)^2}{n^2} + \frac{(\Sigma x)^2}{n^2}$$

$$= \frac{n\Sigma x^2 - (\Sigma x)^2}{n^2}$$

$$= \frac{\Sigma x^2}{n} - \bar{x}^2$$

EXERCISE 2. (a) Draw a flow chart for a routine to read in the number of cards and then the value of each diameter and the frequency of its occurrence. Calculate the number of screws, the sum of the diameter (of the separate screws), and the sum of the squares. Then calculate the mean diameter and the variance of the set of diameters and print the results. (b) Write a Fortran routine to implement the flow chart of part (a).

It has been noted that the frequency distribution of the diameters resembles a normal distribution and that this resemblance is not accidental but is due to the randomness of the fluctuations. This circumstance enables us to make reasonable predictions based on the properties of the normal distribution. In a normal distribution, about two-thirds (68.26 per cent) of the values are within one standard deviation of the mean, as shown in Figure M6.2. That is, they lie in the range from $\bar{x}$ − SD to $\bar{x}$ + SD. If the range is extended to twice the standard deviation above or below the mean, 95 per cent (more exactly, 95.44 per cent) of the values are included. Having determined the standard deviation for the distribution of diameters, we are ready to predict from the table what percentage will have a greater deviation from the mean than any multiple of SD (integral multiple or not).

EXERCISE 3. (a) Write a routine to calculate the frequencies

$$y = \frac{1}{\sqrt{2\pi}} \exp\left\{-z^2/2\right\}$$

for the normal distribution from z = 0.00 to z = 3.00 by steps of 0.01. Also calculate the cumulative frequencies S and the (doubled) ratio R, and type the values of z, y, R, and S on each line. (b) By using the table prepared in part (a), or by interpolating in Figure M6.3, answer the questions posed at the beginning of the problem.

The table in Figure M6.3 refers to a normal distribution for which the deviations z are expressed in terms of the standard deviation, and the total of the frequencies y is equal to 1.0. We apply the table to an actual distribution, as in Exercise 3, by dividing the actual deviations by the actual standard deviation.

This reduces the deviations to standard units; i.e., it expresses them in terms of the standard deviation. We are in effect fitting the actual distribution to the curve representing the theoretical (normal) distribution.

Deviation from mean (z)	Relative frequency (y)	Total within z of mean (both sides) (R)	(above only) (S)
0.0	0.3989	0.0000	0.0000
0.1	0.3970	0.0797	0.0398
0.2	0.3910	0.1585	0.0793
0.3	0.3814	0.2358	0.1179
0.4	0.3683	0.3108	0.1554
0.5	0.3521	0.3829	0.1915
0.6	0.3332	0.4515	0.2257
0.7	0.3123	0.5160	0.2580
0.8	0.2897	0.5763	0.2881
0.9	0.2661	0.6319	0.3159
1.0	0.2420	0.6827	0.3413
1.1	0.2179	0.7287	0.3643
1.2	0.1942	0.7699	0.3849
1.3	0.1714	0.8064	0.4032
1.4	0.1497	0.8385	0.4192
1.5	0.1295	0.8664	0.4332
1.6	0.1109	0.8904	0.4452
1.7	0.0940	0.9109	0.4554
1.8	0.0790	0.9281	0.4641
1.9	0.0656	0.9426	0.4713
2.0	0.0540	0.9545	0.4772

Figure M6.3.　Short table of a normal frequency distribution when the standard deviation is 1.0; $y = \left[1/(2\pi)^{1/2} \right] \exp\left\{ -z^2/2 \right\}$, where $z = x - \bar{x}$

Quality control is a very extensive field, involving continuous procedures to detect deterioration in a product, whether it is sudden or gradual, and to institute corrective measures. We shall consider only one small part of the testing process for the manufacture of screws. Suppose small samples, of about 10 screws, are collected at random times. How can we determine when the fluctuations are no longer due to random errors—that the process is out of control?

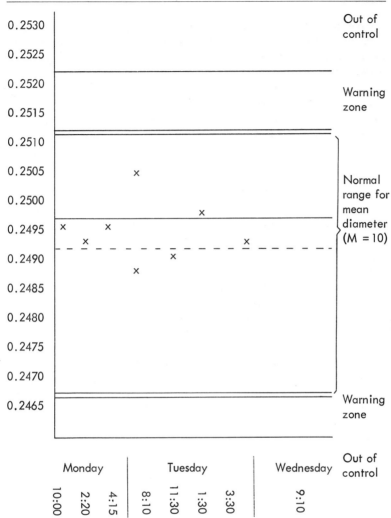

Figure M6.4. Quality control chart with 2SD and 3SD bands

The mean value m of the diameter for successive samples is itself subject to fluctuation. The variance SDM for the mean of n diameters is equal to the variance for the manufacturing operation, divided by the size n of the sample.*

---

*That is to say, the mean of a sample will not fluctuate as widely as the individual diameters.

We can apply to SDM = SD/M the same criterion as before, but this time to the means of successive samples. If only random errors are operative, 95 per cent of the samples should have means lying in a range from $\bar{x} - 2 \cdot$ SDM to $x + 2 \cdot$ SDM. The sample means would ordinarily be plotted on a quality control chart, in sequence, as shown in Figure M6.4. If the means start falling outside the warning lines, the production engineer is alerted to the need for intervention.

> EXERCISE 4. (a) Write a routine to accept from the typewriter the sample size n and the individual diameters, and to type the mean value m and a suitable message such as OK, WARNING, or OUT OF CONTROL. (b) Discuss methods needed to make a program such as that in part (a) an effective unit in quality control.

In the previous discussion, it was assumed that the mean and standard deviation for the over-all process of manufacturing screws could be determined by measuring a very large sample. Then these parameters of the frequency distribution were applied in different ways to smaller samples. The standard deviation is often used in a reversed way to estimate the reliability of values determined for the parameters by a few sample observations instead of by undertaking an extensive preliminary testing procedure.

Problem N1

UTILITY ROUTINES

We frequently need short routines in connection with other routines. For example, we may wish to clear storage, above the arithmetic tables, to zero before loading and executing a long program. Auxiliary routines of this sort are called util-ity routines. It is helpful to have a considerable number of utility routines available at a computing installation. Making such a routine of widest possible application, and document-ing it thoroughly so that it can be used confidently by other persons, offers a real challenge to the student.

A utility routine is especially convenient if it can be con-tained in the loading area, below the arithmetic tables. In that case it can be used with nearly any program. Since such rou-tines necessarily include their own loading instructions, they are often referred to as self-loading routines. One-card rou-tines fall in this class. Routines that require additional storage locations are usually assigned at high addresses, where they are least likely to interfere with any other routine.

> EXERCISE 1. (a) Write a one-card routine to clear storage above the arithmetic tables, 40 po-sitions at a time, without disturbing the record mark at 00400. (b) Write a brief but complete descrip-tion of the routine. Include (1) coded instructions required, (2) estimated time including loading time, and (3) any limitations on use of the routine.

A very useful routine is one to check the arithmetic tables. This is done by adding the signed digits, which should total 741.* With a little ingenuity, such a routine can be compressed into one card.

---

*This is a reasonably good check, but it could be invalid, if, for ex-ample, two correct digits were interchanged.

EXERCISE 2. Write a one-card program that will
check the arithmetic tables and type OK if the sum
is correct.

A routine to load the arithmetic tables can be of the utmost
simplicity. It should, however, also simulate the LOAD CARD
button, so that it can be placed in front of any deck; this increases
the challenge to the student.

EXERCISE 3. (a) Write a five-card routine to load
the arithmetic tables and then simulate the LOAD
CARD button. (b) Write a brief but complete report
describing the routine.

A loader and a dumper would, of course, be useful as one-
card routines. Such routines are described in Problems N3 and
N4. Routines to test for flags or record marks are included in
Problem N5.

We frequently need test data for checking out a new routine.
One very convenient way to obtain such data is to generate and
store an arithmetic progression with a short routine.

The routine should read in from the typewriter as 5-digit
numbers:

X, the field address of the first term of the progression;
A, the value of the first term;
D, the common difference;
N, the number of terms.

All this can be typed in, with field marks, on a single instruction.
By separating the first two parameters from the last two with
code 41 (for NOP), we can store the constants neatly in the middle
of the routine and make the whole routine fit at the bottom of storage, below the arithmetic tables.

EXERCISE 4. (a) Write a two-card routine (to start
at 00000 and fit below the tables) that will generate
and store an arithmetic progression as a table of
5-digit numbers. (b) Modify the routine of part (a),
if necessary, so that it can be used repeatedly by
pressing the buttons INSERT, RELEASE and START.

EXERCISE 5. Rewrite the routine of Exercise 4 as
a subroutine whose calling sequence specifies the
quantities X, A, D, and N.

Problem N2

A UTILITY ROUTINE FOR THE IBM 1620

Problem N1 concerned a subroutine that would generate arithmetic progressions on demand. Of equal use, as a subroutine to use in debugging and testing other routines, is one that will sum a given series and type the sum.

Again, let us first consider a simple restricted case (as with many problems, generalizations can proceed in many directions; the alert student should use his imagination). The terms of the series of numbers to be added are all 5-digit numbers, and their sum can be contained in 10 digits. The calling sequence specifies the address of the first number and the number of terms to be added. The following could be the calling sequence:

Location	OP	P	Q
G	17	$\underline{S}$	$\overline{G}$
G + 12	41	$\underline{A}$	$\overline{D}$

where S is the location of the subroutine, A is the address of the first term, and D is the number of terms. For convenience in extracting A and D for the calling sequence in the subroutine, these numbers should be flagged in the calling sequence.

Notice that we are using the 17 command to form the linkage. The instruction at G in our calling sequence will operate to transmit the number G to the cells just to the left of S (and room must be left for those 5 digits in storage during the assembly of the subroutine). Those 5 cells, then, are now our SAVE register. Just as before, the first task in the subroutine is to transmit that information to the exit command of the subroutine.

The subroutine itself is quite straightforward, as the flow chart of Figure N2.1 shows.

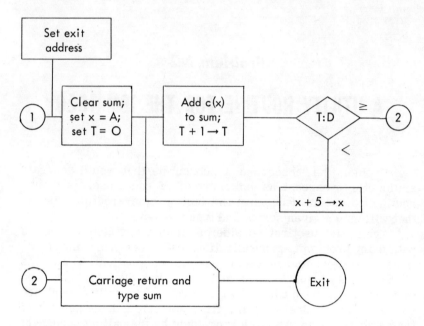

Figure N2.1. Summing a series

Problem N3

LOADERS FOR THE IBM 1620

With a card 1620, a problem that is common to every other problem is that of being able to load storage from cards. Why is this a problem?

First, let us assume that we wish to load only numeric information; i.e., information punched on cards is limited to the following character set: decimal digits, signed decimal digits, record mark, and blank columns. Thus, the execution of an instruction of the form 36xxxxx00500 will effectively cause the card reader to enter 80 characters of information into the area of storage that is addressed on the left by xxxxx. To design a compact routine to repeat this operation for a deck of cards is not a trivial task and must be preceded by many decisions. We have already made one decision, namely, that we are not concerned with alphabetic information.

We will design one specific, rather simple, loader as we go along. It is not as good as it should be. You can design a better one and, in fact, that task is Problem N3. The second decision we have made (for this loader) is this: Our loader will be generalized. This means that it will load information from any card into almost any part of storage. We say "almost" because, obviously, we cannot use a loader to load the portion of storage occupied by the loader itself. (There may be other areas of storage that cannot be loaded by a particular loader.)

The next decision is whether the loader shall be able to load randomly or sequentially. That is, should each card to be loaded bear on it the address into which its information should go? The alternative is to have one address for an entire deck, with the understanding that each subsequent card's information be loaded into some set address higher than the preceding. For example, using the latter method, it would be possible to load 80 characters per card, with each 80 characters loaded into storage at an address 80 higher than that of the preceding card. We will choose the former approach; i.e., each card will contain its own load address, so that each card is loaded independently.

Since an address occupies five card columns, the maximum

we can load per card is now 75 characters. As a matter of convenience, we make an arbitrary decision: Each card will be limited to 60 characters of information to be loaded, plus the necessary 5 digits of address. In fact, we adopt the following format for each card to be loaded.

Columns 1-60: Information to be loaded
Columns 61-65: Address at which column 1 is to be loaded
Column 80 : Transfer control signal

The transfer control signal (in column 80) is a necessary part of a loader; it tells when to stop loading. We adopt another arbitrary convention—namely, that a blank or zero in a column 80 means that the card should be loaded, whereas a nonzero digit in column 80 means that control of the routine passes from the loader to the instruction punched starting in column 1 of the card with the nonzero digit.

Keep track of the arbitrary decisions we are making along the way. In each case, there are other possible decisions that you can make for your loader. Until you know what it is you want to do, of course, you should use a stock loader like the one we are developing.

Now we have another decision to make: Where shall the loader itself be located in storage? One widely used loader, for example, uses the area normally occupied by the arithmetic tables. This implies three things. First, the loader may not use arithmetic. Second, the loader must have cards for the arithmetic tables at the end of each deck to be loaded, in order to restore the tables. Third, the loader is not interruptable; i.e., it cannot easily be used to load part of a deck and then resume for the balance of the deck, since the arithmetic tables wipe out the loader itself. Moreover (though this is not obvious) each card to be loaded must bear two addresses, which is awkward.

For various reasons, then, our loader will be written to use arithmetic and will therefore have to have a location other than that of the tables. We will use location 00402 (another arbitrary choice). We will include the arithmetic tables in the loading package, to guarantee that the tables are in storage and so that the loader will always function; while we are at it, we will also include a routine to check the tables. It may not be apparent, but our loader is getting quite long and will need a deck of ten cards to go in the front of every deck to be loaded. Tacitly, we have made another decision: The loader will be in one part. That is, a deck to be loaded will be preceded by the loader (rather than having the loader both precede and follow the deck).

The over-all pattern we will follow is shown in Figure N3.1.

The LOAD button on the card reader performs the following functions automatically:

1. It moves the first card in the read hopper physically past the read brushes.

2. The information in that card is transferred (as numerical information) by means of the card reader's buffer to positions 00000 through 00079 of storage.

2. Control is passed to the instruction at location 00000.

The LOAD button is thus our bootstrap. It will get one card's worth of information into storage. That information may be used to call in more cards, and so on. So the first cards of our loader will be punched with the information shown in Figures N3.2 and N3.3.

The first few instructions dictate the following cards to be loaded directly into locations whose addresses are 80 apart. The routine proceeds to 00582, where we proceed to check the arithmetic tables. Subsequent cards of the loader contain the arithmetic tables. The flags at 00000 and 00001 are a simple device to flash visually that that card is the first card of the deck.

The table check routine has two possible ends: either the tables check (and the routine should type OK) or they don't (and the routine will type NG and HALT).

If the table check routine ends in OK, a branch to 00402 is executed, and loading of data can begin; for an input area we can use the cells where the table check routine was loaded (namely, 00558 through 00637), since that area is no longer needed. We must now test whether the cell into which column 80 of the card was loaded is (or is not) a zero. If it is not a zero, then this card is our transfer control card, and we branch to the instruction(s) punched in that card, starting in column 1. If it is zero (and a blank column 80 loads into storage as a zero), then the information in this card is to be moved from the input area to the location specified in columns 61-65 of the card. The move will be made by a TRANSMIT RECORD command.

To do this, a record mark must be placed in cell 00618 (i.e., the cell in which column 61 of the data card is stored). Before we can do that, however, the information in 00618-00622 must be used to supply some addresses. Let us illustrate our

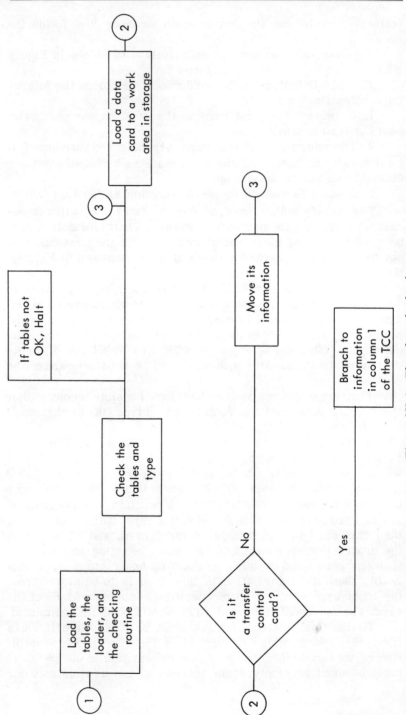

Figure N3.1. The plan of a loader

$$\overline{3}6005\overline{4}600500$$
360062600500
360070600500
360010000500
360018000500
360026000500
49005460

Figure N3.2. The first card of the loader (entering cells 00000–00079 by means of the load button)

00546	360034000500
558	360042000500
570	360050000500
582	$160073\overline{5}04911$
594	$250066\overline{5}00100$
606	210073500665
618	$1400605\overline{0}$
	0399
630	460066601300
642	$110060\overline{5}00001$
654	$490059400\overline{0}00$
666	$140073\overline{5}05652$
678	460073801200
690	$160073\overline{5}05547$
702	340000000102
714	390073300100
728	48000000000$\ddagger$
740	340000000102
752	390073300100
764	340000000102
776	490040200000

Figure N3.3. Cards 2, 3, and 4 of the loader

reasoning here with a specific example. Say a card to be loaded bears five instructions (in columns 1-60 of the card) to be loaded at 02024 (so 02024 is punched in columns 61-65). The card is entered into storage at the input area, 00558-00637, which puts columns 61-65 at 00618-00622.

Eventually we will need a record mark at 00618 (in order to be able to TRANSMIT RECORD),   and the instruction

31020400558 will do the actual loading job. But that will put a record mark at 02084, erasing what was there before. So we must store the contents of cell 02084 temporarily and restore it after the TRANSMIT RECORD takes place.

The complete routine is given in Figure N3.4, with complete remarks. It would be well to study this code carefully.

The loader described here works properly in most cases, but it can be greatly improved. It has certain weaknesses; for example, it will not load information into cells above 19940 (on a 20K machine). It will not load information beyond a record mark on a given card; i.e., if XX ‡ YY is on a card, the XX and ‡ are loaded, but the YY is lost. A single record mark cannot be loaded as the total input on a card. Cards for loading must be in correct order, since later ones can blank out information loaded from earlier ones. A load card that bears one instruction (12 digits) and the loading address will automatically blank out 48 cells with zeros. And so on.

The limitations listed above apply to the loader of Figure N3.4, but every loader has a similar list.

The loader given in Figure N3.4 is serviceable. It takes 10 cards, which must all precede any deck to be loaded. It can be interrupted. Perhaps that needs some explanation.

Location	Contents		Remarks
00402	36 00558	00500	Read a data card
414	43 00558	00637	If column 80 is nonzero, branch to column 1
426	32 00618	00000	Flag the card's address
438	26 00516	00622	Move the address
450	11 00622	00060	Add 60 to the address
462	26 00497	00622	Move (address + 60)
474	26 00528	00622	Move (address + 60)
486	25 00638	00000	Store one character temporarily
498	25 00618	00400	Move record mark to column 61
510	31 00000	00558	Load the information
522	25 00000	00638	Restore the character
534	49 00402	00000	Repeat

Figure N3.4. The load routine

Suppose you have a long routine that occupies storage from 01000 through 05000. In modifying it, you find you need a divide routine that is coded to occupy 01000 through 03000. The problem can be solved, of course, by reassembly or relocation. However, it is also a simple matter to load the divide routine (at 01000) and move it, during the loading process, with one instruction, to 17000. A transfer control card is inserted in the load deck to do this; it bears the two instructions:

```
31 17000 01000
49 00402 00000
```

and a nonzero character in column 80. After that card, the balance of the loading can continue.

Consider a similar problem that arises if the loader of Figure N3.4 is used to load storage above 19940. It won't work (be sure you understand why it won't). Again, the solution may be to load somewhere else and move the loaded information to 19940-19999.

If you use the loader of Figure N.3, check it out for yourself thoroughly. Cards 5, 6, 7, and 8 contain the arithmetic tables. Alter any 1 digit in those cards, and check that the resulting error is, indeed, caught. Find out what the loader does if a deck does not contain a transfer control card. Find out what action results if a data card lacks its load address. (Both these errors are common).

Figure N3.5 shows the complete code for an entirely different loader.

START	RNCD	AREA
	TDM	AREA+12,RM
	BNF	STØ,AREA+64
	TF	STØ+6,AREA+68
ST	TR	20000,AREA
	AM	STØ+6,12
	B	START

Figure N3.5. A one-card loader

As it stands, this loader is designed to load decks bearing one instruction per card; the loader itself fits in one card. It can readily be modified to load more than 12 digits per card.

This loader is neat and ingenious and has many advantages for certain work. It assumes that the arithmetic tables are in storage and that a record mark is stored somewhere. Only the first card of the deck to be loaded need have a load address; subsequent cards will automatically load at positions 12 higher. Every card <u>may</u> have a load address, if desired; the load addresses are not flagged. The transfer control card is one having a flagged address in columns 64-68.

We have shown two extremes in loaders. There can be many other versions. The best loader is the one <u>you</u> write to do <u>your</u> work.

Problem N4

DUMPERS

In Problem N3, we considered the theory of routines that would enable us to load storage from card decks. Several different loading schemes were suggested. In particular, a routine was outlined that would load card information in the following format:

1. Each data card bears up to 60 characters of numeric information (i.e., information restricted to the basic character set of the machine) in columns 1-60.

2. Each data card bears, in columns 61-65, the loading address of the information that begins in column 1. This address may or may not be flagged.

3. Each data card is either blank or punched with a zero in column 80.

4. Immediately following the last data card in the deck to be loaded there will be a card—the so-called transfer control card—punched with any nonzero character in column 80; this card will bear instructions (starting in column 1) to be executed immediately. The commonest and most obvious use is to execute the branch to the starting instruction of the routine being loaded.

Now, the whole idea of using cards for input to a computer revolves around the <u>unit record</u> concept. The cards are normally prepared off-line on a keypunch. Corrections to them can be made the same way, and usually are. So the normal procedure is this: The instructions and data for a routine are punched into cards; the transfer control card is added; the deck is loaded, and the running of the routine is attempted: errors are discovered, and corrections must be made.

We are dealing at this point with the running code, which is always in machine language. If the error is corrected back in the source language (SPS, Fortran, or what have you), then a reassembly or a recompilation will automatically correct the running code deck, by furnishing a new one. If the code was written in machine language, or if we wish to patch for a while in machine language, then we have three choices:

1. The load cards can be duplicated and corrected (on a key punch), and the deck can be reloaded.

2. Patch cards, bearing the corrected instructions, can be placed at the end of the load deck. The correct information will then "stamp out" the incorrect information during the loading process. This course of action has the advantage that the corrections leave a trail behind them that can be retraced. If, for example, it turns out that a "correction" was incorrect, its action can be withdrawn by removing its corresponding patch cards. (This latter situation is not at all uncommon.)

3. Corrections can be made directly in storage, by manual insertion. This situation applies only when console debugging is allowed at all.

We are concerned with the third situation (in debugging work), plus a situation somewhat akin to it—namely, any situation in which we wish to preserve on cards the information contained in some area of storage. The area could contain a routine that has been altered from the way it appears on its load deck (the patching situation with console debugging), or it could contain a section of data, such as a table. In any event, we wish to punch out stored information. We assume that the area to be recorded ends in a record mark. Obviously, we would like to record it in the proper format to be readily reloaded—namely, in the format prescribed by the loader itself. Following the pattern of the main loader of Problem N3, for example, we would want to record in the following format on each card:

> Columns 1-60: Information
> Columns 61-65: Load address
> Column   80 : Blank or zero

So we need a dump routine, or dumper. This should be a routine that can itself be loaded in some area of storage other than the area to be dumped. If the dumper is written in assembly language, it should be assembled at two or more different origins, say, at 01000 and 18000. If written in machine language, it must be relocated to do this (see also Problem N5).

To make the description clearer, let us assume that the dump routine will be located at 18000, and an area to be dumped is located at 08012 and ends with a record mark at 09157.

The first task of the dumper is to call for typewriter input of the starting location to be dumped (for example, 08012). The routine should then proceed to punch a deck of cards.

The first card should bear the information from cells 08012 through 08071 in columns 1-60 and the number 08012 in columns 61-65. Card 2 should bear the information from cells 08072 through 08131 and the number 08072, and so on. The last card bears the information from cells 09092 through 09151. The last card has six columns of information (taken from 09152 through 09157), plus a record mark in column 7, plus the number 09152 in columns 61-65.

The punching should halt when the routine senses a record mark and should branch back to its first task: accepting the location of another routine or area in storage to be punched out.

Details of writing a good dumper are left to the student. We suggest some points to consider:

1. We have assumed that all dumping is done numerically (the commonest use). Would it be useful, perhaps under switch control, to arrange to punch alphabetically as well?

2. The first test of your dumper should be to dump itself, thus reproducing its own load deck. Will your routine do this?

3. Would it be more useful to you to have the input information to the dumper be two addresses—namely, the starting location and an ending location? That is, instead of having the punching end with a record mark, arrange to punch record marks, too?

4. What will your routine do if the starting location you give it is the address of a stored record mark?

5. What will your routine do if there are no record marks in storage? Will it stop at 10000? Should it?

6. It might be convenient to arrange for your routine to be able to find its starting location on the transfer control card of its own load deck. There are situations in which a fixed area of storage is to be punched out after each running of a given problem. To be sure, in that case the dump routine should really be incorporated in the problem itself, but there can be many excellent reasons (shortage of storage space, for example) why that is not possible.

EXERCISE 1. Write out the characteristics of a dump routine, taking into account the points listed.

EXERCISE 2. Draw a flow chart for a dump routine. Then code it, debug it, and test it.

EXERCISE 3. Document your work carefully, giving complete and clear instructions for its use. Be sure to consider all limitations on your routine, i.e., those situations (if any) for which the routine may not function properly.

Problem N5

SEARCHING STORAGE

Storage of the IBM 1620 computer is separated into blocks, or records, by record marks. A whole block can be moved by the single command, TRANSMIT RECORD, TR, Code 31. It is sometimes convenient, during debugging operations, to check the location of all record marks in storage. The flow chart in Figure N5.1 specifies a program that will type out the address of every record mark, and then stop.

The search starts at the top of storage and continues to address 00000. The typewriter skips to the next tabulator stop before printing each address. If some other starting point is desired, or if the addresses should be typed on separate lines to make a vertical list, the appropriate changes are easily made.

It is more convenient, in using a search routine of this kind, if the routine is written for the input-output area at the bottom of storage. Then it can be used for any situation without itself displacing the part of storage above location 00400 that is to be searched.

> EXERCISE 1. Write a routine to search all of storage for record marks (including the one at the end of this routine) and to print the address of each one. Place the routine in the input-output area, below address 00100. If card input is to be used, write the routine so that it can be punched in a single card.

Other searches of storage can be very helpful in debugging routines. Since a missing flag in a TRANSMIT FIELD IMME-DIATE, TFM, Code 16 instruction or in any immediate arithmetic instruction is likely to cause a routine that has just been stored to be quickly destroyed, it is helpful to search the instruction area for missing flags. The flow chart in Figure N5.2 describes a routine to check immediate commands for the presence of a

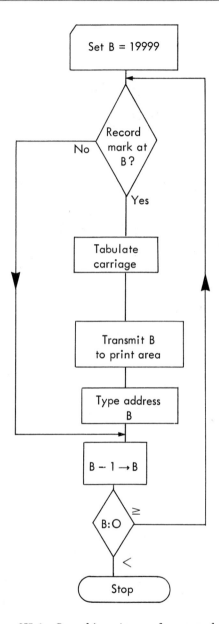

Figure N5.1. Searching storage for record marks

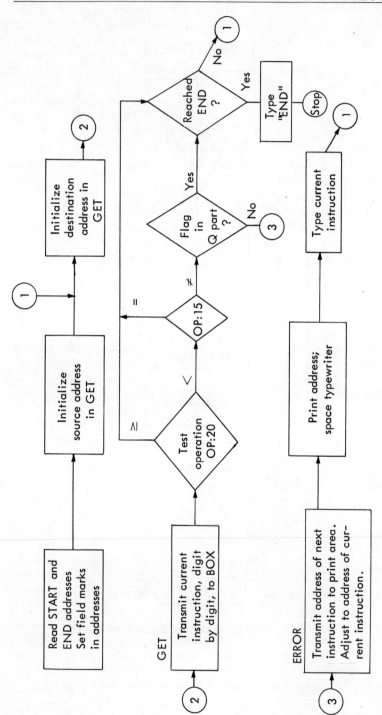

Figure N5.2. Checking immediate commands for field marks

flag in the Q-part. The START and END addresses are to be read in from the typewriter. It is good practice to set a field mark in any address read in from the typewriter, rather than to rely on the operator to supply it. This is done in the first box. The current instruction is transmitted digit by digit so that flags do not interrupt transmission. If the operation code is less than 20, the operation is an immediate one; it is tested to see that it is not code 15, TRANSMIT DIGIT (which requires no field mark). Every digit of the Q-part must be tested for a flag. If there is none (for codes 11, 12, 13, 14, 16, and so on), the address and the instruction are typed out. The address of the next instruction is available; it must be reduced by 12 to obtain the address of the current instruction.

> EXERCISE 2. Write a routine to check immediate instructions for a field mark. Place the routine high in storage so that it will not displace the routine it is intended to check.

A utility routine such as the field mark test may interfere with the routine it is intended to test. One way to solve this nuisance is to write the routine in <u>relocatable form</u>. When a routine is moved from one area in storage to another area, all the addresses that refer to the routine itself must be changed, but other addresses must not. As one way to handle routines in relocatable form, a flag is used in the first position of the operation code to indicate that the P-address must be adjusted; a flag is used in the second position of the operation code to show that the Q-address must be adjusted. Then a special loading routine can be used to place the routine wherever desired.

The flow chart in Figure N5.3 shows how the one-card loading routine of Problem N3 can be elaborated into a relocator routine. A work area of 140 positions is used. Each card to be loaded is read into the last 80 positions of this work area. If a location is punched (with a field mark) in columns 61-65, this address is set into the destination (P-address) of the STO command. If not, the card is loaded into the next consecutive positions. If a digit 1 is punched in column 62 to indicate that the card contains constants only, no adjustment is made in the card. For cards containing instructions, column 62 must be zero or blank. The "base" is the number, positive or negative, that is used to adjust the addresses. If the relocatable program is written so that it appears to start at

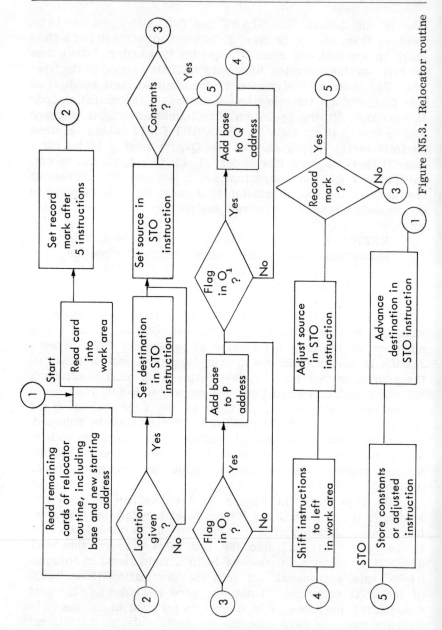

Figure N5.3. Relocator routine

00000, then the base is the location where the first instruction is to be loaded. After each instruction is adjusted, all five instructions are shifted 12 positions to the left in the work area, in order to adjust the next instruction.

The relocator routine is interrupted by placing a card at the end of the relocatable routine with a location in columns 65-68 equal to START of the relocator. This card should place the standard instructions 4800000 00000 49xxxxx 00000 in locations 00000-00023 and branch to 00000. In locations 00014-00018, the xxxxx represents the new starting location of the relocated routine. The relocator routine itself can be relocatable, but it is convenient to have two or more decks on hand, using different areas of storage.

EXERCISE 3. Write a relocator routine along the lines of Figure N5.3, using the relocatable form.

Problem N6

CODE READING

The student will find it interesting and profitable to practice reading well-written codes. It is an excellent way for him to improve his own programming techniques. The code given in Figure N6.1 will count all the nonzero, 5-digit numbers, $x_1, x_2, \ldots, x_{100}$ stored from 19000 to 19499, and also it will form their sum and the sum of their squares. This is a preparatory step to finding their arithmetic mean and their variance, which are of basic importance in statistics.

EXERCISE 1. Study the code carefully. Then fill in the remarks column, making your explanation detailed and explicit.

It is far easier to understand a code when the numbers are replaced by alphabetic abbreviations, as in the 1620 Symbolic Programming System (SPS). Thus, code 16 is replaced by TFM, TRANSMIT FIELD, IMMEDIATE. In a similar way we substitute x for the first of a series of data addresses. We can refer to an instruction by some easy abbreviation, such as COMP for "compare," ADD for "Add," or SUB for "subtract." We limit the number of letters to 5, or 6 at most, so as to conform to the standard SPS. This will make it easy to use the assembly program later, if desired.

EXERCISE 2. Rewrite the code in SPS, using N for the number of nonzero x's, SUM for sum of the x's, and SUMSQ for the sum of their squares. Invent other abbreviations as needed.

The flow of control is shown more easily if the remarks are placed in boxes connected by lines with arrows, i.e., if the remarks are arranged as a simple flow chart.

EXERCISE 3. Construct a simple flow chart for the code in Figure N6.1.

368

Location	OP	P	Q	Remarks
05000	26	05209	05189	
5012	26	05219	05180	
5024	16	05199	$\bar{0}$0000	
5036	16	05059	$\bar{1}$9004	
5048	26	05194	$\bar{0}$0000	
5060	14	05194	$\bar{0}$0000	
5072	46	05132	01200	
5084	11	05199	$\bar{0}$0001	
5096	21	05209	05194	
5108	23	05194	05194	
5120	21	05219	00099	
5132	11	05059	$\bar{0}$0005	
5144	14	05059	$\bar{1}$9499	
5156	47	05048	01100	
5168	4$\bar{8}$	00000	00000	
5180	$\bar{0}$000000000			ZERO
5190	$\bar{0}$0000			BOX
5195	$\bar{0}$0000			N
5200	$\bar{0}$000000000			SUM
5210	$\bar{0}$000000000			SUMSQ

Figure N6.1. Sum and sum of squares

It is often necessary to relocate a routine in another part of storage, perhaps as part of a longer routine. Since this procedure often leads to many errors, the student should adopt a systematic approach. The first requirement is to study each address carefully, to see whether it must be changed. If it refers to another instruction of the routine being relocated, this should be noted. One way is to mark a flag over the first digit of the operation code if the P-address of an instruction must be changed; mark a flag over the second digit of the operation code if the Q-address of that instruction must be changed. This marking is called relocatable form, as described in Problem N5. Then, after the marking has been checked, rewrite the code completely, adjusting each designated address by adding or subtracting the difference between the original location of the first instruction and its relocated location.

EXERCISE 4. (a) Mark the routine in Figure N6.1 with flags over the operation code to show which

addresses must be adjusted when the routine is relocated. (b) Rewrite the routine, relocating it so
that it starts at 06148. One of the very common errors
in coding for the 1620 is to omit the field mark for
the Q-part of an immediate command. This sort of
error is so aggravating (since it often destroys the
program in storage) that a routine is often used to
check it, as described in Problem N5.

EXERCISE 5. (a) Study the code in Figure N6.1
and predict what would happen in each case during
attempted execution of the routine if just one flag
were omitted. (b) Make a list of the results, including those cases where no harm would result.
(c) If you are not certain of some result recorded
in (b), try it on the machine.

Problem N7

DIVISION BY SUBROUTINE

When circuits are not provided in the computer to accomplish division automatically, a subroutine is used to perform this fundamental arithmetic operation. The complete coding for a division subroutine of very wide utility is given in Introduction to Electronic Computers.* That subroutine may be used freely for solving the problems in this book. This problem suggests the desirability of the student's writing his own division subroutine.

The experience gained from this problem will be of great value to the student in situations where an abbreviated division routine is needed as part of a larger routine, or where a process similar to division is needed, as in Euclid's algorithm for extracting a square root.

We shall simplify the problem at first by asking for an independent routine, instead of a subroutine. The dividend and divisor are to be integers of 10 digits or less, with the dividend stored at field address 19989 and the divisor at 19999.

Division is normally performed in a computer by repeated subtraction. We shall therefore need a loop that subtracts the divisor repeatedly from the dividend. We start in the middle of the loop. That is, we assume that we are already at some position in the dividend where the subtraction is taking place. Call the address of this place in the dividend P. Then we ask, Can the divisor DVS be subtracted from the dividend DVD at that point? If so, we subtract it; if not, we move to the right in the dividend. The plan is shown in Figure N7.1. We use MIN (for "minuend") for the address in the work area where the dividend is stored. If the divisor is subtracted, without "overdraw," the quotient Q is increased by one. Otherwise the position P is increased.

Here we add a word of explanation concerning P. There

---

*Fred J. Gruenberger and Daniel D. McCracken, John Wiley & Sons, Inc., New York, 1963, Appendix 2.

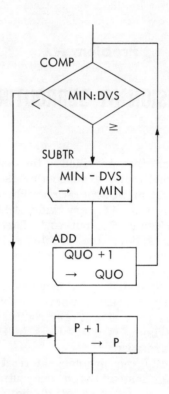

Figure N7.1. Working section of division subroutine, DIV

is no need to reserve a separate place in storage for P, since P indicates only the <u>position</u> in the dividend field where the comparison and the subtraction are taking place. It therefore represents the P-address of the instructions marked COMP and SUBTR. We "advance P" by adding 1 to each of those addresses.

A convenient working area in which to carry out the division is the so-called product area, from 00080 to 00099 (this is, in fact, where the division is accomplished by the special automatic divide feature when that feature is installed in the machine). This area can all be cleared conveniently by multiplying a "10-digit zero" by itself. It is convenient to use the dividend area (19980-19989) for a quotient area, clearing it to a zero field as soon as the dividend is placed in the product area.* Then the dividend should be added to the product area (at 00099) so that no field mark is introduced that would interrupt the subtractions . A little thought or experiment will show that the subtractions should start at 00090 to produce full-length quotients with possibly 10 digits.

> EXERCISE 1. (a) Write a short routine for the working section of a division subroutine, following the plan of Figure N7.1. Supply suitable test data, and debug and test out the result.

When P reaches 00100, the division is complete. We could test for this condition by comparing either of the addresses representing P with 00100. Since this routine is to be used many thousands of times, however, it is especially worth while to consider whether the test can be accomplished in a simpler way. Since the address P is advancing toward 00100, we could test on the unit's digit of P, using the BRANCH ON NON-ZERO DIGIT operation (code 43).

Since the addresses in the three instructions COMP, SUBTR, and ADD are modified during the execution of the loop, they must be preset before the loop is started. Thus far, we have a plan as in Figure N7.2.

> EXERCISE 2. Extend the program of Exercise 1 so as to complete the division loop. Reassemble and check out the new program.

We need to consider now how to determine the sign of the quotient and the remainder, since our loop is written for positive operands only. An ingenious arrangement to make use of the conditional branch operations for doing this is shown in figure N7.3. If the dividend is positive, a trigger is set equal to 1; otherwise it is set equal to minus zero. If the divisor is positive, no change is made in the trigger; if the divisor is negative, 1 is subtracted from it. Now the sign of the quotient can be determined by a single test. If the trigger is zero, the signs of dividend and divisor were unlike and the quotient is consequently negative; otherwise the quotient is positive. Similarly, the sign of the remainder can be determined by a single

---

*Eleven places must be cleared to place a field mark to the left of the first quotient digit.

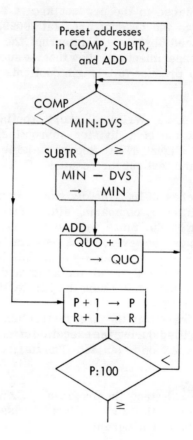

Figure N7.2. Loop to accomplish division by repeated subtraction

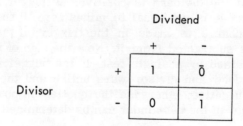

Figure N7.3. Four-way trigger for sign of quotient and remainder

test. If there is a flag in the trigger, the dividend was originally negative, and therefore the remainder is negative, being of the same sign as the dividend.

> EXERCISE 3. (a) Add a section to the routine of Exercises 1 and 2 to determine the signs of the quotient and the remainder and then make the dividend and divisor both positive in storage before division is started. (b) Add a section that will set the signs correctly for the quotient and remainder after the division has been completed. Check the sections of routine for parts (a) and (b) on the computer separately and in combination with the rest of the routine.

When the routine is converted into a subroutine, it should give results equivalent to those expected from the special division circuits. That is, when control is returned to the main routine, the arithmetic indicators should be set correctly according to the quotient obtained. This should therefore be done as the last instruction before leaving the subroutine.

In one respect the division subroutine can be made superior to the special divide feature. In case of attempted division by zero, the subroutine can type an appropriate message.

> EXERCISE 4. (a) Insert instructions to test for zero divisor and to print an appropriate message if necessary. Convert the routine to a subroutine, DIV, by adding one instruction at the end to set both arithmetic indicators and by supplying the linkage and return instructions. (b) Write a short routine to read operands into storage, call upon the subroutine DIV, and print the quotient and remainder. Devise test values to cover as many possible special cases as you can think of, and test the subroutine thoroughly.

The division subroutine may be elaborated to permit the programmer to specify where the dividend is to be placed in the product area and where the divisor is to be subtracted for the first time. This allows the programmer to specify the length of the field for the quotient and to control the number of decimal places in it.*

> EXERCISE 5. (a) Adapt the calling sequence for the division subroutine so as to allow the flexibility described. The subtractions all take place at addresses below 00100, each address yielding a digit (or zero) of the quotient. The first subtraction is therefore performed at the address 00100 minus the length of the quotient field prescribed. (b) Rewrite the subroutine, making the small changes necessary to provide control of the length of quotient field and the number of significant figures in it. Devise additional test cases and test the subroutine thoroughly as in Exercise 4(b).

> EXERCISE 6. Consider the changes that would be necessary for your program to be made completely general. For example, nothing has been done about 1-digit quotients (in the 1620, a field must be at least 2 digits long). Again, the program described here allows for dividends up to only 20 digits. What should be done for longer dividends? We have not considered all the possible error conditions either, although some of them must have shown up during the test phases.

---

*The computer routine does not keep track of the decimal point, except in floating-point operations. This is done by the <u>programmer</u>. In the division of integers by hand, we add zeros to put decimal places in the answer. The equivalent procedure for the subroutine is to leave zeros between the dividend and 00100. For the division of numbers with decimal places, the usual rule still holds: The number of decimal places (counted by the programmer) in the quotient is equal to the number of decimal places in the divisor. A convenient way to remember this is to think of the division process as the inverse of multiplication.

Problem N8

MAKING DECISIONS WITH FORTRAN

How do you make decisions in a Fortran routine? For example, how do you stop at the end of the page?

EXERCISE 1. (a) Write a Fortran routine to calculate and print a table of cube roots of consecutive integers, 100 roots to the page. Print two double-columns of N and $N^{1/3}$ making N consecutive in each column.* Use an IF statement to stop automatically at the end of each page and resume when the START button is pressed. (b) Suggest a different method, using a DO loop to make the page tally for part (a).

A common way of making decisions in Fortran is by using the IF statement with a counter as in Exercise 1. A three-way decision with a single IF statement is illustrated in Exercise 2.

EXERCISE 2. Determine and print the number of intersections of two given circles, using a single IF statement in a Fortran routine. Read in the coordinates (x_1, y_1), (x_2, y_2) of the centers and the radii r_1 and r_2. Return after printing the results to read in new data.

The comparison of absolute values can be accomplished with two IF statements. Part (a) of Exercise 3 is a challenge to the student to analyze the problem carefully and to devise the simplest logical solution. Part (b) is a deceptively simple problem that has a great deal to offer the student in clarifying his concept of simple, straightforward logic.

---

*In your routine, N must be replaced by XN for example, since letters I to N are restricted to variables representing integers.

EXERCISE 3. (a) Write a Fortran routine to read in
two numbers and to type the one whose absolute value
is largest. If their magnitudes are equal, type them
both on the same line provided their signs are different; otherwise type neither. After typing the decision,
the routine is to return for more data. (b) Read three
numbers and type them out first in order of increasing
value and then in order of increasing magnitude
(absolute value).

The numbers are, of course, not necessarily all of the same
sign. The student is urged to make a flow chart for this problem
now, before studying the plan in Figure N8.1.

EXERCISE 4. (a) Make a flow chart for the preceding
problem. The flow chart in Figure N8.1 presents a
natural approach to the first half of the problem:
to print the numbers in order of value. The logic in
this plan is correct, and may seem at first to be as

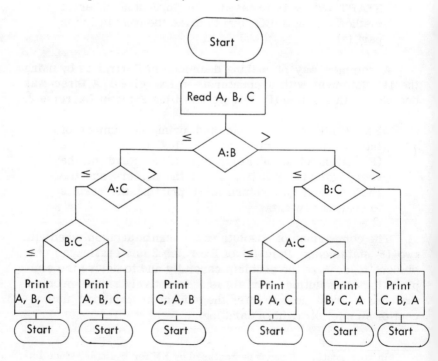

Figure N8.1. Beginner's flow chart for sorting 3 numbers

simple and straightforward as possible. This apparent simplicity, however, is deceptive; it is due to the circumstance that there are few numbers to be compared. If even one more number is added, the complexity of the logic is clearly displayed. Adding two more numbers shows strikingly the limitation of this method. Again, the student is urged to construct a flow chart according to this plan before proceeding to the following discussion. (b) Make a flow chart for the first part of the problem when there are 4 numbers to be arranged. (c) Write a Fortran routine for the plan of part (a) that refers to only 3 numbers.

The complexity displayed by Figure N8.1 is due to the numerous parallel branches. When the number of numbers increases, as in Exercise 4(b), the number of branches increases in geometric progression. We therefore seek to reduce our plan to a straightline flow chart. It will turn out that this kind of flow chart facilitates the formation of loops and is therefore of fundamental importance in computer routines.

We think of the numbers A, B, C as arranged in a sequence. We compare the first two, A and B. If A and B are in order of ascending sequence, we go on to compare B with C. If A is larger than B, we interchange A and B. Then, again, we go on to compare the number that is now B with C. This second comparison may also result in an interchange. Finally, we compare the numbers that are now A and B, making an interchange if necessary to put them in order. We are thus led to the straightline flow chart of Figure N8.2.*

EXERCISE 5. (a) Write a Fortran routine of about 18 instructions according to the plan of Figure N8.2 to sort 3 numbers into order of ascending sequence and type them on the same line. (b) Modify the routine of part (a) so that the numbers are sorted according to magnitude but are still typed with their original signs; three more instructions are required.

Another way to make decisions in a Fortran routine is to use the so-called computed branch statement: GO TO (1, m, n), i.

---

*A further, more complete, discussion of this method of sorting is given in Problem L3.

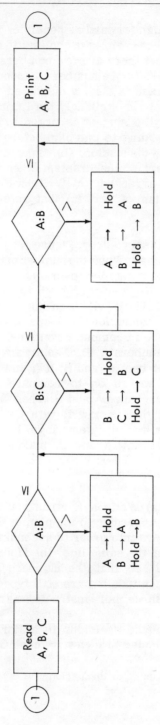

Figure N8.2. Plan for sorting 3 numbers

This method can be used to combine the routines of Exercise 5, parts (a) and (b). The index i is set to 1 on the first execution and then to 2 for the second execution. In this way the second half of each comparison is bypassed on the first execution.

EXERCISE 6. Elaborate the routine of Exercise 5(a) so as to include the routine of Exercise 5(b).

Sets of numbers are easily handled in a Fortran routine by making use of subscripts. These are written in parentheses after the letter referring to the variable. If there were 10 numbers to be arranged in the preceding exercises, instead of 3, they could be manipulated more easily if they were all written as A(I), where I could be changed successively to 1, 2, 3, and so on, up to 10, in a DO loop. A DIMENSION statement is required to reserve consecutive locations in storage for the set of numbers.

EXERCISE 7. Write a Fortran routine to read in a set of 10 numbers from separate cards with a DO loop and to determine the smallest number SML and the largest number LRG of the set and the difference DIFF=LRG—SML. Type out the values of SML, LRG, and DIFF, and return to read in more data.

The Fortran programming system, as its name implies, is very well adapted for solving problems involving mathematical formulas. It is also satisfactory for sorting problems of the kind just considered, provided the problem is small enough so that the additional time required by the Fortran routine is not important. However, Fortran is not at all suited to such problems as the following: Read a number xxxxx.yyyyy, and interchange the decimal and integer parts, typing the number as yyyyy.xxxxx.

It is clear that such a problem is not of frequent occurrence in the applications for which Fortran was designed. To solve such a problem with a Fortran routine, resort must be had to tricks. These tricks may occasionally be useful, of course, in genuine Fortran problems.

The problem here is to separate the number, which is represented in storage as a floating-point number, into two parts. We make use of the fact that the floating-point subroutines must shift the coefficient of a number to the right before adding it to a number with a larger exponent. The least significant digits are thereby lost.

EXERCISE 8. Write a Fortran routine to read in an 8-digit number with four decimal places, interchange the decimal and integer parts, and type the result.

An analogous method can be invented for isolating single digits of a Fortran integer, making use of the fact that such integers are limited to 4 digits. If additional digits are produced by multiplication, the most significant digits are lost. Similarly, a fractional remainder is lost during division.

EXERCISE 9. (a) Write a Fortran routine to read a positive 4-digit integer N from a card and to count the number of times the digit 7 appears in N. Type the integer N and the result before returning to read in more data. (b) Solve the same problem as in part (a) by writing a routine in machine language. Compare the two methods for this particular problem with respect to the number of statements and also with respect to the number of instructions.

The following problem refers to particular storage locations, and therefore is meaningless in Fortran.

EXERCISE 10. Write a routine in machine language to determine the number of times the digit 3 appears in storage from address 00561 to address 00720, inclusive. Read in the two addresses from the typewriter as 5-digit numbers with field marks.

If it is desired to make Fortran available for routines involving much data to be read in or punched out in cards, special subroutines can be used to simplify the programming. An example of such subroutines is the FORCOM (for "commercial FORTRAN") package available from the IBM program library.

Problem N9

CODE CHECKING

You put a new deck into the feed hopper and push the LOAD CARD key. Cards fall into the stacker and then the machine stops. <u>What should you do?</u> Or the machine continues to run. <u>What should you do then?</u>

There is no complete answer to questions such as these. We can give some suggestions, however, that may help to guide the student into logical and systematic procedures for checking codes. We shall introduce our suggestions by means of questions.

WHAT DID YOU EXPECT TO HAPPEN? The absolute requirement for checking any code is to know exactly what you want the machine to do and what result you can expect. The student should therefore always have a neat and complete copy of his routine and the results of a test case, calculated by hand or with a desk calculator if necessary. These should usually be supplemented by a flow chart and a symbol table showing the location of constants, variables, and instructions to which reference is made. Suppose that you expected the machine to type a number as an answer to your problem. Have you actually given the machine an instruction to do so?

DID THE MACHINE EVER GET TO YOUR ROUTINE? The answer to this question is of first importance. It is usually obtained by having the loader stop when the routine has been loaded. Then you can tell when the execution of your routine is started. If your loader or its transfer control card contains such a halt, you should have expected the machine to stop. Knowing what to expect is part of the preparation necessary to do effective code checking.

IS THE STOP A PROGRAMMED HALT? IF SO, WHICH ONE? When the machine is stopped by a HALT instruction, it returns to the MANUAL mode and turns on the MANUAL light. The last preceding reference was made to storage, in order to obtain the 12th digit of that instruction. The address of that digit will still be shown by the MEMORY ADDRESS REGISTER, MAR. The standard arrangement is for a loader to stop in location 00000, hence with 00011 in MAR. Suppose you have used such a loader and MAR does show 00011 with the machine in MANUAL mode. Then you are right on schedule, so far.

The next step could be to press the START key. For a beginner with a short routine, a wise choice is to press the STOP key instead. When the machine is already stopped, this key is the SINGLE INSTRUCTION key (SIE, for "single instruction execute"). If you press it once at this time, the code 49 (for BRANCH) should appear in the OPERATION REGISTER, OP, and the address of the first instruction of your routine should appear in MAR, showing that this address has just been stored in the INSTRUCTION REGISTER, IR-1.

We suppose now that the address in MAR actually is the address of the first instruction of the routine, and that the student continues to press the SINGLE INSTRUCTION key for the code shown in Figure N9.1. This short section of routine is intended to add the 3×3 matrix whose first element is A, to the 3×3 matrix whose first element is B, by adding the nine corresponding 10-digit elements. The following is observed:

	OP	MAR
After	49	00900
We read	21	09000

This is correct, for the first element A is stored from 08000 to 08009. It is added to the first element B, which is stored from 09000 to 09009, by working from right to left, so that the last storage address referred to is 09000.

ADD	A	B,A	00900	21	09009	08009
	AM	ADD+6,10	912	11	00906	0̄0010
	AM	ADD+11,10	924	11	00911	0̄0010
COMP	CM	ADD+11,A+90	936	14	00911	08099
	BL	ADD	948	47	00900	01300
	H		960	48	00000	00000
			972	41	00000	00000
			984	41	00000	00000

Figure N9.1. Addition of two matrices (for code checking)

We press the SINGLE INSTRUCTION key once more. The CHECK STOP light comes on as the machine stops. The light indicates an error. The MARSCHK indicator light shows where the error was detected (MARS for "MAR storage"). The beginner asks, "What bug (goblin, defect) is in the machine?" Many millions of dollars have been spent in an effort to make the computer reliable, i.e., to do every time exactly what the instruction specifies. Modern computers will do that with fantastic accuracy. There is a bug here, but it is in the routine, not in the computer.

We ask now, Where has the computer stopped? To answer this question we note the operation code and MAR address as before, but this time we write them down for a Record of Code Checking.

Indicator	OP	MAR	IR-1
MARSCHK	11	003≠0	

The AUTOMATIC mode light is on, showing that the computer has not completed the instruction. Because of the error, it cannot complete the instruction. We therefore press the RESET key. This clears OP and MAR and turns off all the indicators, the CHECK STOP light, and the AUTOMATIC mode light, returning the computer to MANUAL mode. The operation is terminated without having been completed. We turn the rotary MAR DISPLAY SELECTOR switch to IR-1 and press the DISPLAY MAR key.

We read	OP	MAR
	OO	00924

The INSTRUCTION REGISTER, IR-1, is a counter that contains the address of the next instruction. That address has been transferred from IR-1 (which is one of the storage registers used to set MAR) to MAR by the DISPLAY MAR key for inspection by the operator. The computer must therefore have stopped in the middle of the instruction located at 00912, whose operation was noted as 11 (for ADD IMMEDIATE).

> EXERCISE 1. (a) Punch the routine shown in Figure N9.1 and load it into storage, together with suitable data. (b) Carry out the checking procedure described, verifying that there is an error in the instruction at 00912.

The programmer intended to advance the destination address of the ADD instruction, by adding 10 to it. What, exactly, does the instruction actually demand? It requires that 00010 be added to the field whose address is 00906, starting at the right, but continuing to the left until a field mark (flag) is encountered in that field. The operation is not—and must not be—terminated by a field mark in the addend because there might be a "carry" to be combined with additional digits of the augend. The operation continued, therefore, supplying zeros for the addend all the while, until it reached the record mark in 00400. This record mark appeared in MAR. Since no digit can be added to a record mark, the operation was interrupted by the error.

The student can gain a number of important ideas from the preceding discussion:

1. The "bug" is in the routine (99.9 per cent of the time)—not in the machine.

2. The student should prepare himself thoroughly, with coding sheet, flow chart, symbol table, and test case, so that he knows exactly what he expects the machine to do.

3. The operation code and MAR address should be written down at once, together with the error indication, MARSCHK. Then the machine must be reset, and the address of the succeeding instruction may be placed in MAR.

4. The machine performs the instruction as given, not as intended.

5. Even if no one else is waiting to use the computer, the student should get off the machine at once: He has studying to do.

After studying the routine, the student will see that a field mark is missing at position 00902, but that is not all. The student usually needs to get away from the machine in order to analyze an error completely. He could easily insert the flag with the console typewriter. There is another flag missing at position 00907. This could easily be inserted, too, but this is still not enough. There is an important question to ask here, Why did these errors occur? It is futile to attempt to patch a routine until the reason for the error has been determined. Unless he finds out what caused the error, the student will go on making more mistakes.

In this case, the errors arose because the routine loop was not initialized by instructions. The check stop could easily be eliminated; even a single field mark (flag) at the beginning of the routine, say, at 00900, would suffice. Suppose we insert one there. We press the INSERT key, type

32   00900   00000

and press the RELEASE AND START (RS) key. The machine executes the new instruction, which is at location 00000, and then the BRANCH instruction (that is still stored at 00012). The patched routine is accordingly restarted at 00900. The instruction there, however, no longer reads

$$21 \qquad 09009 \qquad 08009$$

but reads instead

$$\bar{2}1 \qquad 09019 \qquad 08009$$

so that two new errors are introduced: the first element in the second matrix is skipped, and the elements being added are no longer the corresponding elements in the two matrices. The student should rewrite the routine so that it is initialized by two preliminary instructions. The field marks will then be placed by those instructions.

> EXERCISE 2. (a) Rewrite the the routine so that the loop is initialized by programming. Include the two matrices as simply 18 10-digit constants, stored from 08000 to 08099 and from 09000 to 09099. (b) Punch the corrected routine and check the coding.

The instructions in Figure N9.1 represent only a fragment of a longer routine that would probably include input or output instructions and perhaps other calculations. Console debugging is best done in short sections of ten instructions or so. These sections should be separated from each other in storage by a HALT and space for two or three instructions, so that the student can add additional instructions if they are needed, as in this example, without rewriting all the other sections of the routine. The space between sections can be filled with NO OPERATION instructions, code 41, or a BRANCH instruction can be used to skip over it. The HALT instructions can be changed to NOP instructions after the checking is complete.

When the short section of coding in Figure N9.1 has been corrected and executed and the computer stops in location 00960, the results should be examined to see if they are correct. This is testing the routine, and it should be started during the code checking. It is easily done, provided the sum of the two matrices has already been calculated by hand or with a desk calculator.

EXERCISE 3. Test the results obtained with the routine of Exercise 2.

The testing procedure may be built into the routine itself by including output instructions under switch control at various significant points in the routine.

We assume now that the routine has been checked and tested up to (but not including) 00996, as in Exercise 3, and we give the succeeding section of the routine in Figure N9.2. Now after the results have been tested, we can continue with the instruction at 00996.

The CHECK STOP light comes on; the students adds to his code checking record:

Indicator	OP	MAR	IR1
MARSCHK	34	003‡2	

Then, with RESET and DISPLAY MAR, he reads 01008 for IR-1. He inserts the location in his written record. The first instruction in this section (at 00996) is in error. Again the student should leave the computer; he has more desk work to do. There is a record mark in that instruction at 01004, which could be eliminated easily, but why is it there? Address 01003 is referred to as the PRINT area in the succeeding instructions. The intent of the programmer was to make use of the unused part of the CONTROL instruction, code 34, for a print area, since he wished to print only the first 5 digits.

	RCTY		00996	34	0̄0000	0‡102
	TFM	OUT+11,A-5	01008	16	01031	09004
OUT	TFM	PRINT,0	01020	16	01003	00000
WR	WNTY	PRINT	01032	38	01003	00100
	AM	OUT+11,10	01044	11	01031	00010
	CM	OUT+11,A+90	01056	14	01031	09099
	BNE	OUT	01068	47	01003	01200
	H		01080	48	00000	00000
	NOP		01092	41	00000	00000
	NOP		01104	41	00000	00000

Figure N9.2. Output for addition of two matrices (for code checking)

He needed a record mark to stop the typewriter. However, position 01004 is part of the code 01 (for typewriter) in the instruction. The print area must be moved one position to the left, if it is to be left in this awkward position. It would have been far better to assign an address for it that was separate from the instructions. Not only this instruction is affected by the change but also the instructions OUT (for "output") and WR (for "write") are affected. It should be clear that work in changing a code is better done quietly and accurately at a desk and not in haste at the console.

> EXERCISE 4. (a) Punch the instructions of Figure N9.2, and combine them with the routine of Exercise 3. (b) Carry out the checking procedure that has been described, showing that the instruction at 00996 in indeed in error. Then make all three corrections.

After these changes have been made in the deck, it is reloaded. The machine stops in 00000, as before. This time the student may press START instead of SINGLE INSTRUCTION because the first section of the routine has been checked and tested. The machine stops in location 00984. Here the student resumes SINGLE INSTRUCTION operation. The carriage now returns properly on the next instruction; after the following instruction the student records:

Indicator	OP	MAR	IR-1
	16	01011	01020

The intent for the instruction was to transmit the number 09004 to 01027-01031. If that had been done, MAR would have read 01027. Since there was no field mark in the number 09004, the transmission continued all the way to the first flag. The routine has been destroyed from 01011 to 01031.

It is now clear that the routine was not adequately prechecked at a desk before it was brought to the computer. A careful desk-check will reveal that each of the succeeding instructions contains an error.

> EXERCISE 5. (a) Carry out the checking procedure as described. Verify that the routine has been partly destroyed, by typing this section of it. (b) Correct the rest of the routine. Would the instruction at

01056 have been adequate if the instruction at 01068 had been BRANCH ON LOW instead of BRANCH ON EQUAL? (c) Correct the deck of Exercise 4 according to part (b) and check the code. Test the routine by choosing suitable values for the elements of the matrices, including negative and zero values, and comparing with hand calculated results.

Additional important ideas about code checking have been illustrated in the discussion and in the exercises, and should be combined with the previous list:

6. The cause of an error should be determined; the result of that error should not merely be patched. In other words, cure the disease, not the symptom.

7. Every loop should be initialized by programming.

8. A routine should be written as sections separated by a HALT with space for corrections.

9. SINGLE INSTRUCTION operation and the AUTOMATIC mode may be combined advantageously in code checking.

10. After a section is checked (to see if it will run) it should be tested by comparing the results with the expected results, perhaps a hand calculated test case.

11. A careful record should be made at the console of the steps taken in checking the code.

12. Coding should not be condensed by placing constants inside instructions or in other ways.

13. One change often makes other changes necessary, so that the whole code should be reviewed after any change.

14. Every routine should be subjected to a careful desk check before any attempt is made to execute it. The desk check should include the following questions:

(1) Do immediate instructions (except TDM) have a field mark?

(2) Do input and output instructions and transmit record instructions refer to the left-hand character?

(3) Do arithmetic instructions and transmit field instructions refer to the field address (right-hand character)?

(4) Are operation codes correct?

(5) Have BE (BRANCH ON EQUAL) instructions been replaced where possible by BL or BH instructions to increase the chance of failing safe?

(6) Are immediate operations confused with storage reference instructions?

(7) Have inserted instructions changed any address that are referred to later?

(8) Are record marks missing where required for record transmission or for output?

(9) Have the variables been confused with their addresses?

(10) Do transmit field instructions obliterate their limiting field marks, or do transmit record instructions destroy their limiting record marks?

> EXERCISE 6. (a) An input section for the routine to add two matrices is shown in Figures N9.3 and N9.4. Subject the coding to a careful desk check. (b) Simplify the input section of part (a) greatly by rewriting it. Combine it with the routine of Exercise 5, check the coding, and execute the complete routine. (c) Compare the routines of parts (a) and (b) with respect to (1) length (2) time, for execution, (3) code checking time, (4) clarity of logic, and (5) freedom from coding tricks that might confuse another programmer who might have to use or modify the routine.

Now we return to the second question at the beginning of the problem. If the machine does not stop, but continues to run without any output, then what should you do? We respond, as always, with the question, What did you expect to happen? The programmer should have estimated the time required for execution. When a very long time is expected, he should provide for the output of intermediate results. Suppose that the running time greatly exceeds the time required to execute the routine and still there are no results. Then the program is probably executing a perpetual loop. The situation is handled differently for long and short loops. We assume first that the program is in a very short (tight) loop of 6 or 8 instructions.

We stop the computer by pressing the STOP key. Then we advance with the SINGLE INSTRUCTION key (which is the same key) until we have executed the same branch instruction twice in the same way. This verifies that the loop is short. The relevant indicators should be OFF. We press the RESET key and then the DISPLAY MAR key with the rotary MAR DISPLAY SELECTOR switch turned to IR-1. Then MAR gives us the address of the next instruction so that we can refer to the coding sheets to identify the section where the loop is situated. We examine the condition

	TF	RD+6,A,8	00768	26	00786	0̄8009
RD	RNCD	0	780	36	00000	00100
	A	RD+6,30	792	21	00786	00030
	CM	RD+6,A+90	804	14	00786	08099
	BE	RD	816	46	00780	01200
	BNF	STOP,RD+3	828	45	00864	00783
	TFM	RD+7,B,7	840	16	00786	0̄9009
	B	RD	852	49	00768	00000
STOP	H		864	48	00000	00000
	NOP		876	41	00000	00000
	NOP		888	41	00000	00000

Symbol table

RD	00780
STOP	00864
A	08000 − 08009
	08000 − 08099 (matrix)
B	09000 − 09009
	09000 − 09099 (matrix)

Figure N9.3. Coding to be checked for input section of matrix addition

that causes the perpetual return, typing out data where necessary.

In the case of a moderately long loop it may not be convenient to advance by single instructions to the end of the loop. Another way that is sometimes effective in identifying the loop is to advance until an unusual instruction appears. A quick scan of the coding sheets may then make identification easy.

When a routine is perpetually repeating a very long loop, perhaps with many inner loops, it is usually too slow a process to analyze the loop with single instruction operation. In such a situation, we modify the routine by inserting a halt in front of the conditional branches affecting the long loop. Good programming procedure would have provided nearby space for making the insertion. If space is missing, then the technique described as "out to the woods and back" may be used to make a patch.

A useful technique for following the progress of long routines is to have the routine print an identifying number as each phase of the problem is completed. In case of breakdown, the location can then be determined quickly.

EXERCISE 7. (a) Place a perpetual loop in the routine of Exercise 2 by (again) omitting the field mark
in the COMP (for "compare") instruction. Then
follow the procedure described for eliminating a
perpetual loop. (b) Form a team with one or more
other students. Then each student is to alter some
long routine (which has been checked out) by introducing a perpetual loop. The other students are to
compete in checking the code separately, keeping a
careful record of their procedure. By comparing
their records, the members of the team can help
each other to increase their skill in code checking.

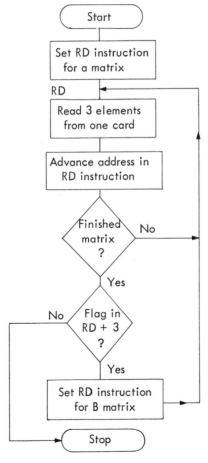

Figure N9.4. Flowchart for the debugging problem of Figure N9.3

It sometimes happens that a routine fails in a section that has previously been checked. Suppose the computer stops in the AUTOMATIC mode with the operation code equal to 40. Since this code represents no machine operation, the original instruction has been altered. A quick dumping of the neighboring instructions may show that a large part of the routine has been destroyed. This destruction is frequently the result of an attempted modification of an address, as in the example given previously. If a field mark is missing, the coding preceding the address in changed completely ("clobbered"). We therefore find the first instruction that is still unchanged. The address modification was probably attempted in the instruction immediately preceding that instruction. We therefore examine (for a missing flag) the instruction used to modify the instruction in question.

In some cases an instruction becomes changed and then it in turn destroys instructions in a distant part of the coding. Such changed instructions are sometimes very hard to find. One technique that has been used successfully is to store an illegal character in the section being altered, perhaps by reading an alphabetic character into an even-numbered address. When the offending instruction tries to alter that section, the illegal character causes a check stop.

Another way to find an altered instruction is to dump the part of storage containing the code, using a routine from Problem N4. Comparison can then be made visually with a similar dump of the unaltered routine. If the dump is into cards, a special routine may be used to make the comparison and type out all the altered instructions so that the offending instruction can be picked out quickly.

A very effective way to divide a long routine into segments is to write it as if it were composed of subroutines, even though each may be called on only once. Then the master routine will consist chiefly of a series of calling consequences. Variables and constants referred to by more than one segment are placed at the top of storage. These can be set equal to suitable test values while each segment is being checked separately. This kind of segmentation is especially suitable for group projects, where several students are working on the same routine.

The student will understand by this time that skillful code checking depends on locating the errors quickly. Even after an error has been restricted to a short section of coding, however, it will occasionally defy detection. Such errors can always be revealed by examining each instruction in detail, together with the result of its execution, using for this purpose an interpretive tracing routine.

Every computer has its own peculiarities. (See Problem N10.) Some of these may be encountered during code checking and appear to be machine or routine bugs. For example, a puzzling stop of the IBM 1620 in AUTOMATIC mode may occur with code 39 (for WRITE ALPHAMERICALLY) in the OPERATION REGIS-TER, OP. One possibility is that the typewriter is locked in numerical shift. No signal lights give any clue to the reason for this kind of stop. Another possibility is that the first character to be typed is a record mark. This last situation will stop the machine in AUTOMATIC mode for code 38 (WRITE NUMERICALLY) as well. If the record mark is encountered after the first character is typed, the operation is terminated normally. It is only when the <u>first</u> character is a record mark that this peculiarity is exhibited.

Problem N10

1620 CHARACTERISTICS

Figure N10.1 shows part of the information given in the manual for the IBM 1620, Model I. It suggests some questions about the operation of the machine that might require some exploration by you.*

1. There are about 40 valid op-codes. Do all the invalid codes have the same action if an attempt is made to execute them? What, precisely, is that action? Can you ever recover from an attempt to execute an invalid op-code without resetting the console?

2. The timing given for the various operations suggests a rough rule: Allow 160 microseconds to decode an instruction, plus 80 microseconds for each digit's worth of arithmetic performed. How accurate is the clock that controls the action of the machine? If we had 1,000 multiply instructions in sequence (easily created in storage with a loop), each calling for 5 x 5 multiplication, the execution of them should take 4.56 seconds, precisely. Or, ten executions would take 45.6 seconds. Try it.

3. The manual is silent concerning various oddball things that might occur during execution. Find out the action that results, for example, from SET FLAG and CLEAR FLAG, addressing a cell that contains a record mark. What happens on TRANSMIT RECORD if you address a record mark?

What, exactly, is the action of the machine if any arithmetic operation is attempted on a nonfield (possible only when there is no flag in all of storage, which is unlikely, or when a record mark intervenes before a flag).

What is the action of the machine when a WRITE instruction addresses a record mark? Is this action the same for both numeric and alphabetic WRITE commands?

Op-code 43 (properly called BRANCH ON NON-ZERO DIGIT) allows us to test a single storage position for the distinction between a zero and any other digit. A flagged zero is treated as

---

*Corresponding research into the pathology of other computers is as easily generated.

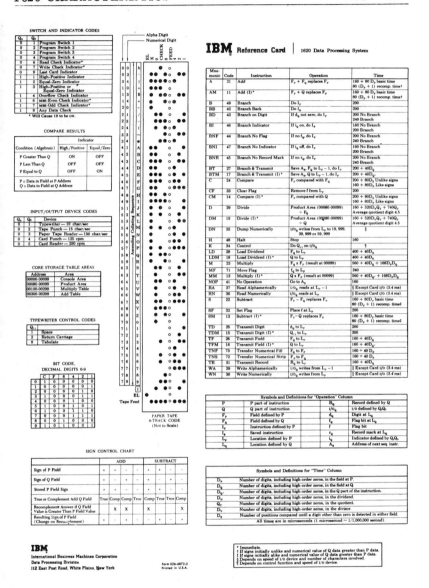

Figure N10.1.

zero; what action is taken when the addressed digit is a record mark?

The machine takes certain actions when it meets illegal or invalid characters in storage. The distinction is this: An invalid character is one that fails the parity check (i.e., the check bit is not correct), whereas an illegal character is a bit-combination not in the machine's character set. Thus, the character stored as 000011 is an invalid 3 (the check bit should be 1); the character stored as 101100 would be valid but illegal; the character stored as 101101 would be both illegal and invalid. The question now is, How can we test the action of the machine —i.e., how can we produce illegal or invalid characters in storage?

The alphabetic storage feature of the machine allows for just 49 valid alphabetic characters, counting the combination 0‡. Thus, the pair 54 is M, the pair 13 is $, and so on. This implies that there are 52 number pairs that are not valid alpha codes (for example, 01, 02, 05, 06, 38, 50, 60, 61, 80, and so on). Is there the same machine action for each of them? Will the action be the same when addressing the typewriter and the card punch?

To what extent can the operation TRANSMIT FIELD involve overlapping fields and the operation TRANSMIT RECORD involve overlapping records? Suppose, for example, there is a record located in cells 10000-10100, with the record mark at 10101. The instruction 31 15000 10000 is normal; what about these two:

$$31 \quad 10050 \quad 10000$$
$$31 \quad 09950 \quad 10000$$

4. The CONTROL operation allows for the digits 1, 2, and 8 in the last position of the instruction (Q11). There must be a 1 in Q9. Do nonzero digits in Q7, Q8, or Q10 have any effect? If Q11 is a record mark, it contains both a 2 and an 8. What action will this have?

5. The MULTIPLY operation clears cells 00080-00099 automatically before multiplying. If a product greater than 20 digits is called for, what happens in the area of storage below 00080? What would happen if that area contained a record mark?

INDEX